"GLITTERING AND
EXTRAORDINARY."
Chicago Tribune

"It is impossible in a short space to give credit
to the scope and color of this book . . . the
whole glittering, flamboyant world of Victorian and Edwardian England."
The Columbus Dispatch

"A STORY FULL OF HISTORICAL
PLUMS."
The New York Times

"DAZZLING . . . SENSUAL . . .
TRIUMPHANT!"
Newsday

Also by James Brough

AN UNTOLD STORY: THE ROOSEVELTS OF HYDE PARK
(with Elliott Roosevelt)

The Prince and The Lily

James Brough

BALLANTINE BOOKS · NEW YORK

Library of Congress Catalog Card Number: 74-79684

ISBN 0-345-28477-1

This edition published by arrangement with
Coward, McCann & Geoghegan, Inc.

Manufactured in the United States of America

First Ballantine Books Edition: April 1976
Second Printing: May 1979

First Canadian Printing: June 1976

For C. J. B., S. R. B.,
and E. K. B.

Acknowledgments

The needed keys to the contradictory nature of the man whom his family called Bertie were found primarily in Sir Philip Magnus' flawless biography, *King Edward the Seventh,* Sir Frederick Ponsonby's *Recollections of Three Reigns,* and the letters of Queen Victoria. Similarly, Georgina Battiscombe's *Queen Alexandra* was indispensable in understanding Bertie's wife, who was known as Alix.

Lillie Langtry proved to be a more elusive subject for study. Her memoirs, *The Days I knew,* were a curious blend of evasiveness and an irresistible desire to hint at her secrets in terms readily understandable by the few people in whom she confided. Interviews conducted in London and Jersey proved to be rewarding. Two Jerseymen in particular, H. T. Porter and Philip Ahier, deserve special thanks, as does the staff of St. Helier's public library. Noel Carson's *Because I Loved Him* served as a useful reference work in establishing the chronology of Lillie's career in the theatre. Victor Malcolm's generosity included permission to quote some "A. E." letters to Lillie.

The background of the island on which she was born is largely drawn from islanders' reminiscences, Edward Le Quesne's *Fifty Years of Memories,* and Raoul Lemprière's *History of the Channel Islands* and *Portrait of the Channel Islands.*

An incomplete listing of other source works includes: Margot Asquith, *Autobiography* and *More Memories; The Diary of Lady Frederick Cavendish;* Sir George Chetwynde, *Racing Reminiscences and Experiences of the Turf;* Lady Randolph Churchill, *Reminiscences;* George Cornwallis-West, *Victorian Hey-Days;* Alden P. Hatch, *The Mountbattens;* Mark Kerr, *Prince Louis of Battenberg;* Anita Leslie, *The Marl-*

borough House Set; Sir Philip Magnus, *Gladstone;* Ian Malcolm, *Trodden Ways* and *Vacant Thrones;* Mary Malcolm, *Me;* Edward Michael, *Tramps of a Scamp;* Harold Nicolson, *George V;* Arthur Sebright, *A Glance into the Past;* Edward Harbord, Baron Suffield, *My Memories 1830–1913;* Frances, Countess of Warwick, *Life's Ebb and Flow;* Richard Hough, *Louis and Victoria.*

Recourse was also made to the files of *Illustrated London News, The Times, Tht Morning Post, Town Talk, Liberty Magazine, Reynold's Weekly Newspaper, Truth,* and *The Sporting Times.*

Margaret Davies served as a tireless and resourceful researcher, notably at the Bodleian Library, Oxford, and Janet Ashton typed the manuscript with errorless skill and grace under pressure. Of all those offering their thoughts in the course of interviewing, the greatest gratitude is due to Sir Basil Bartlett, who supplied the key to the climax.

J.B.

I

A Kingdom by the Sea

❧ I ❧

A day like this was bound to come sooner or later. The interior, undiscussed circumstances of the family made that inevitable. Before nightfall, she would be impelled to grow up. Moving forward so abruptly towards womanhood would be difficult, but she was tough-fibred and her survival was not in doubt. The patterns of her thinking would be disarranged by the demands of maturity, not at the pace of her body's changes these past months, but instantaneously and irrevocably.

In appearance, the girl had already crossed the threshold of adolescence. Full breasts, a straight back, and clear skin the color of cream gave evidence of that. But, on this morning, she was still a child in her thinking, a chrysalis safe in its cocoon.

In an everyday button-through dress of plain wool, she sat alone by the window in the bare schoolroom of the old deanery, passing the moments in daydreams about the boy whose company she was aching to enjoy. The gentleness of the feelings he aroused were unique to her. She could not understand them, nor did she choose to. With the narcissism of the young, she loved him because he was so much like her.

She had reached the age when respectable people considered it unthinkable for a girl of her class to be allowed out of her home unchaperoned. The marriage market set a high price on romance, but damaged goods were heavily discounted, and it was damaging to be found alone with any man other than a close relative.

Risks made up an essential part of her life. The danger of scandalising her father's congregation added spice to all her pleasures. Six brothers had seen to

3

it that she was brought up as a hoyden, inured to the ways of rowdy males. But this new companion had to be put into a different category. He was younger, for one thing, than any brother except perhaps Reggie. He was at least as handsome as her father, the dean, in her judgement, who came close to being a paragon among men. Her new love's hair was the same Titian brown as hers, his eyes bold and violet-blue like those she had taken to staring into, reflected in a mirror. He was far better looking, she felt, than she could hope to be.

As she let her fancy tell her what they might say to each other when they met later in the day, her forefinger touched the leaded windowpane. The meandering curlicues of her initials appeared in the haze on the glass: *E* for Emilie after her mother; *L* for Le Breton. She omitted the *C* for Charlotte. She disapproved of her middle name even more than she disliked the first. To the family, she was "Lillie" for some forgotten reason, perhaps because that was how a child first tried to say "Emilie." Leaving her mark on windowpanes was one of the habits she did not outgrow. If she included the year, it would be 1868.

There was time to spare before Reggie and Clement came home from school, their boots skittering over the loose stones of Deanery Lane, leading down from Father's church at the top of the hill. She taught a children's class there on Sunday mornings, and she had started to take over some of the duties expected of a dean's wife now that her mother complained of feeling less than well and spent more and more time in privacy.

Today called for no visits to the sick; no bazaars; no climbing into a horse-drawn charabanc with a load of shouting children off on a Sunday School treat of lemonade and obstacle races in some farmer's field; no handing out of Bibles or *The Pilgrim's Progress* to conscientious attenders on a prize day. She could pursue her dreams about the inexpressible nature of love.

Before Reggie and Clem followed them, all her

other brothers in turn had gone to the same school—first Francis, then Trevor, Maurice, and William. The uniformed boys who attended Victoria College were not supposed to mix with lesser breeds, most particularly not with the barefoot urchins of the ragged school down on Cannon Street, who relied in large part for their existence on donations of hot soup and cast-off clothing from the good ladies of St. Saviour's and the other churches. The Le Breton boys had been taught to ignore the rules in that respect. The dean was no believer in manifest discrimination.

By the implacable standards of the church, he came suspiciously close to being an impractical visionary. A man of the cloth had no business advocating universal education when book learning could only encourage the poor to sedition. A girl smitten with the fanciful idea of serious studying could scarcely fail to lose the essential innocence of mind and spirit which was so dear to every man. The dean, however, felt that a woman had a right to knowledge beyond the prescribed reading, writing, simple numbering, and embroidery. The problem was that Victoria College was a school for boys only. The island lacked all facilities catering to his eccentricity concerning a girl's claims to be educated.

Certainly Miss Le Vesconte's prim Establishment for Young Ladies on Royal Bay Terrace did not meet the need. Miss Straight's similar accomodations on Colomberie, whose curriculum included lessons in making wax flowers, were no more promising. So his only daughter had been taught, of necessity, at home, in the schoolroom, where she idled away these moments, of the deanery whose grey granite walls contained a stone-cut with a date of 1100. Red, pink, and white damask roses climbed the walls toward the pantile roof. Cherry and pear trees scattered petals on the lawn, contained between the two wings of the house, reaching out like enfolding arms.

Madame Bisson, who wore a frilled cap with mauve ribbons in token of her position as combined housekeeper and part-time governess, gave the girl her first instruction in reading and writing in English and madame's native French. She also filled the child's head with her tales of invading Frenchmen landing by night on the beaches that girded three sides of the island, intent on recapturing it from the British crown. Men-of-war had not crossed the fourteen miles of water that separated the island from the coast of Normandy since the days of Louis XVI, on the eve of the French Revolution. Old Madame Bisson's vivid tongue made it seem as though only yesterday Baron de Rullecourt, a soldier of fortune, led his men into the heart of the town of St. Helier, which lay at the foot of St. Saviour's Hill.

"My own father saw the end of that affair," she used to tell Lillie. "Your great-grandmother had to take her children and flee for their lives."

King George III's designated Lord of the Islands, Major Moses Corbet, was in his four-poster bed when the French burst into Le Manoir de la Motte. "We are the masters now," they said. He quickly signed the document of surrender which they forced into his hands. His senior officer, Major Francis Peirson, refused to obey. Instead, he called out the militia to reinforce the 78th and 95th regiments fighting under his command.

On a dank January evening, battle was joined on the stone seats of St. Helier's Market Place. Peirson and de Rullecourt died together, but the French were driven into retreat. Time and time again, the old housekeeper told the tale of delicious terror until the girl would lie awake after her candle was blown out, straining to catch the clash of swords and the rattle of muskets signalling a new invasion. All she could hear was the distant surge of the sea.

On the island of Jersey, the only corner of the world she knew, it was impossible to escape the tang of salt in the air or the murmur of waves pounding the northern cliffs, green with lichen, and rolling over the yellow sand that filled the shoreline bays. Jersey, largest of the Channel Islands, was punier in size than the least of the counties of England, the beckoning, commanding matriarch one hundred and more miles away. By concentrating hard, Lillie could picture the island in its entirety, nine miles long and five miles wide, in a single instant in her mind. In her childhood, it bore most of the marks of heaven.

There was more fun to be had, of course, when all the brothers lived at home and she and Reggie could tag along after them on their escapades. They impressed on her what a miserable handicap it was to be a girl. They would not tolerate a silly, tearful little creature spoiling everything. The price of being allowed to join in with them called for steadying her nerves and biting her lips when she suffered hurt. "You must look at things from a boy's point of view," they insisted. Doing her best to conform, she climbed trees and vaulted fences with the rest of them.

The graveyard of Father's church was a favourite playground, under the towering elms and oaks, among the tombstones of pink granite and softer sandstone, quarried on the island and impervious to the ravages of weather. Some of her ancestors were buried there. Well-to-do neighbours on St. Saviour's Hill grew accustomed to the sight of an exuberant little girl, with uncut hair streaming past her shoulders, scrambling over the stone walls of the cemetery to race after her brothers on the road to town. It was no way for the dean's daughter to behave, but perhaps it was only to be expected. They found him sadly lax in disciplining his children. Surprisingly few girls of her age were encouraged to play with her, considering the Le Bretons' place in society. Those who made the attempt met with her customary sullen stare.

"Girls," she repeated to herself in her brothers' words, "are silly, easily scared, full of qualms." Being a boy was far superior.

Only occasionally her guard fell and she permitted sentimentality in herself. In their schooldays, her brothers made the deanery a menagerie for their pets. Rabbits, guinea pigs, and ferrets scurried around in cages in the disused west wing, which housed the remains of a cider mill. Lillie kept a canary, which

7

only she was supposed to care for. When she discovered it dead from starvation in its cage one morning, she buried it in her mother's flower garden, weeping as she set into its grave the wooden cross she had nailed together.

A seagull replaced the canary in her affections. Her mother came across it on the beach of Grouville Bay, thrashing the sand with a broken wing. The great grey and white bird was given the name "Jacko" when Mrs. Le Breton brought it home to splint the broken bone. The family learned to stay clear of its cruelly hooked bill until it was slowly tamed. Then it would stalk the walled garden, where a fig tree grew to the east of the house, and the flower beds, which were Mother's special pride. Jacko's staccato cries were added to the background of domestic sounds around the deanery, the cackle of chickens in the yard, the whinnying of horses from the stables.

One spring Mrs. Le Breton brought in a brood of young partridges. The sight of them undid the training in docility which Jacko had received. The gull's slashing bill killed every one of them. When she saw the havoc, she lashed at the bird with her riding crop. Lillie saw him stretch his wings and take off into the open sky, heading for the sea, gone, as she thought, forever.

She was mistaken. Another spring came, and Mother packed a picnic basket and drove the children in the carriage to Grouville Bay with their greyhound, Hawk, running behind. The dog was chewing on a bone left over from the meal when a gull swooped to fight for possession of it. Jacko had returned. He picked at scraps from Mrs. Le Breton's plate, while Lillie and her brothers watched, making no movement. She remembered the moment all her life. When she reached out a hand to stroke his back, Jacko took wing. He sailed out over the water, and that was her last sight of him.

She became too much of a handful for Madame Bisson to manage. The old woman went into retirement, not at all satisfied with the achievements of her pupil. Lillie was bright enough, but bored with lessons. *"I'vaut mûs all ou ongri l'bras qué l'co,"* her teacher might well mutter—"Better stretch the arm than the neck"—in the ancient Norman-French of the islands, where the language, *le jerriais,* endured unchanged from the time the first Dukes of Normandy conquered them.

Lillie started her education over again at the hands of tutors, who came in the evenings to drum extra Latin and mathematics into the resistant skulls of the dean's half-dozen sons. Mr. Draper put in regular appearances to instruct her in the ladylike arts of drawing and dabbling in watercolors when his classes in the Masonic Temple were over for the day. Speaking French presented no difficulties; in the practise of the island, the dean preached alternately in that language and in English at the services which, morning and evening, lasted for two hours and more. His more devout parishioners attended both.

History, especially family history, intrigued her. For close to a thousand years, Le Bretons had lived on the island, nobody being certain of the exact span of time. Perhaps they did not reach as far back as the years of St. Helier himself, who sailed from Normandy to bring the Christian faith to the barbarians. He was slain by a Saxon pirate's ax A.D. 555 and his body tossed into the sea. She had joined the processions which, every July 16, wended out at low tide across the causeway stretching from St. Helier to the massive rocks beyond the mediaeval Elizabeth Castle to commemorate the anniversary of his death at the walls of the crude, spray-drenched stone shelter which was the martyred hermit's dwelling place.

There was no doubt that Le Bretons had established themselves on Jersey before the bastard-born Duke William of Normandy invaded England to make himself king. A Le Breton fought in the Battle of Hastings beside the Conqueror, whose domain included Jersey. Her ancestor was pictured in the Bayeux Tapestry. Lillie went to see it for herself one day and was disappointed to see no family likeness discernible in

9

the woven face of a helmeted warrior dead for eight centuries.

The Norman kings of England were well served by Le Bretons, whose rewards in the shape of fields and orchards spread across the island. The vassals who laboured in the warm sunlight and gentle rain amassed wealth for the family. A manor house was soon to rise at Noirmont, to be one of the finest of its kind in Jersey, looking across the water to the battlements of Elizabeth Castle.

Edward I ruled England when the Seigneurs of Noirmont fell into a dispute over rights to their property. They were challenged by the abbot of Mont St. Michel, the speck of sanctified, fortified rock off the nearby French coast. The family, which had conserved its wealth through centuries of attack by invading French and marauding pirates, lost its place in the ranks of the richest seigneurs of the island, the De Carterets and the rest.

Now Noirmont Manor was the enviable home of Mr. Pickering, a businessman, who was still struggling to build Jersey's first railway after twenty years of frustration. In the opinion of the gentry, it was scandalous that the island had to rely for public transportation on carriages rented from Gregory's, Fanvel's, or the Paragon livery stables, either that or the so-called buses, which amounted to no more than an airless box set on a farm wagon, with straw littering its floor, and luggage roped on the roof under a tarpaulin. England had miles of track even before Victoria was crowned. Coaching there was quite passé, except as a sport for gentlemen. Only a handful of stauch traditionalists shared the view of the lately departed Duke of Wellington that railways were a dangerous evil because they "encouraged the working classes to move about."

Lillie occasionally dreamed about the glories of Noirmont, just as she liked to conjure up for herself the most valiant among her forebears, Raoul, "a man after my own heart," as she described him. King John was memorable for her not so much for signing Magna

Carta as for providing a Le Breton with the chance to slash a path up along the Seine with a few hundred retainers to capture Paris from his liege's rival for the throne, Arthur of Brittany.

Le Bretons turned to the professions after they had been humbled as feudal lords. One of them became a *jurat*. The office dated back to the time of King John. It combined the functions of magistrate and permanent juror, sitting with the presiding judge when a defendant was tried before the Royal Court. Justice was stern and punishment swift, another tradition which kept its hold up to this day when Lillie daydreamed in the schoolroom. In 1868 parents still hurried their children up to Westmount to watch prisoners hanged outside the town gaol. A man or woman condemned to the pillory in the marketplace might be pelted with oyster shells until blood oozed down the victim's face. The diehards concluded that England was softening that year when they heard that public executions had ended at Newgate in London, where nineteen-year-old Alexander Mackay, found guilty of murdering his mistress, Emma Grossmith, was allowed to swing in private.

Superstition as well as a dark streak of cruelty marked Lillie as a Jersey girl. For two or three years now, she had been dabbling in spiritualism, convinced that she had a gift for conjuring up mysterious spirits. The cult had arrived in Jersey belatedly, as such novelties usually did, after it had laid its spell in England. The astonishing accounts of the rappings and inexplicable movements of furniture in the house of the two Fox sisters in Hydeville, New York, had spread by this time across Europe. Eager sitters were holding séances everywhere, except on the island, to summon the spirits of the dead, who would obligingly rap once for "yes," three times for "no" to answer questions posed to them. Any true believer might conceivably be a medium, capable of inducing tambourines to shake, chairs to topple over, and ectoplasmic faces to float in the darkness of a curtained room. There were rumours that Queen Victoria's

11

drunken Highland gillie, John Brown, had occult powers that kept her in touch with her dear, departed husband, Prince Albert, and explained the servant's bewildering influence over her.

Lillie enrolled two of the handful of girls she knew to join her in an experiment with table-turning in the deanery's drawing room, which had been built as an addition to the cramped, low-ceilinged rooms of the house by her father. As she expected, he raised no objections to her séances. At the girls' first session, she convinced herself that the table did indeed provide intelligent answers in the rappings it produced to her touch.

"I really *was* the cause," she assured the dean. A fascinating future might open up for her. She would be a medium, acclaimed as a living, international marvel, respected by men of reputation and scientific distinction as she conjured up the past and perhaps foretold the future.

Late one night, when the three girls sat together in darkness on the sofa, she felt panic stir. Moonlight gleamed through the windows. Suddenly, she related afterwards, she heard "a weird rustling like the whirring of huge wings." The sofa moved sedately across the floor from one end of the room to the other. That could only be proof that, as she chose, she could command the mysterious forces of the universe. She would continue her experiments even if her friends were scared half out of their wits.

By this time, prosperity had been restored to the Le Breton family for a hundred years and more. They made their money in trade with the colonies of Englishmen which sprang up along the coasts of South America and the land that was to become the United States. Links between the Channel Islands and the New World were first forged when Jersey fishermen sailed to the waters off New England to fish for cod.

The Le Bretons themselves did not put to sea. Their way was to engage ships and crews among the islanders, who had followed the sea since the beginnings of remembered time as mariners, fishermen, privateers, and smugglers. The ships were fitted out in St. Helier's bustling yards. They carried woollen goods, clocks, and furniture to the faraway pioneers.

Le Bretons joined, too, as ships' masters in the profitable, three-way trading, which sent fishing boats first to net cod off the towering coasts of Newfoundland and Massachusetts, then to head south to sell their catches, dried and hardened, in the markets of Latin America for Friday and fast-day eating. Or they would recross the Atlantic to find other Catholic customers in Italy before they sailed into harbor with cargoes picked up on their season's voyaging.

In late March or early April, Lillie and her brothers would skip down to watch the wooden vessels being fitted out for the next sailing. The waterfront of St. Helier echoed with the tapping of caulking hammers as tarred hemp was forced between the planking of hulls laid up in dry dock. The decks of ships tied up at the piers swarmed with sailmakers, chandlers, and carpenters. Crewmen staggered aboard with barrels of salt pork, fresh water that would soon turn brackish, biscuits six inches wide and an inch thick from the bakery at the foot of Pier Road. Soaked in hot water, they had to last for half a year, weevils and all.

Mrs. Le Breton would fret unless her daughter came home punctually on the eve of a sailing day. Crews were paid a month's wages in advance as a gesture towards providing for the families they would not see again until November. Their wives did not always see the few gold sovereigns passed in wages. The seamen's bars were crowded to the doors on those nights. The police hand truck was kept busy trundling drunken sailors to the dockside, to be sobered up with buckets of salt water before dawn arrived.

On the next morning's tide, the Le Breton boys helped man the capstans at the end of Albert Pier, hauling the fleet one by one out of harbor into open water. Then the sails were hoisted to the wind, and Lillie would see the ships set careful course between

Oyster Rock and the craggy pile called the Dogs' Nest before they swung west like a strange flock of water fowl towards the great ocean.

Her great-uncle, Sir Thomas Le Breton, held the supreme appointment of *bailli* of Jersey, outranking the noble Lord of the Islands himself, when Lillie was born on October 13, 1853. In his crimson robes and cap of office, he presided over the island's lawmakers as Prime Minister, chief magistrate, and plenipotentiary combined, with a unique responsibility as spokesman and defender of the free-spirited islanders in their ceaseless struggle for a measure of privilege and immunity from the dictates of England.

No man on the island in his generation won such honours as his. He would talk of the day when, as a young law student in Caen, Normandy, he was presented to the Emperor Napoleon. As Colonel Thomas Le Breton, he had commanded the militia on the sparkling September morning when Her Majesty the Queen came ashore from her yacht *Victoria & Albert* and dubbed him Sir Thomas before the day was over. After such a triumph, the Le Bretons regarded themselves as superior to any family on Jersey.

Lillie's father did not fit comfortably into the mould. She could not always reconcile herself to the difference. It might have been easier for the whole family if Father had been more ambitious, a Le Breton who pursued rank and honours, instead of an easygoing priest.

He had the presence of a leader, standing a majestic six feet tall, ruddy-cheeked, broad in the shoulders, with the unfailing courtesy of a gentleman, which was a rarity among some seigneurs. Good humour gleamed in his piercing blue eyes, though one or two of his parishioners fancied that perhaps he carried geniality too far, past the point of slipperiness.

He liked to tease them with his quotations, more often from the classics than from the Bible. "I am a man and therefore consider all that belongs to man akin to myself." Not many of them would recognise the source as Publius Terentius Afer, pre-Christian writer of comedies to amuse the Romans, or sympathise with the point of view.

In the schoolroom of the quiet house that day, Lillie could find herself listening for the crunch of his carriage wheels as he turned into the deanery yard and his cheerful good-bye to a passenger he had carried. He seldom failed to stop at the foot of St. Saviour's Hill to pick up a peasant woman, in calico bonnet and clattering sabots, laden with baskets on her way home from the glass-covered market with its fountain playing in the central hall. That, too, set him apart from most men of his station in life.

Pride in the family's achievements ran strong in Lillie, and she was proud of everything she knew about her father. William Corbet Le Breton was baptised in St. Helier's Church the month after Napoleon escaped from Elba. Like most boys of his position, he was sent off to school on the mainland. It was a full week's journey by ship and then by mail coach to Winchester in Hampshire.

He displayed every sign of Le Breton studiousness when he followed his Uncle Thomas' path to Pembroke College, Oxford, and took a degree there. Sir Thomas' practised hand showed in the help extended towards his nephew's further education. William Le Breton, bachelor of arts, received one of the fellowships to Exeter College reserved for Jerseymen under the terms set forth by King Charles I in a moment of gratitude for the island's fealty to him in his war with Oliver Cromwell.

After William, with a master's degree, was ordained deacon and then priest, he had no inclination to hurry home. London fascinated him, though it was a hard day's journey by coach from Oxford, where he served and continued to study, and he fascinated his daughter with his tales of the life he found there. Even on Piccadilly, people turned to stare at the vigorous young clergyman striding past the mansions of the rich and the shops that catered to their extravagances in food, clothing, and wine.

Listening to Father's actor's voice relate his personal history was a special delight of Lillie's childhood. She heard time and again how in London he met and courted Emilie Martin, a widow's daughter, who lived in Chelsea at 3 King's Parade in circumstances made more modest by her father's death. William took lodgings a brief walk away in one of the rows of houses that formed Robert Terrace. Uncle Thomas could not approve his nephew's choice. Surely he would have been far better advised to find a suitable Jersey girl, preferably of seigneurial blood, so that a useful dowry could again be added to the Le Breton fortune in accordance with the custom of their forebears.

But little blue-eyed Emilie had auburn curls and a fascinating smile. The heart of the Reverend Mr. Le Breton was easily stirred by such charms. Emilie felt an evident weakness for men of the faith. Mr. Kingsley, rector of the Chelsea parish of St. Luke's in which the Martins lived, had two sons. Charles, a theological student at Magdalen College, Cambridge, spent hours in the Martins' sitting room, choosing poems for her enjoyment under her mother's gaze. He spoke so enthusiastically of the girl's charms to his brother Henry that Henry determined to marry her. But William captured her first, in the year that Charles Kingsley graduated, putting himself on the road to fame as a preacher and author of *Westward Ho!* and *The Water Babies,* written later for his own children. He remembered Emilie as "the most beautiful creature I ever saw."

She became William's bride on July 8, 1842. The rector performed the ceremony in St. Luke's in the presence of a bevy of her family but with no Le Breton in the church except the bridegroom. Within the year, she gave birth to her first son, christened Francis for his great-grandfather. She was twenty-two. In the next twelve years, she would bear six more children, no more than was expected of a sturdy woman, but a drain on her health that thickened her figure and tempted her to seek more passive company than that of William, with his lusty Jersey ways. At the time of Francis' birth, an offer came, possibly inspired by Uncle Thomas, for William to return to Jersey, where a church could readily be found for him. The islanders looked on St. Saviour's as something of a Le Breton bailiwick. Two earlier generations of the family had each provided a rector there, and one of them had been Dean of Jersey. But William, nearly twenty years away from the island by now, refused the invitation.

His preoccupation with the sights of London did not stop with the modest privileges he enjoyed as a Le Breton in Society. One of the stories he told his children had him at a levee of Queen Victoria's, where the laides fluttered over the ripple of his shapely calves in black silk stockings over buckled shoes, beneath knee breeches. A blustering army general in the audience complimented him, too. "Do you know, sir," he barked, "that when you joined the church, there was a deuced fine sergeant-major spoilt?"

The Reverend Mr. Le Breton's compassion was stirred by other aspects of London, where beggars huddled in their rags in the side streets. An imponderable will to survive drove flower girls to sell themselves for any purpose for the price of the daffodils and violets they displayed in their wicker baskets. The roads he crossed were swept clear of mud and horse dung by grime-encrusted boys, who otherwise dozed on wisps of straw in alleyways with their arms around one another for the only comfort they could find. The clothes on his back, like the crinolines and fur-lined pelisses on the ladies who caught his eye, were stitched together in one-room East End tenements, where families bred and died. The matches he bought from barefooted children were made in shanties where the sulfur which produced the flame ate into the bones of their makers.

The job to which he was appointed as curate put his fingers on the pulsebeat of poverty. St. Olave's stood in Southwark on the far bank of King's Reach of the sombre-brown Thames, at the unfashionable

17

end of London Bridge. A frenzy of railway construction had demolished much of the parish, forcing its people into tenements already overcrowded. Trains rumbled in and out all day to the shriek of locomotive whistles and the reek of smoke.

The maze of narrow, sunless streets housed a horde of itinerant workers who scratched a living where they could as porters, dock labourers, hawkers, pickpockets, rat-catchers, cess-pit cleaners, and a hundred other pariah trades. His parishioners included mudlarks who delved in the slime of the river for bits of jetsam that might be sold for a penny or two. There were chimney sweeps among them, whose livelihood depended on employing "climbing boys," sent clambering on calloused knees up soot-clogged stacks at the risk of suffocation or burns that never healed.

In his first year at St. Olave's, Le Breton's name was dropped from the Oxford Calendar's alphabetical listing of past and present members of the university, never to reappear. Perhaps it was that he simply neglected to pay the small annual fee. He offered no known explanation. He remained a curate for five years, in which time Emilie bore him three more sons, William, Trevor, and Maurice. Then old Dean James Hemery died on Jersey, and William overcame his scruples about making his return.

He was not a popular choice among the clergy on the island. He had been gone too long, for one thing, and some hint of his disturbing views may have reached the ears of his future colleagues. They unanimously signed a petition urging that the new dean should be one of themselves instead of a virtual stranger. Family influence prevailed over this rebellion. Two months before his thirty-fifth birthday, William was named Rector of St. Saviour's and Dean of Jersey in January, 1850. The people of St. Olave's presented him with a silver salver to mark his leaving, engraved in terms of glowing praise for his attentions to the poor "whereby he has endeared himself to all who knew him." Lillie was proud of him, though no matter how hard she tried, it was impossible for her to picture the horrors of the slums whose people thought so highly of him when she had not so much as set eyes on a railway train.

To a visiting stranger, Jersey was paradise compared with the fetid slums the new dean had left behind him. Orchards covered the gentle slopes of the hills. On Saturday's market day, the stalls were piled with fresh-picked grapes, plums, cherries, apples, and autumn chestnuts. Turbot, whiting, mackerel, cod, and conger glistened with the rainbow colors of the sea. As early as January, the fields glowed with narcissus, jonquil, hyacinth, wallflowers, and mignonette. Acre upon acre of wheat, oats, and rye rippled in the summer sunlight. The island virtually fed itself. Shiploads of farm-made cider, vegetables, butter and cheese went off to the mainland. Every country lane was fragrant with the scent of honeysuckle and wild geranium.

Yet poverty existed as stark as anything he had seen in his years away. Field workers took home no more than a few shillings a week to the one- and two-room cottages, where families lived in fear of pestilence, which was endemic among them, when buckets carried from a pump provided their only water and cesspools their only sanitation.

The contrast between the poor and the prosperous struck more forcibly than in a teeming city, where sheer distance segregated the two societies. Here, seigneurs and labourers rubbed shoulders every day. It was commonplace for housewives of Emilie Le Breton's station to go to market to bargain in person with the country folk for butter and fresh vegetables, rather than send down a servant to carry out the haggling, as London ladies did. Distinctions between the classes were rigid, nonetheless. Seigneurs mixed only among themselves and with professional men. Professional men held themselves aloof from tradesmen and barred them from their clubs. Tradesmen confined their dealings with the poverty-stricken to those hours when their shops were open. Employees must raise their hats to their employers and address them invariably as "sir."

19

Those blessed with money maintained a close watch on their wealth. The population of St. Helier's gaol was kept down, along with the taxes, by the expedient of encouraging malcontents to slip off to France or England to escape arrest. Old men seeking workhouse relief because they were too frail for farm labour were put to work cracking stones for road repairs.

For all that, most islanders, rich or poor, were imbued with a strong sense of political independence, always ready to fight for the rights which they had wrested from a succession of English kings. A Jerseyman was reluctant to work for hire if he could avoid it, so many an estate-owner had to import English, Irish, or French labour. If a Jersey girl was employed as a servant, she would not kowtow to a master or mistress, who often turned to bringing in domestic help from America. One perceptive traveller of the day saw a clear parallel with the style that prevailed in the United States: "The spirit indeed, which animates the mass of the people—more especially, the inferior classes, is strongly republican; and the blunt independence of character and manner, as well as other evidences of this spirit, bear no small resemblance to the traits which attach to our brethren across the Atlantic."

One more brother, Clement, was added to the family before Lillie entered the world. The dean had lost the hair from the top of his head by then, but the clusters of white curls over his ears only increased his look of romantic virility. His sermons made him popular wherever he preached. "Be bold for God" was his repeated rallying cry from the pulpit. It was a slogan calculated to appeal to the men who came to hear him in threadbare Sunday frock coats and mouldering green top hats. "The struggling of your soul against the torrent of iniquity" was another catch phrase of his, though he was careful not to spell out in detail all the forms of iniquity that came to his mind.

The first winter of Lillie's life brought rare frost to

the island and an old-fashioned Christmas of snow and dense fog to England. With temperatures down to twenty degrees and more below freezing, only the warm and well-fed had cause to celebrate. A resurgence of cholera had already taken a toll of thousands. The price of food soared everywhere. Even bread was scarce. The queen, passing the holiday in accordance with her custom at Balmoral Castle in Scotland, had occasion to be much exercised by the extraordinary impudence of the government of France, which intercepted ships laden with corn intended for her hungry subjects within telescopes' sight of Jersey. That was as provoking as the behaviour of her firstborn son, twelve-year-old Bertie, Prince of Wales. In uncontrollable rebellion against the careful education to which he was being subjected, he had a habit of snatching up anything he could lay his hands on and smashing it against a wall or pitching it through the nearest window. Then he would stand in a corner to stamp and scream.

Though the dean's brood sometimes needed discipline, they were angels compared with Bertie. Their father's definitions of iniquity did not coincide with those of the imperious little woman who sat on the throne of England and reigned as temporal leader of the church in which he had been ordained.

He turned a blind eye when his sons and daughter played ghost in the graveyard, stumbling out of the trees' shadows on stilts with sheets over their heads, to scare belated strollers on St. Saviour's Hill. A letter to the island's newspaper from an outraged parishioner, threatening to end the haunting with his shotgun, put a stop to that.

The dean did take exception to his children's pastimes of stealing door knockers or stretching a string across the driveway leading up to the house at a height carefully calculated to knock off the hats of his evening callers. He was stirred to real or pretended anger when his nearest neighbour overcame his reticence one night to lodge a complaint at the deanery. Mr. Wilkins, a retired tradesman, lived with two un-

21

married sisters in the white house at the top of the lane. He made an unexpected appearance at the doorway which led to the dean's study and the schoolroom —one of Mrs. Le Breton's rules was that the main entrance, with its flowering plants under the glass portico, should be reserved for herself and invited guests.

"Forgive me, sir, but your boys and your little girl tied a string to my knocker and have kept me running to my front door for hours," said Mr. Wilkins. "I caught them at it when I chanced to hear their giggling."

It was a trick cunningly designed to put fear into Mr. Wilkins' heart. On Jersey, the superstitious took the rapping on a door or window after nightfall as an omen of impending death. *"C'est un avertissement—* a warning," they said, a signal as dreaded as a bird flying in through an open window, which foretold certain disaster within a year.

The dean assured him that the children would suffer suitable punishment, which meant no more than being sent off to bed without supper.

As his sons grew older, the audacity of their tricks increased. At the top of the marketplace, where witches had once been burned and prisoners whipped as they staggered from the courthouse to the gaol, there stood a statue identified for inquisitive newcomers to the island as a memorial to George II. The curiously imprecise "George Rex" was carved on its plinth, but set on top was a mincing figure, in buskins and toga with a laurel wreath on its curls, who resembled a homosexual queen rather than the obstinate Hanoverian king. Lillie preferred to believe the hearsay which named it as a latter-day Roman relic that a Spanish sea captain had intended as an ornament for his garden before his ship was wrecked on Jersey rocks and the cargo looted by scavengers.

She stayed at home the night her older brothers crept into the square to tar and feather the statue. The deed outraged the respectable citizens and delighted the more sacrilegious among them. The culprits were easy to trace by the tar on their hands.

The resultant scandal exploded over the dean's head. By her later account, all his children suffered at his hand for that.

Her own escapades showed signs of greater abandon as time passed. She had learned to swim at the age of four and ride when she was six. At ten she was a "pretty little girl," as one approving seigneur, Sir John Le Couteur, noted in his diary. In a community where rumour ran rife, stories piled up about Lillie. She was scurrying home with her brothers long past her bedtime, according to one tale, when they all scrambled ahead of her over the iron entrance gates of the deanery. In her haste to catch up with them, her petticoats caught on a spike of the gate. To escape her parents' scolding, she dangled there all night until the postman arrived early next morning. As soon as he had freed her, she darted across the lawn to clamber up to her bedroom window, where white jasmine and a climbing crimson rose clung to the wall of the house.

No Jerseyman doubted that the dean's daughter was a headstrong creature. In early adolescence, when her body was beginning to shape itself, she took a spill from a racehorse that she was exercising, bareback. Sir John called to see how she was progressing. "Imprudent," his diary recorded, "to allow a girl of thirteen to ride a racer without a snaffle." The following year he escorted Lillie with her parents "to examine the lads at the Industrial School in St. Martin's for my annual prize." The old seigneur pursued his interest a little later: "Took Mrs. D. and pretty Lily to the dressmaker."

The story spread that the girl, whose face and figure an increasing number of men admired, had outdone herself when she accepted her brothers' dare. If she was as bold as she pretended to be, they said, let her prove it by taking off her clothes and running naked along Deanery Lane. Everyone who knew her believed that she did not hesitate to do just that.

She was outwardly calmer now that her four older brothers were no longer there to taunt her. Francis was to sail to India to join the Bengal Pilot Service. Trevor had enlisted in the Royal Marine Light Infantry. Maurice had become a civil servant, due to serve with a measure of glory as Deputy Postmaster General of Rajputana. India, too, attracted William, a staff officer-to-be in the Royal Field Artillery in Bombay. Clement planned to go to the royal military army college at Sandhurst, England, before being commissioned as an ensign in the Northumberland Fusiliers.

There would be only young Reggie left, born when his mother was thirty-four and weary of childbearing. He found it hard to understand the changes that had come over his sister. Once she had been his best playmate. Now she spent much of her time, as she did on this particular day, dreaming about the first young man to come her way whose affections she felt stirred to return.

She skipped out of the house to meet him as they had arranged that evening. They were sauntering together, like a matched pair of pedigrees, down Patier Lane, a brief walk from the deanery, when her father saw them. A glance was enough to tell him the warmth of their regard for each other. He seemed unnecessarily perturbed when he abruptly ordered her home.

He closed the study door behind her, then turned with unaccustomed sternness in his eyes. "I forbid you ever to go out again with that young man," he said. She asked—not timidly, because that would be contrary to her nature—why he objected with such violence to a boy who had so many qualities like his own. The dean at first only repeated his instruction. This was alien to the way her adored parent had invariably treated her until this moment. She pressed him for an explanation. When it came at last, it was given reluctantly.

"Because he is your own half-brother. You must endeavour to understand. He is another son of mine."

It is unlikely that her composure deserted her. She was adept by now at controlling her feelings. Her brothers' training had taught her to think more like a man than a weeping girl. She accepted her father's

24

order, though the implications underlying his reason may have taken longer to analyse. She did not know at that time that there were others on the island like her forbidden admirer.

Perhaps only the Very Reverend Dean Le Breton could guess at the full score, but Jerseymen of the next generation included among his bastards one man, the aristocratic Mr. Perchard, who delivered the day's mail.

A visit to England was not to be undertaken lightly. Most of the fifty thousand islanders lacked the means and any inclination to travel down to the St. Helier dock and board a boat for the mainland when the return fare cost twenty shillings and a mechanic, carpenter, or mason earned no more than eighteen of those silver coins for a fifty-nine-hour week.

Most families never left the island. They were tethered as closely as the doe-eyed Jersey cattle, whose blood lines, as pure as any racehorse's, were protected by the law that prohibited the return of any one of them once the animal had been shipped away.

A journey to England meant arising at dawn to catch the steam packet's sailing at six forty-five. On Mondays, Wednesdays, or Fridays, there was a paddle steamer waiting, the *Fannie, Brittany,* or *Southampton.* On Tuesdays and Saturdays, one of the new screw steamers, the *Honfleur* or *St. Malo,* set off for the mainland with its siren exulting, belching a black cloud across the sky, scattering flakes of soot from its smokestack.

The situation at home made it essential to get away for a while. The chance of drowning in shipwreck was not to be thought of. Her mother, a less hardy soul, may have had qualms about the trip. It was she who had become the more special parent, no longer the dean, who had spoiled his daughter in all but one vital respect. Mrs. Le Breton agreed that Lillie must visit London, and she must go with her. Relatives there could be relied on to put them up during their stay.

Self-assurance was bred into the girl. Yesterday could be discounted because tomorrow always beckoned. She fancied that the mark she made on London would match the mark it would leave on her, not as the city of squalor which her father remembered but as the seat of power and glory, the capital of all the known world. "Precocious" was her own word for herself when she looked back on that year.

Mother and daughter needed new clothes for their adventure. They went together to shop on King Street. They pored over the silks at the Louvaine House, the calicos at Colebrook's, the shawls and bonnets, velveteens and merinos at Noel & Porter's, then turned the corner to Madame Boielle, the dressmaker on Bath Street, with the results of their hunting. Lillie was allowed only one new party gown. More lavish spending was impossible on the dean's income. She hoped that London would find it as beguiling as she did.

For a year and more she had been allowed to taste what entertainments the island had to offer. The choice was limited but enjoyable by the standards of a girl who had experienced nothing more sophisticated. Perennially mild weather made a picnic on the beach something to look forward to for more than half the year. Or she would ride up to Sorel Point, where ceaseless wind rippled the water four hundred feet below. Gulls wheeled behind the ploughman's team when spring came. Autumn blackberries waited for the picking in hollows among the bracken. She would stand at the cliff's edge, staring out towards England, out of sight over the horizon.

At weekends, the draughty, dilapidated, corrugated-iron arena known only as the Tin Shed usually offered a concert, a dance, or some boxing bouts. Poole's wondrous diorama made an appearance in Oddfellows' Hall, and she sat in the audience watching sea battles unroll on gaudily painted canvas cylinders while the pianist rattled out "Rule, Britannia" and the drummer supplied thunder and the cannons' crash.

She went with her family, as duty demanded, to the Grand Review held on the pale sands of St. Aubin's Bay to honour the queen's birthday every May. Her Majesty's representative was ranked these days as lieutenant governor, now that the old titles of Lord of the Islands and Governor had passed into history. The bewhiskered English general who invariably occupied the post was obliged to camouflage his disdain at the motley parade that passed before him in the march past and console himself with the thought that his term lasted only five years. The first of the marchers, red-coated soldiers of the queen from the battalion of army regulars stationed on garrison duty, always passed muster, thanks to days of preliminary spit-and-polishing under the corporals' steely eyes. But the horse artillery that followed could be counted on to run into problems when the limbers' wheels dug into soft sand, and the russet-cheeked militiamen who brought up the rear were a sorry story. Discipline was no better than could be expected when sergeants were chosen on the strength of their willingness to donate a five-pound note for beer on the annual outing.

After half a century of peace with France, the British army remained a powerful factor in island living. Lillie heard the military bands' faithful performances of Myerbeer and *La Vie Parisienne* at the musical promenades which brightened winter evenings at the Imperial Hotel. She asked every season for a new dress to wear to the supreme event on the social calendar, the militia ball.

Oddfellows' Hall was made over with potted palms, bunting, and banks of flowers for the momentous night. Outside, Don Street was choked with rented carriages. Some of the coachmen and footmen showed the polish of having been trained in the service; others among them were labourers and apprentices, as evidenced by their broad grins and misbuttoned livery. General Guy, in corsets and gold braid, would take the arm of a lady of seigneurial quality and lead the grand march. Lillie's ambitions soared to the point where she could picture herself occupying that dazzling role someday. Then the violins of the uniformed musicians struck up the lively bars of a schottische or a quadrille—never a waltz. For all the reputation of Johann Strauss as an uncrowned king in Vienna, his music had not yet reached Jersey's shores.

The cream of society that mixed in Government House had once been almost exclusively Jersey-bred. It was adulterated more and more by the English product. Other Le Bretons had the entrée; the dean's family, possibly by his choice, was not so privileged. They were not to be excluded, but there was something outré about the children's behaviour, and whispers about the dean could not be entirely ignored.

With its sentry mounted in the entrance lodge, Government House stood in its grounds off St. Saviour's Hill, a few minutes' walk from the deanery. The style of the lieutenant governor set the tone for the seigneurs and milords who moved in his circle. Few other families were invited. Ceremonial at a levée or a banquet was every bit as rigid as at the court of the queen herself. Gentlemen bowed to him, ladies curtsied, hands were kissed. The dining table was set with flowers, nameplates, and serried silver. Etiquette called for a toast to be drunk to "The Duke," which meant the sovereign, though she chanced to be a queen, and "Duke of Normandy" was never listed as a royal title.

As Lillie made her preparations to visit London, she had never sat down to dine among the starchy splendours of Government House. Major General Philip Melmoth Nelson Guy, who had just started his term of office, was a remote autocrat to her. She had an idea of his vice-regal importance from the homage which tradition said must be paid to him as representative of the queen at the *cour d'héritage,* held twice a year.

The dean's attendance was an obligation which he

could not ignore. In the palmier days of the relationship between them, his daughter was proud of the part he had to play as the preeminent church dignitary of the States of Jersey. A garrison guard armed with pikes and halberds lined the corridor and the staircase leading to the courtroom. Between their ranks filed a procession headed by the undersheriff bearing the massive silver-gilt mace presented by Charles II "as a proof of his royal affection," in the words of its Latin inscription, "toward the Isle of Jersey (in which he has been twice received in safety, when he was excluded from the remainder of his dominions). . . ."

The new *bailli,* John Hammond, who succeeded Uncle Thomas, followed immediately behind, ahead of the lieutenant governor himself in token of superior office. Red-robed judges, bemedalled officers of the Crown and the lieutenant governor's staff followed. Every formal word of the ceremony was in French. After opening prayers, the roll was called of the seigneurs owing allegiance to the queen. Loyalty was not the only reason for their being there. If they neglected to pay homage on three consecutive occasions, their land holdings could be forfeited.

As he heard his name, each seigneur rose and made a deep bow to the lieutenant governor. His fief was his to hold without challenge for at least six months more. The law of the island added a bonus for its lords. With the act of fealty taken care of, the *prêvots* and *chef sergents* reeled off the names of all islanders who had recently died without leaving heirs. The seigneur of the district concerned drew the rents from the dead man's property for a full year.

Not only the pageantry of the *cour d'héritage* impressed Lillie at an impressionable age. Jersey law which gave the seigneurs these privileges of inheritance applied only to men. A woman had no such rights. A woman could never rank as a seigneur or own property in her name. A woman was little more than a chattel, like a plough or a stick of furniture, in spite of her father's fine words about a place in the sun for her sex.

Breakfast on sailing day had to be a hurried affair of porridge, bread and butter, and homemade jam, not unusual by standards at the deanery, where meals were plain and often sketchy. In her smart bonnet and bustled skirt, Lillie drew her expected share of attention as she and her mother boarded the steamer. The reek of hot oil and coal dust drifted up from the engine-room companionway. Lillie continued to think of her mother as the better looking of the two of them. The dean discouraged vanity in Lillie. "Oh, you should have seen her mother when she was young" was his usual reply to any compliment about his daughter.

Mrs. Le Breton had different thoughts. Materially, she had bettered herself by marrying above her mother's social rank. Perhaps Lillie could do the same, not on Jersey but in England. She had already been favourably noticed by a most distinguished gentleman, Lord Suffield, who had just been appointed lord-in-waiting to the queen. The bearded middle-aged baron, whose first wife, Cecilia, had borne him two sons and seven daughters, was one of the new category of Jersey estate-owners. He had been introduced to Lillie at a well-chaperoned summer picnic.

Her mother had caught his remark: "Do you know, Miss Le Breton, that you are beautiful? You ought to have a season in London." When he had heard of their visit, he invited them to dine at his London house at 46 Upper Grosvenor Street. Who could tell what such an introduction to society might lead to? Mrs. Le Breton indulged her dreams of splendour for Lillie.

It would be too much to expect the honour of actually seeing the queen, who rarely showed herself in public, insisting on the seclusion of Windsor Castle, seven years a widow and "invisible" in the opinion of Mr. Gladstone, who had recently succeeded Mr. Disraeli as Prime Minister and First Lord of the Treasury. But it might be possible to catch a glimpse somewhere of the Prince of Wales, who, everyone said, was quite unlike his mother in character and habits. He was out and about all over town whenever he and his admirable wife, Princess Alexandra, were in residence at Marlborough House. But the princess was occupied with plans to accompany him on a forthcoming tour of Europe and the Near East now that her fourth child had been successfully delivered. His circle was as remote as the moon from the everyday London rounds of a provincial dean's wife and daughter.

Her mother's reminiscing about the city in which she had grown up had given Lillie little idea of what to expect. Her own fertile imagination had fallen far short of the reality. St. Helier's streets were so narrow that one cart could not pass another along most of them. Here the avenues appeared as broad as fields, yet they were clogged with a dozen varieties of spic-and-span private carriages fighting for the right of way with four-wheeled growlers and hansom cabs.

On the island, dresses were long, but hoop skirts impractical except for the *haut monde*. Here, the fashionable ladies were encircled in crinolines as wide as their owners' height, making them look oddly like inverted, legless cones as they fussed along the smart shopping streets. Island milliners on King Street prided themselves on the true French style of the bonnets they sold, but Lillie gasped at the incredible confections of feathers and lace which perched on the upswept curls of London women.

Lillie was overwhelmed. Nothing had prepared her for this. She had to admit to herself that her hope of leaving a mark on this uncaring, incomprehensible city should be dismissed as a childish fancy, like wishing that a sand castle would withstand the incoming tide. She could scarcely understand the idiom of the language whined by cockney hawkers at the street corners and drawled in the salons where the two Le Bretons were asked to tea.

She appreciated nothing of the subjects she heard discussed: the rivalries between Mr. Gladstone's Liberals and Mr. Disraeli's Tories; parties that lasted for days at the great estates of the peerage; the scandals endemic at the apex of the social pyramid in which, it was whispered, even the prince was embroiled. The newspapers, including *The Times,* had hinted at an affair of his with an actress, Hortense Schneider, and everyone knew what kind of woman made her living performing on the stage.

Lillie's despair reached its nadir on the evening they dined at the Suffields'. The baron fitted the mould of the English aristocrat. He owned twelve thousand acres of Norfolk, where he commanded the militia artillerymen in their red tunics and pillbox caps. His country house there, Gunton Park, hung with historical paintings said to be worth a fortune in themselves, made him a neighbour of the prince at Sandringham. Suffield was master of the county foxhounds and staghounds. He had married another baron's daughter, Revelstoke's, and his brother Walter's wife was a Rothschild. It was understood that Walter's name was not to be mentioned. "He would do anything dirty for a five-pound note" was one of the kinder remarks made about him.

The invitation to dine took Lillie and her mother to their first London ball. From the moment the butler announced their arrival at Upper Grosvenor Street, Lillie realized that her new gown would beguile nobody. It made her feel like a clumsy peasant, inferior to the Suffields' maids in their smart black dresses and starched white caps and aprons. She did not even know how to make a graceful entrance into the dining room, or that young ladies, as a matter of course, did not eat cheese at dinner parties.

The array of silver knives, forks, and spoons set at her place at the dinner table among the paraphernalia of roses, candlesticks, and epergnes bewildered her. As one course followed another—strange tastes of fish and fowl and meat, blended with rich sauces— she survived only by peeking at her neighbours to see what items of silverware to pick up next.

The worst disgrace came when the guests moved into the ballroom. Everybody in London waltzed, except those in the closed circle surrounding the queen, who frowned on all dancing as irreverent frivolity, unworthy of the memory of the prince consort. Lillie could not follow her partners' steps as they tried, with coattails flying, to whirl her around the gleaming floor. She stumbled as awkwardly as a colt, murmuring blushing apologies, unable even to manage her skirt to keep it clear of her slippers. She gave up and sat out the rest of the evening on a sofa beside her mother, a gauche, embarrassed wallflower, waiting impatiently for the humiliation to end.

❧ II ❧

She reconciled herself to making the island a permanent home as soon as she returned there. Visions of conquering London were put aside, together with the pitiful clothes she had packed for the trip. Most days, she took out a horse to go riding with Reggie on the beaches and down the lanes to the cliffs. She curled up on the window seat of the library to read by the hour until her mother told her, "I do think it unwise to spend so much time with your head in those books. You must not ruin your eyes, dearest." She paid no more attention to that than to most of Mother's fluttering.

Nothing in her nature could turn Lillie into a recluse. The irresistible subject of men continued to occupy her. If she had no choice but to live according to the standards to which she had been born, she may as well be married. An early suitor combined two of the characteristics which the Le Bretons normally regarded as worthy—a strong church upbringing and an army career. Arthur Longley, aged twenty-three, joined the garrison on Jersey as a staff paymaster. His father, the Right Honourable and Most Reverend Charles Thomas Longley, occupied the highest rank in the English church as Archbishop of Canterbury after having held the lesser office of Archbishop of York. His mother was the Honourable Caroline Sophia, daughter of Lord Congleton.

Arthur Longley, paying his respects to the dean, met Lillie and was captivated immediately. Sparing no time to tell his father of his intentions, he took the first opportunity to propose marriage to the girl. Perhaps, for all his speed, she found him less exciting, too poor, or lacking the looks of the forbidden half-brother. She gave him no firm answer but enough encouragement for him to plead his case with the dean. Longley was crushed by his reception. "Are you aware that my daughter is not yet fifteen and far too young to marry?" her father said. Disappointment and the death of the archbishop from bronchitis combined to prompt the young man to apply to be transferred off the island.

There was no shortage of callers ambitious to court Lillie. None of them appealed to her until another young soldier came to light as the man she wanted for a husband. Edward Hemery Le Breton was an ensign in the Royal Irish Regiment, stationed at Aldershot barracks, Hampshire. He and Lillie shared the same great-grandfather in Francis, the first of the family to become Dean of Jersey.

Edward and Lillie announced their engagement, with no thought that the family would do anything but congratulate them. They received a saddening surprise. After conferences with his relatives, the dean delivered the verdict: "Edward would not be a suitable husband for you. There has been too much marrying between cousins already." That made three romances stifled for one reason or another. Lillie had cause to wonder whose bride she might eventually be.

She may have been tempted to try finding an answer in the witchcraft which most islanders believed in. Witches and warlocks, goblins and ghosts, kelpies and nixies haunted the minds of the peasants, and Lillie knew the tales. Witches conjured up storms at sea and danced in their covens at Rocqueberg Point, where the devil's deputy, *Le Tchézoit,* had left the print of his cloven hoof on the rock.

Les petits faîtiaux, the little people, lived in underground mansions all over the island, as greedy as magpies and rich enough to shoe all their horses with silver. A woman who once saw one of them steal a silver knife of hers had an eye plucked out in vengeance by the pixie. It was only by the grace of God, or an oversight of the Infernal, that means existed to ward off evil. Turning your jacket inside out protected you from a goblin's tricks. Wearing a piece of herb-of-grace root on a white ribbon around your neck cured any illness and broke a sorcerer's spell.

If Lillie was anxious to learn when she would marry, all she need do was follow the custom of local girls, who went to the dark cave near Bonne Nuit Bay to drop a pebble in the water. Counting the ripples told the number of months that would pass before marriage. It was a perilous undertaking. The kelpie who lived in the cave could read thoughts. He stirred up the sea like a seething cauldron whenever he went swimming and shrieked with delight when he sank a boat. Islanders related the fate of Anne-Marie, a girl as handsome as Lillie, who was seized by the kelpie and carried off by him to the depths of the cave as his bride. By a miracle, the crow of a cockerel sounded from a farm nearby, driving the creature to flight. At the point of death from drowning, Anne-Marie was saved.

Lillie's superstitions did not carry her as far as Bonne Nuit Cave. A pebble let fall from her fingers would produce too many ripples to be tallied. Marriage for her lay some five years ahead. Her future bridegroom had only recently arrived on the island, to wed another girl.

Edward Langtry, a morose young man of twenty-two, hailed from Belfast, where his grandfather George had made himself the city's wealthiest shipowner, who pioneered the service to Liverpool across the Irish Sea and whose vessels sailed regularly to London. On his death, his son Richard succeeded him in the business, but Edward had been fatherless now for eleven years, and the family was considering selling the seventeenth-century Fortwilliam House and its grounds that stretched down to the shore from Buttermilk Lane.

Edward had supposedly "come down from Oxford," where he claimed to have studied law. Some of his associates, skeptical about his attainments as a scholar, concluded that he had done no more than come down by train. He had no profession and showed no interest in any kind of career. Richard Langtry had spoilt his son. Edward could only be categorized as an amiable ne'er-do-well, content to spend his days aboard his eighty-foot yacht, *Red Gauntlet,* which carried a white-suited crew of five as well as a captain.

The climate and lazy living ·that Jersey offered his kind, with sailing and fishing to his heart's content, enchanted Edward Langtry, reared in a Quaker household in dank Belfast. *Red Gauntlet* spent more and more time at anchor in St. Helier Harbour. The sun-tanned girls of the island attracted him, too, but he chose as his wife a pale, languid beauty, Jane Frances Price, who was British, born like him in Belfast. Her father, Francis, had retired from the civil service of Ceylon to live in "Bel Air," a house in St. Saviour's parish. Edward and eighteen-year-old Jane were married in St. Mark's Church the year after Lillie had made her disillusioned return from London. His brother Richard and one of Jane's four brothers were their witnesses.

Lillie was too young and too exuberant to suffer the pangs of hurt pride indefinitely. The dream of life in England stirred again in her. The snippets of news from London printed in a daily column in the *British Review* were fuel for her fancy. The queen had opened a new bridge over the Thames at Blackfriars. Charles Dickens, who mocked the values Lillie believed in, had been buried in Westminster Abbey. Princess Alexandra was expecting her fifth child. The prince himself had been served with a subpoena to appear as a witness at hearings to determine the sanity of Lady Harriet Mordaunt, whom he had known since her childhood; now she claimed that he had slept with her more than once.

"Has there ever been any improper familiarity or criminal act between yourself and Lady Mordaunt?" he was asked in court before Lord Penzance. "Never!" came his emphatic reply, and the spectators cheered.

That summer, the lords and ladies who visited Jersey whispered that His Royal Highness might be called to court again. Rumours in Westminster had it that he would be named as a corespondent when Lord Sefton sued his countess for divorce. In fact, that scandal never broke. The proprietor of one newspaper that published the canard, William Lang of the *Sheffield Daily Telegraph,* was hauled before Leeds Assizes and fined 50 pounds for libel.

Before the year ended, with thick frost blanketing the fields in the coldest weather any Jerseyman could remember, the first of a series of tragedies struck home at the deanery. The news came by telegraph, which tied the island to the mainland unless the cable broke in winter storms. Lieutenant Trevor Le Breton lay dead in Toronto at the age of twenty-five. His mother took the loss harder than anyone else in the family.

It was unthinkable for her to share in the celebration that marked the trial run of Jersey's long-awaited railway on a late afternoon ten days afterwards. Mr. Pickering of Noirmont Manor had finally felt compelled to put up most of the capital. Hardheaded professional men jeered at his foolhardiness, when the necessary Act of the English Parliament to permit the laying of track set the maximum fare at only sixpence first-class and twopence for an open coach ride on the seventeen-minute journey between St. Helier and St. Aubin.

The dean was invited to add his presence to the inaugural ceremony conducted by General Guy. Lillie would go with him in her mother's place. Flags fluttered over the roof of the little station that hugged the stone seawall at St. Helier. The militia had turned out in a guard of honour at the other end of the line. A few rousing words from General Guy were capped by a thirteen-gun salute by a battery of the Royal Jersey Artillery. The whistle of the locomotive *Haro Haro* shrilled out in triumph, and every gull in sight took off in protest.

The guests of honour piled into the four first-class carriages, shipped in from Liverpool, to be trundled along the track to St. Aubin and a champagne buffet at the home of Mr. Pickering. Lillie was intrigued to enter the house which long ago had been Le Breton property. A succession of owners had enlarged the place and added the white columns on either side of the front door. Most of the furniture was new and stylish. Something akin to envy flickered in her, which was rare in this girl who felt increasingly that somehow she would make her own way in the world, indebted to no one, an independent being, subservient to no man.

Two years and seven months after his marriage, Edward Langtry was a widower. In spite of the sunshine and the gentle, flower-scented air, pale-skinned, childless Jane fell victim to tuberculosis in her father's house, where she and Edward lived. The disease struck indiscriminately at rich and poor, like the fever which surged through the population periodically, with no one suspecting that contaminated well-water might be the carrier. He buried the memory of her beauty for future use as a yardstick against which to measure all women. There was no change in his pursuit of idleness.

Another of Lillie's brothers died in the service of the queen. Francis Le Breton, of the Bengal Pilot Service, would never again leave Calcutta, capital of British India, more than seven thousand miles away. His name on a memorial stone in St. Saviour's churchyard would commemorate him. It was Mrs. Le Breton who once more felt most keenly the pain of bereavement. Sometimes it was hard to "be bold for God."

Edward found a new companion when William Le Breton came home on leave with a mind to marry.

Among their children, Mr. and Mrs. Price had another daughter, Elizabeth Anne. She was William's choice. His newfound friend decided that the wedding of William and his sister-in-law must be as spectacular an affair as the island had seen in years. Lillie would be one of the four bridesmaids, Reggie one of the equal number of groomsmen, the other three being brothers of the bride.

St. Helier buzzed with anticipation for weeks in advance. The dean's son had been gone from the island long enough to pique the town's curiosity to discover what the young rascal had succeeded in making of himself. Elizabeth Price's family had money to spare, so the bride was bound to be worth seeing. The ceremony would be held in the evening, so any workingman with a mind to do so could find time to attend the show. There were rumours that a torchlight procession was going to lead the bride and groom from St. Saviour's church.

Lillie went back to Madame Boielle's to be fitted for her new white grenadine dress and ruby satin tunic. Madame Nicolle of Halket Place made up the bridesmaids' hats of the same red fabric, trimmed with pearls and long ostrich feathers—"in the style of Louis Quinze," she announced. It would all be as fashionable as Jersey society could aspire to, something certain to draw a crowd. The dean, of course, would conduct the ceremony, with the support of his vicar, the Reverend Mr. Rey, the organ, and the choir. Edward was to serve as best man.

The spectators had already begun to gather on St. Saviour's Hill when the ushers led the first wedding guests to their places in the church at four o'clock. Soon afterwards, carriages blocked the driveway and stood in line halfway down the hill, horses snorting impatiently, postilions chatting with each other. Ninety minutes later, with another half hour to wait before the service began, the mob of sightseers overflowed the rear pews of the church, filled the churchyard and stood on its walls, shutting the road completely. The handful of paid police called in the parish's volunteer *centeniers, vingteniers,* and constable's officers, who, in descending order of seniority, always had a role in maintaining law and order. An affair like this might well follow a sturdy Jersey tradition and develop into a full-scale melee.

When, with fifteen minutes to go, Lillie and her companion bridesmaids made their appearance, the groomsmen had to elbow a way for them into the church. By now, the congregation was climbing on top of the pews and clinging to the pillars for a better view. Only the organ, played fortissimo, could be heard above the din. In the vestry, Edward had to wonder whether perhaps he had been responsible for stirring up what threatened to turn into a riot.

As November darkness fell, crewmen from *Red Gauntlet* lit carriage lamps to hang from the churchyard trees. A roar from the crowd announced the arrival of the bride, not a minute late, wearing white silk over a satin quilted petticoat. The dean, his congregation agreed, had never been in better voice as he stood in the pulpit, gaslight shining on his leonine head. Some of them murmured about the emotion they detected when he uttered his blessing on the first of his children he had married. *"Quel sentiment de ferveur!"* noted the account in the *Chronique de Jersey* in the following Friday's issue.

Trouble broke out as soon as the ceremony was over and the bride and groom tried to leave the church porch. Edward's carriage waited for them in the darkness, marked by the ship's lanterns glowing red and green. His crew, with other lanterns held above their heads, struggled to hold their places in the surging mob that fought to get a closer look, while the congregation struggled to follow behind the bridal pair.

Like everyone else in the wedding party, Lillie was lost in the frenzy. One woman in the crowd screamed as she was crushed against the graveyard wall and pinned there, face against the stone, blood flowing down her cheeks. Another had her hat snatched from her head and, with it, the switch of false hair she wore as a chignon. A third felt her earrings ripped

40

away and suspected that was no accident. Dresses by the dozen were torn to rags. One spectator told the police that he had lost a boot. Altogether, in Jerseymen's opinion, it was as exciting as the new railway and superior as an entertainment to Poole's diorama, since it had not cost a penny.

Dinner started late at the Prices' house. The wedding party had been held up at the church until the police cleared away the crowd. After dinner, Edward took the guests on to his own contribution to the festivities—a ball at the Jersey Yacht Club. Lillie was impressed by his hospitality, which compared well with anything she had seen in London. Pennants and bunting festooned the walls. *Red Gauntlet's* seamen, changed into spotless white, were put to work again with their lanterns, lining the staircase. The tables were spread for supper with dishes almost as elaborate as those she remembered at the Suffields' five years ago. The evening persisted in her memory, rose-tinted like an entertainment from the *Arabian Nights*. Perhaps Edward, a widower for two years now, could be counted on as a donor of similar gifts to her. He was a man worth considering as a suitor. As a final mark of esteem, he lent William *Red Gauntlet* for his honeymoon. Lillie set out to capture Edward as her own.

Before the week was over, he asked to speak privately with the dean. He would like permission, he said, to propose to Miss Le Breton. Her father was no more enthusiastic about this insipid young Ulsterman than he had been about the others who had sought to take away his only daughter. She had already accepted a diamond ring from Edward, though that was a secret from her parents. She could see in him just the kind of man she needed—someone she could easily dominate; a husband who would supply her with the key to escape from the island; a generous, unassuming provider of the material things she wanted, who would enable her to establish herself in England.

"You are too young, my dear, to be married," the dean told her once more, but she was past twenty

41

and insistent on her rights, as he had taught her to be. She also claimed as a matter of course that she loved Edward Langtry, but there was no evidence of that.

Her father commissioned Clement, the hardest-headed of his sons, to look into the prospect's background. Clement, a lieutenant now in the Royal Fusiliers, would resign from the army pleading ill health the following year and take up the law.

If Lillie chose to marry for money, then the dean and his son would see to it that she was comfortably provided for in advance. The Langtrys did not object to settling the sum of ten thousand pounds on the future daughter-in-law. She would draw the income immediately and inherit the principal in the event of Edward's death. The Le Bretons had an instinct for business when the occasion arose. The deal struck with the Langtrys showed the touch of the girl's shrewdness. It had shown itself before. At fourteen, she had taken a spiritless mare, Flirt, bought by the dean for something less than two pounds, then had fattened and ridden the animal to win as a racer in order for Flirt to be sold for twenty times more than her purchase price.

Details of the marriage settlement were resolved by the middle of January, when Edward asked Lillie to be his wife. She had known for six weeks what her answer would be. Her father and mother maintained their arguments against the marriage. "I had wanted you to see rather more of life before you became any man's wife," the dean said. "If only you might have just one season in London first," said his wife. With Lillie gone, she would have only Reggie of her seven children left at home. Pleading only strengthened her daughter's determination that this engagement was not going to be broken off.

Even Reggie, the closest of her brothers, took sides against her. Possibly he knew her better than anyone. There was a sensuousness in her which she had inherited from their father. In her case, it was held under tight control, but it was irrepressible, a determining factor in her nature. Edward, by comparison, seemed strangely passionless. In Reggie's judgement, he would make a poor mate for his sister.

She refused to listen to her brother. The engagement was officially announced. With the diamond of her ring, brought out of hiding, she carefully cut her initials in the pane of the schoolroom window where she had once traced them in the mist made by her breath. Now they served as a memorial to the past and a token of what she wanted from the future. "I'm going to be married," she gaily told the cook.

"How soon is the wedding?"

"Oh, not yet. Mother says I'm too young. But I can wear my engagement ring."

She was willing to wait only two months more. The dean, by special licence, married his daughter to Edward Langtry on March 9, 1874, five years all but a day after Langtry had taken Jane as his wife. In after years, Lillie used to say starkly that she fell in love with *Red Gauntlet,* not with her husband. "To become the mistress of the yacht, I married the owner. . . ."

She had acquainted herself in advance with every inch of the vessel on the occasions when Edward invited her to go cruising with him to the French coast and back. Mrs. Le Breton could not overcome her fear of the water. The memory was too fresh for her of the disaster of the London & South Western paddle-wheeler *Normandy,* making full speed through heavy fog when she collided with a freighter at the cost of thirty-four lives. The dean gladly filled his wife's place as chaperone, amused to see how his firm-jawed daughter set about capturing Edward's attention. Seasickness was unknown to her in all the years she had gone sailing, but aboard *Red Gauntlet* she was careful to show just a trace of ladylike *mal de mer*.

Her motives were well concealed on her wedding day. To avoid the turmoil of William's marriage, the ceremony was held almost secretively early in the morning in St. Saviour's Church. Clement was her only brother to attend. The Langtry family was

43

noticeably absent. Reggie refused to be part of what he regarded as a mockery. Instead, he went riding on the cliffs. Lillie was not to see him alive again.

There were some odd inconsistencies about the events of that day. She remembered her husband as having been "about thirty years old." He was, in fact, twenty-six. He was born, he said when he was married to Jane, in Belfast. Now he claimed Islay, Scotland, as his birthplace. He had formerly listed himself as a "gentleman." Now he was "independent."

His new wife made a show of conserving his money. "I hated the idea of a big wedding," she said later, "and the conventional bridal array." She wore her going-away dress at the altar. After a wedding breakfast at the yacht club, they sailed immediately aboard *Red Gauntlet,* which had served before as honeymoon quarters for Edward and Jane, William and Lizzie.

It was an unemotional send-off, with the bride as calm as the flat, blue sea. On the beaches, the carts of the seaweed gatherers stood waiting for loading with the *vraic,* which was spread on the fields every season at this time to enrich the earth. Fishing nets were spread to dry in the sun alongside boats hauled out on the tide.

A more tender being might have been moved by the thought of leaving the island birthplace or else exulted in the feeling that prison doors were opening at last. Whatever else she was, Lillie was not sentimental. The question that occupied her mind was simply what might happen next.

Marriage for both of them fell short of giving the satisfactions they had looked forward to. If one was more disappointed than the other, it was Edward. Lillie was incomparably different from the wife he had adored—wilful where Jane was compliant, demanding where Jane had been delicate. Before long, he dropped into the habit of measuring one against the other and turned aside all compliments he heard paid to the new Mrs. Langtry's looks. "Oh, you should have seen the first girl I married," he would say.

What physical joy Lillie found in the relationship centred on *Red Gauntlet* and the sea. She was disturbed to discover Edward to be "extremely shy," as she described him. Resignation showed itself in his melancholy face and hunched shoulders. The ends of his trim, brown moustache seemed to droop in frustration.

She remembered their honeymoon pleasures in terms of crowding on sail and cresting through broken water, drenched with salt, never of warmth or so much as mild affection for the man she had chosen to marry. They spent a month's cruising, then sailed into Belfast to give his mother her first sight of Lillie.

She passed inspection. The Langtrys were eager to convert the son to their own patterns of good works and respectability. Edward was invited to join in running the steamship business. Domestic life in Northern Ireland played no part in Lillie's formidable plans. Edward turned down the offer.

She had no inkling of an idea about running a household. Sewing and cooking had never interested her, and her mother had given her no training. There was no heritage of French cooking to intrigue Lillie on Jersey, where conger-eel soup was a staple of diet and tubs of salt pork served through the winter as a substitute for beef. Practical experience in housecleaning was out of the question for a girl brought up in her circumstances, when servants were cheap and plentiful, with a kitchen-maid counting herself lucky to be paid eight pounds a year, since scrubbing pots and pans was a lot easier than toiling in a field or sweating in a factory. More than one and a half million men and women of all ages worked as servants on the mainland.

Though she had no definable objective in mind, she had faith in what the future would hold for her in spite of her present discontentment. Good things were bound to happen sooner or later if she willed them to come about. There was a growing streak of mysticism in her, mixed in with her belief in her powers of summoning the spirits. Even skeptics were impressed by a recent manifestation in the assembly rooms at Birmingham. A spiritualist medium there, Benjamin Hawkes, a toy dealer by trade, told his audience how he had once felt his hand clasped by the Apostle Paul.

The magical touch made it simple, Hawkes said, to understand how Thomas at the Crucifixion thrust his hand into the gaping side of "the Personification of Divine Love." At the instant he spoke that phrase, Hawkes toppled dead on the platform. A doctor at the inquest concluded that congestion of the lungs had killed the medium, but the jury would have none of that. "Died by the visitation of God" was their verdict. If the Lord exercised such power, Lillie decided, there was no knowing what He might do for her.

Edward's income of three thousand guineas a year had served him handsomely on Jersey, where an English shilling was worth not twelve but thirteen pence and seventeen and a half ounces made up a pound's weight. One shilling bought a pound of best local beef, not the cheaper cuts shipped in by schooner from Spain; or a dozen eggs, a pigeon for a pie, two pounds of pork, a pair of crabs. A cabbage or a lettuce cost no more than a penny, a hundred Havana cigars less than a pound.

But in this new marriage, he urgently needed more capital. Rents from the properties in Belfast which Richard Langtry had previously put in his son's name would not suffice. Edward had to sell *Red Gauntlet* and two other boats he owned, retaining only a racing yawl, *Gertrude*. Lillie expressed no regret over the loss of the yacht which only a few months earlier had typified splendour to her. The past could be left to take care of itself.

They spent most of the summer on *Gertrude,* sailing from one regatta to another from Cowes to Le Havre. It was a sport that even princes could not always afford. The biggest racing cutters could weigh as much as three hundred tons and carry a crew of close to thirty. The new millionaires delighted in out-doing each other in the size, speed, and luxury of their toys. Even *nouveaux riches* Americans like John Pierpont Morgan, aspiring to old-world grandeur on pyramiding profits from his American railroads, were permitted to join in. "You can do business with any-body," Mr. Morgan allowed with new-world candour, "but you can only sail a boat with a gentleman."

Lillie kept her husband's enthusiasm warm for yacht-racing. The Langtrys had to be classified as poor re-lations at the tables of the yacht-club rich, but there a certain camaraderie among sailing men that blurred sharper distinctions of wealth. "I gained an appreciation of the power exerted by the owners of large yachts," she recalled later. "One day, I decided, I would become one of them."

Gertrude, a mere eighty tons, chalked up some vic-tories in her class. Edward might have won more of-ten if he had not indulged his wife's whim of taking to her bunk when excitement faded. The wind died one evening in a race up the Thames from the Nore lightship and she retired to bed in disgust. Early next morning, the incoming tide carried the yawl first past the winning post, with Edward at the helm. He hesi-tated to fire the mandatory cannon to announce his arrival for fear of waking her. By the time breakfast was served from the galley and Lillie was ready for a new day, two other boats drifted clear of the mud-banks on which they had been caught. One of them was declared the winner, because Edward had dis-qualified himself out of deference to his wife.

She set her sights high in the choice of their first home. On Langtry money, she intended to regain some of the high ancestral style of the Le Bretons. Noirmont Manor would make a fitting background for her and Edward. The place stood conveniently empty after the departure of the Pickerings, his schemes for a prosperous railway shattered by winds and tides which had devastated the seafront track.

She felt a glow of satisfaction every time the car-riage turned into the narrow lane between craggy banks grey with lichen leading down towards Belcroute Bay. Another turn past a woodland waterfall under arched sycamores brought her to the wrought-iron gates of the big square house on Ghost Hill. A chimney stack soared at each end, a porch stretched across its front. From its westerly windows, she could see the spires of St. Helier.

A steep, cobbled path wound alongside the brick wall of the ornamental gardens in the shade of chestnut trees, taking her down to a pebble beach, broken by pink rocks, and a slipway, where a small boat could be launched at high tide. Or she could walk by the mile over the rising cliffs to Noirmont Point, where tethered cows grazed on the thin grass and the constant breeze carried the scent of flowering yellow gorse.

She spent much of her time alone, not by choice, because she had an aversion to solitude. But Edward did not share her sense of achievement in a Le Breton's return to Noirmont, and Reggie consistently refused to see her. Whenever she drove to the deanery, her brother would be sure to take himself off at the sight of her carriage.

She went sailing from the beach one day with two of Sir Robert Marrett's sons. It could be a hazardous undertaking when the wind was in the wrong quarter; sailboats had been overturned in Belcroute inlet before. A sudden gust tipped the cutter over. Lillie was a powerful enough swimmer to survive, but her companions were drowned. Islanders thought she was lucky to escape alive. She dismissed the idea. If possible consequences always had to be calculated, no risk would be worth taking.

She sharpened the distinction between her new mode of living and the rough ways of the island. It was no longer amusing to do down to St. Helier on Saturday evenings, as she had done with her brothers, to listen to the plaintive music of concertina-players on the street corners and watch helpless drunkards being wheeled down King Street strapped to the police truck, or to go to holiday sports in the park to see the

Punch and Judy show, the greasy-pole climb, the co-conut shy.

The gap between her class of people and the work-ingmen of Jersey had increased, if anything, recently. The island was not immune from the slump in farm prices brought about by the sudden, overwhelming in-flux into Europe of wheat from American prairies. John Pierpont Morgan and his like had organized the laying of thousands of miles of new railroad track across the plains of the postbellum United States. Freight trains carried settlers' crops for less than cost to booming ports of the country's eastern seaboard. Cyrus McCormick's newfangled mechanical harvesters, invented of necessity because labour was scarce, did the work of a hundred field hands. The new oceango-ing steamships made it easy to dump cheap grain in the ports of the Old World.

The steamships' routes across the storm-tossed wa-ters of the world were stitching together the patterns of a new era. Loads of one cheap commodity, grain, were ferried onto the docks of London and Liverpool, Southampton and St. Helier. Another cheap com-modity, mankind, was ferried out. St. Helier suddenly blossomed with advertisements offering bargain-rate tickets for emigrants to America and completely free passage to Australia for willing farmhands and ser-vants.

Deepening poverty helped to harden the hearts of her fellow islanders, who were never renowned for their charity. The courts of St. Helier were about to sen-tence a fourteen-year-old girl, Harriet Gilbert, to a month's solitary confinement on bread and water for a petty theft after she pleaded innocence of the crime. Her punishment was not considered especially harsh when many a child before her had been birched on the day he entered prison and birched again on the day he left. The fact that she died of starvation in her cell aroused little more outcry than a handful of letters to the newspaper.

No protest was heard from the dean. Moulded by change in his own circumstances, he was preoccupied by a move which, in the next few months, would take him from St. Saviour's to the senior parish of St. Helier's itself. The town church—where criminals once raced for sanctuary and cannon for the militia were stored for years after his marriage to Emilie— would be his at last. The only letter he wrote to the *British Review* was a panegyric in favor of psalm-singing, including quotations from John Milton.

The delights of being mistress of Noirmont soon palled on Lillie. She could not tolerate the thought of spending the remainder of her days cooped up on a few square miles of earth as familiar as the back of her hand, among people upon whom she was unlikely to make any greater impression than she had already made. She was sure she was capable of better things, and she had no trouble convincing Edward to believe as she did. They must live in England. Before they left, she scored her name with her ring on a windowpane.

The Langtrys moved into a house he had bought overlooking Southampton Water. From its windows Lillie could watch the London & South Western steam-packets sail up the broad inlet to dock after winding through The Solent at the end of the run from Jersey, one hundred and fifteen miles away. Across the Solent lay the Isle of Wight and the town of Cowes, the center of *haut monde* yachting. Overlooking the water stood the *palazzo*-style towers of Osborne House, where the queen spent half the year in secluded invisibility from her people, fawned over by her ladies-in-waiting, still wearing required black mourning in respect for Albert.

Lillie found no contentment in the new house. Cliffe Lodge's seventeen rooms were spacious enough after the low-ceilinged little boxes of the deanery. She had four servants at her call, and the butler, like many of his kind, was more than willing to keep the running of the household in his hands and maintain his own dominion.

Southampton seemed like a way station to her, two-thirds farther in miles along the road to London, but as distant in spirit as St. Helier had ever been. The sight of passing steamers tantalised her, bringing not nostalgia to return to her birthplace but a sense of deep frustration.

The eight-month-old marriage was starting to founder. Her husband seemed willing to let her dictate the course of their lives, though he complained bitterly about every decision taken. His compliance ended with that. They had so little to say to each other that he ate breakfast alone. On most mornings he left the house to join his friends in Southampton before she was out of bed. At the dinner table, conversation between them revolved listlessly around whatever trivialities the day had brought.

She was instantaneously bored with the pettiness of provincial society, with its rituals of making and receiving calls, of afternoon tea served from a silver tray as solemnly as the Eucharist, of interminable gossip about people of no consequence. She was meant for better things. She kept up a steady correspondence with her mother, but her letters to Reggie went unanswered.

The monotony was interrupted by a microscopic organism which nobody in the world had yet seen, much less recognized, though it had laid waste to man since the time of Hippocrates. Identification of the bacterium *Salmonella typhosa,* which produced typhoid fever, lay half a dozen years ahead under the microscope of the German pathologist Karl Joseph Eberth. When the doctor finally diagnozed the symptoms in Lillie, he concluded, in the medical opinion of the day, that she must have contracted the disease through the breath or touch of another sufferer. In all likelihood, she had drunk milk or water infected by human feces or eaten from dishes similarly contaminated.

The attack came on gradually. At first she felt listless, a condition rare in her. She attributed it to lack of outdoor exercise. Her normally healthy appetite deserted her, and she blamed the tedium of her daily routine. A headache that refused to leave brought on lack of sleep and constant nausea.

Edward, by some accounts, decided that his wife was pregnant. Among her family, there was the unshakable belief that this must be ruled out as impossible. He could not be so totally unknowing as to imagine that a child was to be fathered by a kiss or a caress. Yet the conviction handed on from one generation to another was that Lillie's marriage was never consummated, that Edward never knew the pleasures of his wife's body and the passion he might arouse in her blood.

By the end of a week, her fever mounted far past the hundred-degree mark. Telltale pink spots speckled her smooth belly. The doctor needed nothing more to tell him that this was typhoid, the disease that slaughtered tens of thousands every year, civilians and soldiers, statesmen and kings.

The Prince of Wales had fallen victim to typhoid fever four years earlier, as a guest of Lord and Lady Londesborough at Londesborough Lodge, Yorkshire. He had arrived in customary style with a retinue of courtiers and enough luggage to fill a cart. He had been provided with the most opulent suite of rooms in the house, the cellar's finest wines and the best cooking the kitchen could produce. But a potential assassin lurked in the fouled drains, a colony of bacteria multiplying by the hour. Another guest, the seventh Earl of Chesterfield, died of the contagion. His great-grandfather was that Chesterfield who immortalized himself with letters exhorting his son on matters of etiquette.

Two weeks before Christmas in 1871, hope was lost for the prince. He lay raving from delirium in Sandringham House, singing, whistling, and panting for breath for thirty-six hours until his fever broke. Victoria was convinced that it was a judgement on her heir's wickedness. It was almost ten years to the day since typhoid had struck down his father. "In those heart-rending moments," the Queen confided to her diary, "I scarcely knew how to pray aright, only asking God, if possible, to spare my beloved Child."

The danger to Lillie's life mounted towards its

peak at the end of the second week. The bacteria, following the classic pattern, had penetrated the walls of her bowels and gone into her bloodstream, threatening septicemia. She had the innate physical strength to combat the infection, and that first crisis passed. The nurses who kept twenty-four-hour watch over her struggled to reduce the fever with wet packs on her forehead and sponge baths of tepid water. There were no other treatments, no known drugs to improve her chances of recovery, apart from antiseptics given as intestinal injections. The sickroom attendants could do no more than wait, pray for her when she proved unwilling or unable to pray for herself, and burn the discharges of her body.

If her husband stayed at her bedside as Alexandra had kept vigil at the prince's, or if Edward showed her any special attentions in her ordeal, Lillie was unaware of the fact, or else she erased it from her memory. She made no subsequent reference to any evidence of devotion. He had seen his first wife slip from the world. Possibly he could not face the prospect a second time. Or, in her delirium, Lillie may have unknowingly given him a glimpse of her true feelings, previously kept secret from him. During the course of the prince's illness, his doctors had compelled Alexandra to leave his bedroom so that her peace of mind might be preserved. In his ravings, "all sorts of revelations and names of people" came from his lips, said Lady Macclesfield, who kept watch with the princess at his bedside.

During the third week, her mind cleared as her temperature fell close to normal. This marked the onset of a second crisis. She was close to final exhaustion, with tremors in every muscle and her heart weakening. She refused to allow herself to die. The distant sounds of the steampackets' sirens reminded her of the distance she had travelled and how far she still must go to achieve the indiscernible future she wanted for herself.

Another bitter winter blanketed the British Isles. Snow fell over parts of the country for three days on end. Trains were marooned. The mortality rate rocketed in London, but nothing would keep her from that city. Her convalescence began in the fourth week following the doctor's diagnosis of her disease.

"You will have to be careful with yourself for many weeks more," he told her. "What you need is a complete change of air. I really do advise you to leave Southampton."

"That was all she had waited to hear. She dismissed out of hand his suggestion that she might well spend a month or so on Jersey. For the time being, she had already had her fill of the island. The deanery could be home to her no longer. What was left of her family would shortly be installed in the manse in St. Helier. Her father would no longer offer rides to tired peasant women up St. Saviour's Hill. He would spend more time drinking port with his cronies at the Victoria Club. He would still quote the classics and preach the virtue of being bold for God, and he would not lose his appetite for women.

Lillie chose London as the perfect spot for convalescence. Using all her powers of persuasion, smiling with her full, inviting lips and her bewildering violet eyes, she won the doctor over. He accepted the outrageous suggestion that the capital city, cut in two by its turbid river, its sky never free from a pall of soot, should be the place where she would recover her health.

Edward in the past had been reluctant to venture into the intimidating town to which he was virtually a stranger. He belonged to no clubs and had no friends there. It would be impossible to go sailing or fishing or follow any of the outdoor sports which this placid man enjoyed. But with her doctor to back her, Lillie was adamant. The butler and the rest of the staff were discharged at short notice. Cliffe Lodge was put up for sale and the furniture for auction.

"I have no idea what led us to select the smoky city as a sanitarium," she said afterwards, but that was dissembling. She chose London because it was the hub of the universe.

On a murky January morning, the Langtrys arrived by train under the vaulted glass roof of Waterloo Station, less than a mile from the grime-blackened church where the dean had served his curacy. Softer hearts than Lillie's sank at the sight of the dingy streets, the bitter rain, the pitiful tenements. Another girl who left Jersey for London remembered the initial shock. "The pinched pathetic faces of the ragged urchins who ran barefooted beside the cab, begging for pennies with which to get some food, seemed to destroy all my most cherished hopes," she wrote. "The gulf which lies between the romantic and the sordid was never more clearly visible to me than on that day." That was Elinor Glyn, eleven years younger than Lillie, who played with Ada Norcott, the new lieutenant governor's daughter, in his residence on St. Saviour's Hill, where Lillie had seldom, if ever, been invited.

Her hopes were indestructible. She was blind to the squalor that passed outside the windows of the cab carrying her and Edward to Brown's Hotel, where they would spend a few days. She pictured herself conquering the city where she had failed before. She concentrated on the imagined joys that awaited her— sauntering in Hyde Park and the new Leicester Square Gardens, visiting the mansions of the rich in Mayfair, St. James's and Belgravia, mingling with milords and millionaires.

The Langtrys rented comfortable apartments on Eaton Place, almost within sight of the tall brick wall bounding the queen's gardens behind Buckingham Palace. Lillie scouted a number of sites before she settled on this new address. Every street had its distinct place in the social hierarchy; a few yards could spell the difference between acceptance and ostracism.

Eaton Place did not compare, of course, with Piccadilly, where Nathaniel Rothschild lived at Number 148, or St. James's Square, which harbored Their Graces the Dukes of Marlborough and Norfolk. The Langtrys' apartments must be rated as meagre judged by the standards of the great town houses, like the

Duke of Buccleuch's Montagu House, or Chelsea House, the home of the Earl of Cadogan, or the Marquess of Hartington's Devonshire House, with its soaring marble staircase.

But around the corner lay Eaton Square, with a more than respectable population of the peerage—Lord Chelmsford at Number 7 and Lord Hampton at Number 9, the Marchioness of Headfort at Number 11 and General Sir William Knollys, the prince's Controller and Treasurer, at Number 17, together with his son Francis, the prince's private secretary. Knollys' singular plain daughter, "the inevitable Charlotte," as the gossips labelled her, was Woman-of-the-Bedchamber and dear friend of the Princess Alexandra.

To live on Eaton Square called for an income of at least ten thousand pounds a year, with ten servants and a first-class cook. The square housed seventeen other dukes, earls and viscounts, eight knights, one foreign count, nine titled ladies, a trio of admirals and the same score of generals, as well as nine Members of Parliament, who interested Lillie considerably less than their more distinguished neighbours. All in all, Eaton Place was an eminently satisfactory base from which to start impressing London.

First, she needeed to teach herself much more about the town and its most eminent citizens than she had been aware of as a callow adolescent. She must improve her mind, so that she would not repeat her mistakes. She used her eyes, her ears, and the newspapers to absorb the background information that would enable her to mix at the levels of society she had chosen as her own.

Fashionable London joked that spring about the tens of thousands who beat a path each day to Agricultural Hall in the suburb of Islington, lured by the reputations of Dwight Lyman Moody and Ira D. Sankey, who had arrived from America to preach hellfire and salvation to the British. The rich remained unmoved, and the masses of the poor were too cynical to be stirred by revivalism. The middle classes turned up in the biggest multitudes the city had ever seen gathered under a roof, with men outnumbering women three to one. Ushers with long white wands escorted the celebrants to their seats. While Mr. Sankey, backed by a white-robed choir, pounded his cabinet-organ and roared out gospel hymns, Mr. Moody urged the audience to repentance and drove sinners to their knees. England had seen nothing to equal the fervour, but the ripples did not reach as far as Eaton Square.

The North Pole was a more popular subject there. Its existence was known only in theory—no man had ever succeeded in breaking through the frozen seas to reach it, though uncounted lives had been lost on voyages of exploration. Now two fresh attempts were in the making. The ships *Alert* and *Discovery,* their hulls reinforced against the crushing pressure of ice-fields, were being fitted out at Portsmouth. In South-ampton docks, the *Pandora,* commanded by the ex-plorer Captain Allan Young, was being readied for a separate venture into the Arctic.

What she heard of the personality of Captain Young captured Lillie's fancy. He had tried three times before to reach the Pole and claim territory for the queen. In his forties, he was still a bachelor, a man-about-town, a yachtsman, a companion of the prince. He had spent a fortune on his adventures and made certain in the process that the world knew his name. The newspapers were full of his latest efforts, down to the details of his shipboard quarters, the landscapes that hung on the walls of his cabin, the books he had chosen to read during the months he would be at sea, and the organ he was taking aboard, a battered veteran of four previous expeditions re-furbished for sentiment's sake.

Above all, it was news of the Court, filling a daily column in the papers, that fascinated her. Ever since *The Times* reported in March that the prince was contemplating a visit to India "in the ensuing cold season," Eaton Square had bandied stories of the preparations that were under way and the plotting and counterplotting that occupied the queen and her minis-ters.

The prince was eager to see for himself the fabled subcontinent which his mother regarded as the most precious jewel in the British crown, though she had paid no visit there and had no wish to do so. He hungered for fresh experiences. He wanted to sample the splendours with which Indian princes surrounded themselves, and he intended to fit in some hunting of big game. But he set two major conditions for his tour. It should be paid for by the British government, not out of his own always-strained pockets. And he was not going to have his wife accompany him at any price.

He began by keeping his plans a secret from her, while he had his librarian at Sandringham collect books about India for him to dip into through the previous winter. Then he called on his mother at Windsor Castle to win her assent for his expedition. She gave it willingly after he told her that her ministers had already approved the tour, which was not true at all. Alexandra was infuriated when she learned what her husband had been doing behind her back. She was not especially concerned by the thought of his long absence or the perils of the journey. She could not tolerate the idea of missing a treat as rare as this, of touring "that most beautiful and fairylike country," as she pictured it, which set her imagination on fire.

Disraeli had ousted Gladstone as Prime Minister thirteen months earlier and formed his second Cabinet. He followed the prince to Windsor and found himself in the midst of some royal squabbling. The princess was insisting on going with the prince. The queen would have none of that and blamed herself for agreeing to her son's scheme without first consulting her ministers.

The prince was "our young Hal" in Disraeli's condescending private references to him, though in all correspondence he carefully addressed him as "sir, and dear Prince." Hal's problem, as usual, was finance. "Where is the money to come from?" the hawk-faced leader of the Cabinet asked in a letter to the Secretary for India, the Marquess of Salisbury. "He has not a shilling; she will not give him one. A Prince of Wales must not move in India in a *mesquin* manner. Everything must be done on an imperial scale, etc., etc. This is what she said. . . ."

The prince, a spendthrift where his own money was concerned, was righteously indignant when Radicals in the House of Commons spoke out against allocating a penny of public funds on a pleasure trip. Disraeli, assuming all responsibility in hope of personal glory, engineered a grant of 112,000 pounds, to which the Indian government added a further 100,000 pounds. The prince "was still liable to talk 'big' when among his 'creatures' about 'spending, if requisite, a million,' " Disraeli discovered when he was summoned to Sandringham to listen to the prince's complaints.

The prince, however, proceeded to draw up a list of the men he wished to accompany him on this exclusively male excursion. He wanted Suffield as Lord-in-Waiting, but Lillie heard none of this from Suffield himself—she was not ready yet to renew her contact with him. The Earl of Aylesford, "Sporting Joe" to the prince and the rest of his friends, was named as a personal guest, and hot-tempered Lord Charles Beresford, a lieutenant in the Royal Navy, as an aide-de-camp. Lieutenant Colonel Owen Williams, the Welshman who commanded the Blues, would serve as equerry. Another aide-de-camp would be Sub-Lieutenant Prince Louis of Battenberg, slim and delicately boned, a twenty-one-year-old distant cousin and a Navy man since he enlisted as a cadet seven years earlier. He was a special favourite of the prince's.

The queen reverted to form by ordering that every detail must be submitted to her by Disraeli or Salisbury, taking all arrangements out of her son's hands. He took it as yet another mark of her lack of confidence in him and stormed off to Downing Street to confront Disraeli. The inscrutable Prime Minister had already heard Alexandra's plea to be included in the party. He sidestepped the issue. Her only ally was William Gladstone, now of Her Majesty's loyal Opposition, who kept himself in trim felling trees on his estate at

Hawarden Park and reading the galleys of his new book, a learned thesis arguing that Homer was no mythical creation but the true author of the *Iliad,* which he entitled *Homeric Synchronism.* Perennially occupied with the relationships between man and woman, he thought it shameful for the prince and princess to be physically separated for such a length of time. But his voice, too, went unheard.

Eighteen men finally constituted the prince's personal party. In a state of "extraordinary excitement" possibly reminiscent of his schoolboy outbursts, he had flatly informed Disraeli that he refused to tolerate any changes in his list. His mother objected to Lord Charles Beresford and one other guest, Lord Carrington, "a gay fellow," in the prince's admiring terms. Her smooth-tongued Prime Minister conciliated her by promising to warn the pair of them that there must be no "larks" on this expedition. The prince in turn ceded a point: He would give up his plan to take along a detachment of Life Guards for ceremonial display.

None of the men whose names she heard and read about were known personally to Lillie except Suffield. She had not as yet set eyes on any member of the royal family, but she was acquainting herself with some of the ways of princes. She absorbed the accounts of the forthcoming excursion. The prince would be served by a valet, a stud-groom, a page, three chefs, and the Duke of Sutherland's Scots piper, all ranked as "upper" servants in contrast with twenty-two in the "lower" category. He would embark for Bombay in the ancient, full-rigged troopship *Serapis,* escorted by the frigates *Pallas* and *Hercules,* with the royal yacht *Osborne* in attendance.

Serapis was undergoing a stem-to-stern transformation in readiness. Her hull was painted white for coolness in the tropics and her bow adorned with a crest and motto, "Heaven's Light Our Guide." His Royal Highness was allotted two suites, one on either side of the ship, to be spared the sun on whichever course she sailed. Each consisted of a boudoir, bedroom, and bathroom—portside out, starboard home, indicated by the initials POSH, which consequently acquired its meaning as a synonym for luxury. He would not take the train from Charing Cross Station on the first leg of his journey until October. Meantime, there were other sights for the Langtrys to see.

On Easter Monday, they joined the bank holiday throng that flocked to Hyde Park to watch the procession that marched there under a flutter of banners to the music of the brass bands. It was not in the least like Jersey, where Easter meant Good Friday picnics, with limpets pried from the rocks and cooked on the spot in a *gâche à fouée* and the only music available for a crowd was the annual visit of a six-piece German band, performing on street corners, surrounded by boys sucking lemons in hope of disrupting the cornet player before the hat was passed.

If there was time to spare, she would persuade Edward to take a hansom cab down to Kensington, where she could pass an hour or so among the flora and fauna, including three stuffed African giraffes, at the Natural History Museum. She had a desire to inform herself about all manner of things. Or they might ride to Great Russell Street, so that she could walk around a hall or two of the British Museum and see the Elgin Marbles, Nelson's log book, and a copy of the Magna Carta, signed reluctantly by the king whom her ancestor Raoul had fought for so valiantly.

No matter what, she would not join hoi polloi in traipsing around the Crystal Palace, opened a year before she was born, which could only be regarded as an oversized conservatory, or in feeding buns to the animals in the Regent Park Zoo, where the collection was soon to be increased dramatically by the addition of three tigers, a leopard, a bear, some Brahmin bulls, a midget donkey, four elephants, and other fauna brought back by the prince in cages on the decks of *Serapis* and *Osborne*.

He was installed, and she read about that, as Grand Master of the English Freemasons before a gathering of eight thousand of his fellows one month later, in April. The site chosen for the ceremony was the

Royal Albert Hall—it struck her that almost everything new in England was named either for the queen or her departed husband. Newspaper reporters outdid themselves in describing tier upon tier and loggia after loggia filled with solemn men in gold and white, purple or blue collars, and the insignia of their order.

In May the prince sat on a box seat next to the Duke of Beaufort when His Grace presided over the opening meet of the Four-in-Hand Club in Hyde Park. The duke's gleaming carriage, like most of the twenty-eight others, sported the red-and-dark-blue trim of the club colors. The surrounding roads were lined three deep with spectators on foot and at the reins of their own turnouts. Other sightseers on horseback trotted behind the single-file procession of club carriages as it wound through Cumberland Place, drivers' whips flourished to acknowledge the cheers. But Lillie missed another opportunity to see a royal in person by staying home that day.

The summer was particularly hard on Edward. He had been compelled to sell *Gertrude* to meet medical expenses and the cost of their moves. He sorely missed the old days which had been abandoned. Being cooped up in an alien city grated on his nerves. Southampton would be infinitely preferable to this. Lillie refused to budge, even though they could scarcely endure each other's company. "He was a fish out of water," she said bluntly later, but she was a minnow, bent on mastering her new element.

They diverted themselves occasionally by going to the theatre. She saw Henry Irving's lean-shanked, gentlemanly portrayal of *Hamlet* and wrote home to her parents that she was "thrilled beyond my powers to describe my feelings." Ellen Terry returned to the theatre that year, after divorcing her second husband, to play Portia in *The Merchant of Venice*. Lillie watched her performance spellbound.

Like the rest of the country, the Langtrys glowed with a moment's patriotic pride over the triumph of Captain Webb of the Royal Navy in swimming from Dover to Calais, threatened by rising waves under a storm-grey sky, spending nearly twenty-two hours in the water with no nourishment other than swallows of brandy, coffee, and beef-tea. Lillie would have liked to show another touch of patriotism and go to see the Prince and Princess Alexandra leave by special train for Calais to the jaunty music of the band of the 104th Fusiliers, with Charing Cross Station specially illuminated for the occasion and bagpipes playing, his luggage for India aboard, but Edward could not be coaxed into crossing London.

Eaton Square had more morsels of gossip to enjoy. The princess had been thwarted in her desire, "the one wish of my life," as she said. She was to be at her husband's side only as far as Calais. He would lunch with the President of France, Marshal Marie Edme Patrice Maurice de MacMahon, go to the theatre with the Comte de Paris, then join *Serapis* at Brindisi. For consolation, Alexandra had her father and mother, King Christian and Queen Louise of Denmark, to keep her company at Marlborough House.

Victoria flatly refused to invite her daughter-in-law or her parents to the christening of her latest grandchild, Marie, the daughter of her second-born son, Alfred, Duke of Edinburgh. That would result in too big a crowd at Windsor Castle, she complained. She made her dislike of "the Denmarks" even plainer shortly afterwards by summoning Alexandra alone to Osborne House, leaving Christian and Louise behind in London.

"Of course the Princess of Wales sees this," wrote Victoria's private secretary, General Sir Henry Ponsonby, "and will talk about it and if it gets about that the Queen is unkind to her when she is so very popular there will be a row."

November brought its unfailing shroud of choking yellow fog to the city. The Thames overflowed its banks on schedule as the tides surged, flooding the low-lying houses of the poor, drowning their dogs and cats and chickens by the hundreds. Even Lillie was overcome by depression. On Jersey there would be days of sunshine and the heartening smell of the open sea.

She spent half her days alone in bed to escape the unaccustomed chill and a nagging sense of failure. She had books to pass the time—R. D. Blackmore; Anthony Trollope's new novel, *The Prime Minister;* perhaps even a dip into Algernon Charles Swinburne's *Erechtheus,* just published and applauded by the critics. The newspapers she turned to were full of the prince's tumultuous reception in India, where street signs proclaimed "Welcome to our Future Emperor." He was proving to be the epitome of the British Raj, as impressive to bejewelled princes and native potentates, who showered him with the riches of the earth, as to the hundreds of thousands of scrawny peasants, who flocked to watch him pass in procession, carried sometimes on a golden litter, resplendent in one of a score of full-dress uniforms with his Knight of the Garter badge and the gem-encrusted Star of India, escorted by the massive troopers of the viceroy's bodyguard in zebra-striped turbans and tunics of scarlet and gold.

His party maintained punctilious standards of formality whenever they were on public view. "We are more like a lot of monks than anything else," Carrington had written sadly to his mother, Lady Lincolnshire, as they set out, ". . . No news—all well—no whist and no sprees, or bearfights, or anything!"

The prince, an autocrat with glimmerings of liberalism, was offended by the intolerance he noticed among some Englishmen. He protested to Salisbury about British officers who persisted in calling the natives "niggers." To the Earl of Granville, who had been Gladstone's Secretary for the Colonies, he wrote ingenuously, "because a man has a black face and a different religion from our own, there is no reason why he should be treated like a brute." To his mother, who kept up a flow of telegrams asking about his health, he complained about "the rude and rough manner with which the English political officers . . . treat the princes and chiefs upon whom they were appointed to attend."

Apart from the queen's clucking messages, the only real blot on the expedition to date was an outbreak of cholera in Mysore. It was decided that plans to visit there must be abandoned after tens of thousands of pounds had been spent on preparations. Instead, *Serapis* sailed for Ceylon and elephant hunting with a shipload of newspaper reporters following in her wake. Two weeks or so before Christmas, the prince shot his first elephant and cut off its tail as a trophy. Charlie Beresford had just started to dance a hornpipe on its flanks when the animal staggered to its feet and lumbered back into the rain forest. Not even Suffield, probably the best shot among them, had time to grab a rifle and fire.

Suffield felt it his duty to play watchdog to the prince at no matter what cost in fever or fatigue. He took turns with an equerry in guarding the prince every night, pacing the hall outside his bedroom or the earth outside his tent to keep himself awake. The prince, who scouted the idea of danger, regarded it as touching but quite unnecessary.

In Agra, the royal sprig, Prince Louis, out for wild boar, took a spill from his horse, but alarm subsided when it was discovered that he had only broken a collarbone. Carrington went pig-sticking, too, and met with a worse fate when his front teeth were knocked out by the butt of his lance. The Prince of Wales, suntanned and pounds lighter than when he set out from London, escaped intact, as happy as a sandboy. Before he left Nepal, he was treated to an unbroken week of hunting in the jungles of the Sardah River by Sir Jung Bahadur, the Prime Minister.

Two hundred riding elephants and two thousand coolies were gathered for the prince's party, which numbered fewer than twenty men. With bird-of-paradise plumes and a gigantic ruby in his helmet, Sir Jung had one thousand elephants of his own and ten thousand soldiers ready to give the prince some good days of sport. On his first full day in his rocking howdah, the prince bagged six tigers. That night, as always, he relaxed in a hot bath, changed into evening dress, and gave a dinner party to celebrate. The following morning the kill continued.

One of his party summed up the achievements of her eldest son in a report to the queen. Citing the impression he had given "of manly vigour and power of endurance which pleased everyone, Europeans and natives alike," he thought. "It was like winning a battle and proved he possessed Royal qualities of courage, energy and physical power."

At home, there were always contrary opinions to be heard. Admiration for Albert Edward, Prince of Wales, was far from universal. If Lillie had a mind to do so, she could read a scurrilous, paper-backed publication which had gone on sale some months ago and was still passed from hand to hand. *The Siliad,* written anonymously, consisted of close to a hundred pages of verse in the manner of Alfred Tennyson, the poet laureate, who divided his time between his Isle of Wight estate at Farringford and the new home he had built at Aldworth.

The central character of *The Siliad,* a political satire, was instantly recognisable as the prince. Arch references to his social habits, including his notorious escapades with women, studded its pages. For example:

> Suppose I am all that they say I am,
> I'm better so than live a priggish sham;
> I am not clever; why should I pretend
> To learning that I do not comprehend?

While Lillie spent most of her days with reading, Edward turned to a different method of killing time. By her account, when she took to her bed, he took to the bottle before the winter was over.

☙ III ❧

The capital of the kingdom, and of the empire on which the sun never set, spread like a shapeless, pulsing blob on both banks of the river which first gave it life. Its birth dated back long before the Roman legions came in their slave galleys. Two thousand years later, the river still sustained it. Every year the city's borders swelled farther out over the flat surrounding countryside, ingesting cow pastures, streams and villages, manors and farmhouses. In the past half century, the population had doubled. Now more than four million people lived here, the spectrum and model of civilised society, from beggars to millionaires. London, like the nature of God, was whatever a man imagined it to be. It impressed the rustic reformer William Cobbett only as a tumour on the fair face of England, and he accordingly labelled it The Wen. The original *Encyclopaedia Britannica* in 1771 waxed more enthusiastic. "When considered with all its advantages, it is now what ancient Rome once was: the seat of liberty, the encourager of arts and the administration of the whole world." Anyone who spoke English, or hoped to learn some day, looked to this city for inspiration, commands, appointments, or rewards.

Buried among its stones and its refuse-pits was the history of the Anglo-Saxon race. Alfred the Great ruled here. William the Conqueror granted its charter. Wars and famines stunted its early growth. One hundred thousand died in the plague of 1664. The greater part of the town had disappeared in flames two years afterwards. Every monarch since Duke William was crowned here, except Edward V, who was murdered, and one of them, Charles, was beheaded.

In 1876, it was the biggest, busiest, most prosperous and powerful city in the Western universe and, to Lillie, the most important place on earth. She could stand in Trafalgar Square, alone if need be, close to the core of London's hundred square miles, and thrill to the sight at each point of the compass of Portland stone reduced to grey monochrome by the fall of grit and dust. The smoke of sea-coal still colored London, though as long ago as the reign of the first Edward, efforts to cleanse the atmosphere had made death the penalty for its use.

In the center of the square towered the column to Admiral Lord Nelson, victor over the French in the Battle of Trafalgar, whose perch on its pinnacle was sometimes obscured in winter fog. A good place to stand, she found, was at its base, guarded by the four bronze lions of Sir Edward Landseer, painter of dogs and deer, whose "The Monarch of the Glen" and "The Stag at Bay" hung as steel engravings in the parlors of half the middle-class homes of the country.

Like Horatio Nelson, she could gaze southward down Whitehall, lined with buildings as solid as the empire itself, where the business of governing every territory under the Union Jack was carried on. To the right ran Downing Street, where, at Number 10, Disraeli spent a large part of his time devising fresh schemes for flattering his queen.

At the far end of Whitehall, there was a glimpse of Westminster Abbey; Victoria, as a tremulous girl of nineteen, had been crowned there on an exhausting June day thirty-eight years ago. To the left of the old cathedral, the Houses of Parliament were in session, opened by the queen herself in February, for only the second time in her years of widowhood. She commanded Alexandra to go with her in the prince's absence and take her reluctant place on the woolsack, as prescribed for a royal princess in the ritual, to hear her mother-in-law's brief speech from the throne. "I pray that your deliberations may, under the Divine blessing, result in the happiness and contentment of my people," said the queen.

Westward lay Buckingham Palace, its three hundred and more rooms kept staffed with servants but left untenanted by Victoria. The din of London, she said, was bad for her nerves. She had never invited Alexandra into her private rooms there. Her son felt that she should "go oftener and remain longer in London . . . as the people, not only Londoners—cannot bear seeing Buckingham Palace always unoccupied." In an earlier letter, he had been more specific: "We live in radical times, and the more the *People see the Sovereign* the better it is for the *People* and the *Country*." But Her Majesty was not to be persuaded. She was perfectly satisfied with Windsor Castle, Osborne House, and visits to Balmoral, the sham castle she had ordered built beside the River Dee in Aberdeenshire, where burly John Brown reigned.

A quarter-turn by Lillie brought the National Gallery into view and a fleeting thought into her head of a self-proclaimed Jerseyman whose apple-cheeked wife was known to the dean and Mrs. Le Breton. John Everett Millais' canvases were hung every year in the Royal Academy exhibition, but not yet in the National Gallery, which in any event was closed at the moment and would not be reopened until the summer, with its collection of Holbein, Rubens, and some dubious Raphaels rearranged in new rooms.

Millais' gift of telling stories in pictures had won his fame as a giant among contemporary painters. Lillie thoroughly approved of the mark he had made, first as a leader of the Pre-Raphaelite brotherhood, more lately as his own imaginative master, absorbed with symbolism and his distinctive poetics in paint. Though she had never met him, it was reassuring to think that Jerseymen could conquer London when they tried hard enough. She wished she could have seen the Royal Academy exhibition five years earlier. Two other island artists besides Millais had paintings hung there—C. H. Poingdestre and Walter William Ouless, who, according to St. Helier gossip, earned as much as three hundred guineas for a single portrait.

Another turn and she could look southwest to a

magnificent new tree-lined thoroughfare, Northumberland Avenue, in the final stages of completion before its opening in March at a cost, it was said, of more than six hundred thousand pounds. At its foot, she could see Victoria Embankment and the Thames, winding down to the sea forty miles away through a section of the city, unknown to her, where steamships docked and the air was thick with the reek of Billingsgate fish market and the odors of factory smoke—breweries, distilleries, sugar refineries and tanneries.

In its attitudes of mind as well as in its size, London was bursting at the seams, setting styles for many another city in the nation. For the first time in British history, democratic opinion commanded consideration by the rulers of the land, whose will had seldom been questioned. The rebellious American colonists had lit the way by throwing off the hand of the queen's grandfather, George III. The French had gone further and overthrown the monarchy in their own country in the bloodbath of the Revolution. But only a handful of Englishmen were stirred by events in America and France so profoundly as to dream of similar sweeping change in their native land. It took factory life and the attendant degradation of existence for millions of the English to drive home with the force of a steamhammer the need to transform the institutions of government.

The spirit and temper of masses of citizens were changing in the London that lured Lillie. The futile battles of the old aristocrats to defeat the first reforms of electoral laws, which eroded the power of the peerage by adding tens of thousands of new names to the polling lists, lay in the past, in 1832, her grandfathers' time. For nine years now, as the result of a second Reform Act, the middle classes by and large had enjoyed the right to vote, provided a householder had at least fifty pounds in a savings bank. If he paid one pound a year or more in direct taxes, he was allowed a second ballot. Pressure from the lower levels of the social pyramid was mounting to give every man a voice in putting into Parliament the party of his choice.

"We live in radical times," the prince recognised. But his mother expected to do more than merely reign as a respected symbol of authority, with the right to be consulted by the men the voters had elected. She wanted to *rule*, just as her five ancestors of the House of Hanover had done before her in the tradition of monarchs going back to Saxons and Danes. Duty, by which she set such store, demanded that she fight against limitations on her supreme authority.

The new democratic spirit of the English was reflected in a host of commercial innovations. Profit-seeking businessmen seized the opportunity to coax money from the pockets of the self-respecting, intellectually hungry middle classes. New "palaces" designed to dazzle the common man and his family sprang up in London. They were monuments to the exploring mood of architects and builders in seeing what could be achieved by working with glass and cast-iron girders from the searing hearths and furnaces of the industrial North. They enclosed acres of space in which tens of thousands of ticket buyers could find amusement to entertain and possibly educate them. The Great Exhibition of 1851 in Hyde Park, one of Prince Albert's multitude of pet projects, had set off the vogue. The Crystal Palace followed on similar lines. Soon after the Langtrys arrived in London, ill-fated Alexandra Palace, burned down within a few days of its original opening, had been given a second start on a day of pouring rain which thinned the crowds to vanishing point.

The latest of the pleasure domes, built in Tothill Street, Westminster, and bigger than even the Crystal Palace, was grandiloquently styled the Royal Aquarium and Summer and Winter Garden. There were no fish or any other forms of marine life on display in its tanks and pools on the January opening day. It was to provide the key to Lillie's liberation from despair and the closed company of an alcoholic husband.

Affie, the Duke of Edinburgh, substituted for his

absent elder brother in the ceremonial declaring the place ready to receive the public. Nearly ten thousand ladies and gentlemen of quality came by invitation to hear him speak in the great central hall, bright with flags, hothouse flowers and potted palms. The soft splash of water in the marble fountains provided a *sotto voce* accompaniment. Festooned crimson damask, white lilies, and blue silk hangings trimmed with white lace decorated the royal box.

The duke, out of naval uniform for once at a function of this sort, was received by the chairman of the executive committee of the venture, Henry Labouchère, a man of many parts, Liberal Member of Parliament, distinguished journalist and would-be diplomat. The undertaking, said the welcoming address, was intended for "the encouragement of artistic, scientific and musical tastes." It was to be "not only a popular exhibition, but a means of intellectual enjoyment and educational advantage." No one had the temerity to mention the shortage of fish.

The aquarium, the duke responded, "cannot fail, if properly directed, to stimulate the love of natural history and the acquirement of scientific knowledge." He was delighted, he said, to recognise the same high aims as his father had in view in sponsoring the Great Exhibition. All in all, the attractions of the enterprise "cannot but exercise a most beneficial influence in refining and cultivating the public taste." With this much said to a round of polite applause, he retired to luncheon in a private room behind his box.

The aquatic specimens, including a modest-sized alligator, had been delivered when the Langtrys came sometime later to see London's newest indoor promenade after columns of type extolling its wonders had appeared in the morning newspapers and the weekly illustrated magazines. They found Mr. Macfarren's Festival Orchestra giving its daily concert, playing much the same repertoire as on the opening day: Sir William Sterndale Bennett's Symphony in G Minor and *Procession March* by Arthur Sullivan, who had recently

72

begun to devote all his time to composing light opera with his partner, William Schwenck Gilbert.

Lillie noticed a familiar face in the sauntering crowd, under a glossy top hat tilted at a jaunty angle. Lord Ranelagh, with a flower in his buttonhole, defied his sixty-four years by dressing in the pinched-waist jackets of a young buck. He made a practice of escorting two nubile girls whom he sometimes referred to as "my daughters," though he had never married, sometimes as members of the *corps de ballet* at the Covent Garden opera. The same pair had aroused some amusement at Waterloo Station a day or so earlier by trailing behind him with their thumbs at their noses.

The seventh Viscount Ranelagh, the last of his line, owned a bungalow on Jersey, overlooking Belcroute Bay. Lillie had met the old roué once or twice before. He was known to his friends as the "Brompton Garibaldi" in reference to the location of his London town house, his exercises as a tandem lover, and his feelings towards the former Italian firebrand, now a tame member of the Parliament in Rome. Lillie remembered the Langtrys' former neighbour principally for his encounter with the venerable Jersey procedure of *Clameur de Haro.*

Clameur supposedly originated with Rollo, a Viking chieftain who was recognized as Duke of Normandy by Charles the Simple, King of the Western Franks, in the year 911. A Jerseyman's plea to Rollo for swift justice proved so effective that the tradition, and the law supporting it, survived unchanged on the island. All a man need do to invoke it was to fall on one knee and shout, *"Haro! Haro! A l'aide, mon prince! On me fait tort!*—Help me, my prince! I am being wronged!" "O, Rollo" had been corrupted into *Haro* by the passage of centuries.

A rutted lane divided Ranelagh's bungalow from a Jersey farm. When the Englishman attempted to have its potholes filled to make smoother going for his carriage, the farmer objected that the lane was his, and he chose to leave it as it was. No British peer who had

73

served in the 1st Life Guards would tolerate such churlishness from a social inferior. Ranelagh promptly hired a labourer to carry out the work. Lillie was intrigued to see that overnight the farmer spaded out every hole.

Ranelagh tried again and again on successive days, but every night the ruts were restored. Going back to inspect the battleground one morning, she saw that her determined fellow islander had dug a trench clean across the lane. At the sight of Ranelagh, the farmer knelt and uttered his cry to Haro. The law stipulated that the situation must rest there until the courts could decide the rights and wrongs of the case. Since the workings of Jersey justice were otherwise slow, Ranelagh could only admit that he was thwarted.

It would be imprudent, she knew, to bring up the subject of *clameur* as she chatted at the aquarium with her lecherous old neighbour. The meeting was amiable to the point that, on parting, Ranelagh said, "I insist that we see more of you while you are in London. You must come to see us on Sunday."

Mrs. Langtry was delighted to accept. She could detect a chink opening in the wall that so far had sealed her off from her goal. Edward would accompany her whether he wanted to or not.

Ranelagh's invitation could not be more timely. The Langtrys had come close to retreating from the city where they had found neither friends nor nourishment for their needs. Edward's misery led him to think again about his family's promise to make room for him in the shipping business if they would only settle in Belfast. Lillie would have no alternative then except to go with him, unless she wanted their marriage broken. Neither of them had gone so far as to contemplate that. Divorce was reserved for the profligate rich. In any event, Jersey law and her father's church made no provision for it.

The necessity of making a favourable impression frightened Lillie as Edward rang the doorbell of the creeper-covered house on the bank of the Thames in Fulham one Sunday afternoon. Her social skills and graces had been disused for more than a year. Teatime ritual—a porcelain cup and saucer on the lap, a petit four or an eclair to nibble on—was more exacting than a banquet, where the tablecloth would hide trembling knees. There must be no blunders at Ranelagh House, or London would slip from her strong fingers like a dropped plate.

Edward felt as uncomfortable as she did, perched on the edge of a brocaded chair while the housemaids circulated with silver teapots and the hum of barely decipherable accents droned from the lips of the other guests. He fidgeted with his starched white collar. Lillie's self-control did not fail her. She sat as composed as any lady of fashion, a half-smile on her curved lips, calming herself by fixing the scene in her memory so that she could tell her mother about it in her next letter. She seldom spoke except to answer a question in a guardedly soft contralto. Listening was safer than talking, and there was certainly enough to listen to. Scandal was erupting around the prince's expedition in India, and London relished every detail.

On February 20, at the start of the tiger hunt in Nepal, Sporting Joe Aylesford received an hysterical note from his wife, Edith. She had made up her mind to elope, she wrote, with another friend of the prince's, highly strung Lord Blandford, father of three children, who would abandon his wife, Bertha, the Duke of Abercorn's daughter, for her sake.

The Aylesfords and the Blandfords were members of the prince's inner circle, the Marlborough House set, hand-picked from the five or six hundred families who made up London Society, with a leavening of young officers from the smart regiments. The prince was involved more deeply than that. Edith, who was Owen Williams' sister, was another of the ladies the prince had flirted with in the past. In his romancing, he had written her some frivolous letters treasured and saved by her.

The prince had already approved Colonel Williams' urgent return home to join his dying wife. Now he sent Joe off from camp on a riding elephant, making for the nearest railway station, while he denounced Blandford as "the greatest blackguard alive." As soon as Aylesford reached London, he announced that nothing would stop him from divorcing Edith. He spread the word around the clubs that the prince was on his side. The colonel, for his part, strongly advised his brother-in-law to challenge Blandford to duel, as gentlemen had been accustomed to do a generation earlier, choosing pistols and a misty dawn in Hyde Park, before Prince Albert condemned such barbarity.

The blackguard Blandford, eldest son and heir of the Duke of Marlborough, had grabbed the chance provided by Sporting Joe's departure for India. While Edith moved into one of the country houses her husband owned, Blandford installed himself with his horses in a village nearby. Throughout the winter, he spent infatuated nights with his mistress, letting himself in with a key she had given him, leaving telltale footprints in the snow.

To the disappointment of Colonel Williams, his brother-in-law heeded the counsel of Lord Hartington, Chief Secretary for Ireland in Gladstone's Cabinet, who had a long-term love of his own in Louisa, the sparkling Duchess of Manchester. Calling out a man to pistols was out of date, said Harty-tarty, but he could not talk Aylesford into dropping the idea of ridding himself of Edith as an adulteress. The colonel's enthusiasm for duelling did not extend to divorce. Sporting Joe's notorious reputation was securely based on his weakness for gambling and wenching. "Aylesford," snapped the colonel, "is already so unsavoury that it will not do for him to appear in a divorce court."

A love affair could be carried to any ends but that. Society condoned and often encouraged a man, married or single, overcome by the desire to bed a woman for a night, a weekend or for as long as passion survived. The rules demanded discretion, little else. The prince was outraged only by Balndford's recklessness, not by his liaison with another man's wife. Divorce meant a public scandal that could blacken the names of everybody involved, the prince's included. It would damage the people's confidence in the ruling classes; that could be disastrous in these radical times.

The cast of characters most intimately concerned clung to the pathetic belief that only they, their relatives, and closest friends knew about the upset, yet by early March it was common gossip. The queen prided herself on her infallible sources of information. She thought it was "a dreadful disgraceful business." Hindsight told her that Sporting Joe had erred in going to India. "Poor Lord Aylesford should not have left her," she said. "I *knew* last summer this was going on. Those Williamses are a bad family. . . ."

The storm was blowing up. Blandford's younger brother, Lord Randolph Churchill, saw to that. Randolph, who sat in Parliament as the Member for the Marlboroughs' tied village of Woodstock, Oxfordshire, shared, without knowing it, a thought of the queen's: "Tho' I never believed it, some people said it was Lady A. the Pce admired—as Lord A. was too great a fool to be really agreeable to the P. of Wales."

Pleading with his brother not to elope, Churchill telegraphed the prince, asking him to persuade Joe to forget about divorce. Randolph's suspicions convinced him that Edith had been forced into Blandford's arms by a princely plot that took Aylesford aboard *Serapis* in spite of her begging him to stay with her. The truth was that she had urged him to go. If there was a plot, it was hatched between her and her lover. The prince declined to intervene.

Edith had a sudden change of heart. Her sisters argued with her that a divorce would finish her in Society. Hurt by the prince's refusal to exercise his influence, she handed her precious packet of his letters to Blandford, for use by Randolph in putting pressure on the prince. Churchill straightway announced to his friends that he "held the Crown of England" in his hands.

The Churchills were not renowned for their scruples. Safe in the knowledge that the prince, on his way home, was now staying in the Gezireh Palace,

Cairo, Randolph called on Alexandra at Marlborough House. Neither she nor Victoria knew as yet about the letters. Randolph experimented with blackmail as he broke the news. He felt sure of his ground. He had already consulted his solicitor, W. D. Freshfield. He knew that the memory of the Mordaunt case still haunted the princess. Should Aylesford proceed with his suit for divorce, he told her, the prince would be subpoenaed by Blandford as a witness. If the letters were published, the prince "would never sit upon the Throne of England."

Word of the meeting reached the prince in Cairo. He exploded into a fit of blind rage over the treatment of Alexandra by a man he had always thought of as a friend. He ordered Beresford to sail immediately in *Osborne* to Brindisi, then make all speed to London. Churchill must be challenged to duel. Beresford was to set a time and place on the coast of France where the prince could confront his wife's tormentor at the end of a pistol before *Serapis* reached home port.

There the matter stood on the Sunday afternoon when the Langtrys took tea with Ranelagh, and the company she aspired to was charmed as much by the grace of Lillie's manners as by the beauty of her face. She strolled with Edward on the mossy lawn that swept down under shade trees to the river. She murmured the right words of praise for the daffodils and jonquils that bloomed in the flower gardens, remarking that the viscount's gardeners grew vegetables and strawberries, too. She sat for a while on a wrought-iron chair, hoping, with justification, that she would not go unnoticed.

For a few more days of frustration, it appeared that the lightning was not to strike. The Langtrys fell back on the routine of drinks for him and reading in bed for her, interspersed with more strolling around Eaton Square and up to Buckingham Palace. They returned to Eaton Place one afternoon to find an invitation waiting for them. Would they present themselves at 21 Lowndes Square, the home of Sir John

78

and Lady Sebright, the following Sunday evening? Ranelagh could be thanked for that. Over dinner with the Sebrights he had said, "Would you do me the favour of asking a friend of mine to that reception of yours? She comes from Jersey, I assure you that she is very beautiful, and her name is Mrs. Langtry."

Here was a ladder to help her scale the wall that divided a woman of her limited background from the places where she felt sure she belonged. "I knew," she said simply, "that good things were happening to me." Edward disagreed. He did not want to face another bout of boredom and uneasiness. She should send her regrets, he said.

"If you refuse to come with me, then I shall be left with no choice but to go alone," she answered. That was unthinkable by her husband's standards. For the sake of appearances, he would have to escort her.

Olivia Sebright made up in astuteness what she lacked in looks. She was in the process of ruining her husband by wild gambling on the Stock Exchange. Nevertheless, she was regarded as one of the most fascinating women in London, an enthusiastic amateur actress, whose musical voice and extravagant air drew attention in any room. Upstairs in the nursery, there were a five-year-old son and a baby daughter, who did not appear, of course, when guests were present. They could not be permitted to curb their mother's Bohemian style.

She counted herself a "soul," as the dilettantes liked to style themselves. A reception at the Sebrights acted like a magnet for equally intense fellow-believers. All of them were rebels of sorts against the gross materialism of the age of iron and the tastelessness of its products, from stuccoed streets in Pimlico to squalid workhouses where the destitute lived on thin gruel in verminous rags.

Aestheticism was a fashion, not an organized movement. If anyone could be identified as the founding father, it was William Morris, the bushy-haired dreamer from Walthamstow, Essex. As a child, he used to ride on horseback through Epping Forest in a suit of toy armour, acting out the deeds of his knightly heroes. Nostalgia for a romantic past that existed only in imagination was a mark of the aesthetes. England was never so merrie as they pictured it in their paintings and poems.

Morris first applied his imagination to poetry with *The Defence of Guenevere,* then decided on architecture as a profession. His influence matched his enormous energy. By the time he came into Olivia's orbit, dozens of new town halls, railways stations and hotels, alike in their ponderous neo-Gothic façades, dominated the cities of England.

With another idealist like himself, Edward Burne-Jones, a friend of their Oxford days together, Morris exercised his talents in painting. They were spurred on by Dante Gabriel Rossetti, revered as their master, who had followed the twin paths of his Italian-exile father as a poet and artist. Until he established his independence of them, Millais had joined these Pre-Raphaelites in depicting the stiff, lustrous mediaeval figures of Biblical heroines and forlorn virgins posed, stone-faced, in mysteriously menacing foliage, which had entranced the current generation of *cognoscenti* when they appeared on art-gallery walls.

Morris, who cultivated friendships with workingmen as a matter of Socialist principle, had finally found his destiny in arts and crafts. "I would have nothing in my home," he declared, "that I do not know to be useful or believe to be ornamental." Olivia was one of the educated multitude with money to emulate his doctrine and refurnish the dismal rooms of her house.

The manufacturing company he helped to found turned out a handsome line of simple chairs and other furniture. The fabrics and wallpaper he designed changed the look of her home and thousands more like it. The poor, whose way of life he sought to improve, could not afford to redecorate. The middle classes continued to be captivated by china ornaments mass-produced in Birmingham, antimacassars, and curlicued cast-iron water closets. And London's sewer system, started a quarter-century ago but never completed, was a hazard to everyone.

The aesthetes were scoffed at as lackadaisical, "greenery-yallery" poseurs by harder-headed people, who were as indifferent to vulgarity and ugliness as they were to the fate of the submerged population at the pyramid's base. But aestheticism flourished, and some of its proponents, notably the painters, grew rich on commissions that poured in from the patrons they cultivated. An eye for beauty was common currency among them.

For their ride to the Sebrights, Edward was callow enough to engage a four-wheeler from the nearest cab rank; growlers were shunned by more sophisticated people, who suspected that their use by the poor in taking themselves to the hospitals made them potential pesthouses of contagion.

Lillie had not bothered to dress up. Her wisdom about herself told her that she could not possibly compete with the other women she would meet in finery of dresses or jewellery. Edward had neither the means nor the wish to make her a clotheshorse. She was too restless to submit to a dressmaker's fittings. The few new dresses she owned, she bought from Madame Nicolle on rare visits to Jersey. Her figure had not altered noticably since she was a girl. If anything, the aftermath of typhoid and the frustrations of Eaton Place had narrowed her waist and pared down her moulded cheeks. She put on a gown that had seen previous service. She arranged her long, chestnnut hair in its usual loose knot at the nape of her neck. She was ready to submit herself to another appraisal.

With Edward hesitating at her elbow, she made her way calmly into the drawing room. The Langtrys exchanged a few words with Olivia, but she had more important guests to occupy her. There were lions to be entertained tonight, men who found fame with their talents as actors, painters and writers, the kind of celebrities she admired above all others. Irving was here, and so was Millais. William Morris was no admirer of gilded affairs like this—Lillie made his acquaintance not long after—but the peppery little American, James Abbott McNeill Whistler, had arrived. High-minded Mr. Frederick Leighton, whose associations with the court dated back to the prince's boyhood, also circulated in the throng.

Leading Edward, Lillie walked sedately towards a corner of the room, wondering whether she had made a favourable impression on her hostess. The tones of violet in her great, shining eyes brightened with concealed excitement. Her skin, paled by want of sunshine, coloured with a golden glow. In profile, the high forehead softened with curls, the aquiline nose with the slightest change of line towards its narrow tip, the rounded chin with the suspicion of a cleft, had the tranquillity of a Greek coin. Her full, red lips were half-parted with expectation that could be a child's at the sight of a Christmas tree or a woman's waiting for a lover. Her gown was humdrum, but the body beneath it was statuesque—tall, shapely, as broad in the shoulders as in the hips.

Any man of aesthetic sensibility would have noticed her, and the room was filled with them. Here was Guenevere incarnate, an unknown face, an air of innocence, seemingly unravaged by the pressures of competing for attention in the *salons* of the city. This was no languid, consumptive maiden, but a sensuous woman. The hint of melancholy in her face was as tantalising as the promise of passion in her body. To a score of men in the room, she appeared like a vision of the golden age that glittered in their fantasies.

Millais edged his way over to his hostess to ask to be introduced. Like everyone else in his genre of painting, his mind was alert to the significance of flowers. Red roses spoke of sensuality, forget-me-nots of remembrance, yellow rue of grief. The lexicon contained a hundred such examples. Perhaps he already sensed that a lily would symbolise this woman, pure in its look, seductive in its scent, equally suitable in a bride's bouquet or a funeral wreath.

He was nearing fifty, but was handsomely rugged as if he were half that age. Effie Gray had become his contented wife after her first marriage to the righteous pundit of the arts, John Ruskin, was annulled because he could never be induced to sleep with her. "May I present Mrs. Langtry, who comes from Jersey?" said Olivia, ignoring Edward as did Millais.

In the corner where she sat, Lillie, by her account, had been feeling "very unsmart and countrified." Millais' enthusiasm swept away her self-doubt. He was delighted to hear that they had the same island as their background—his father, he said, was a Jerseyman. He must paint her portrait. Would she sit for him? On the spot, she agreed.

The élite of the company took their cue from Millais and pressed in on her. Leighton, who had an unofficial position as decorator to the Marlborough House clique, envisaged her in marble. She promised to model for him, which ranked as a social triumph; he was due to be president of the Royal Academy the following year. Edward continued to be overlooked by her admirers and unconsulted by her.

Her instantaneous success drew men like dogs to a fight. Irving waited to be introduced, his hollow cheeks creased in a practised smile, his eyes sharp behind his pince-nez. Edward Montagu Stuart Granville Montagu-Stuart-Wortley-Mackenzie, advanced from a baron to an earl that same year and one of the richest men in England, made a mental note that she must be invited to dine. In the middle-aged crush that surrounded her, the only man to spare a moment for Edward was Whistler. He was also the only man egocentric enough not to be wearing a white tie, starched shirt, and long-tailed coat.

The youngest in the circle around her had sidled in after exhibiting signs of being overwhelmed on sight. "Who *is* she? Who is the Grecian goddess in the black dress?" asked George Francis Miles for the benefit of anyone listening. He made a further effort to impress by pulling a tailor's bill from an inside pocket and quickly sketching her in pencil. Seventeen months older than Lillie, he was no more than a cadet in the ranks of master artists, but he was an apprentice "soul" and a pet besides. Frank Miles, as he signed his name, was a Nottinghamshire clergyman's son who made his living by turning out illustrations for the magazines, as well as portraits in pencil or oils of his patrons.

Society and Bohemia met in his shabby apartments at the top of a creaking staircase in an old house on the corner of Salisbury Street, overlooking the Thames. Princess Louise, the queen's daughter, unhappily married to the Marquess of Lorne, was a regular visitor. Violet Fane, who wrote poems with a flavour of Elizabeth Barrett Browning, was an habituée. Ellen Terry called; so did Whistler and Johnston Forbes-Robertson, who was distinguishing himself as an actor with Irving's troupe.

Among his worn furniture and Japanese prints, Miles was a confirmed exhibitionist. Like Victor Hugo, who went into exile on Jersey after Louis Napoleon's coup of 1851, Frank had a weakness for exposing himself to small girls. His friends overlooked this foible, though they sometimes remarked on the child, known only as Sally, whom he picked up on the pavement outside Victoria Station, where her mother sold flowers, and kept her in his apartments to preside at tea parties. Sally also served as a model for Miles—the prince himself bought "A Flower Girl" —and for Frederick Leighton, who painted her as the subject of a sentimental canvas that he called "Daydreams."

As soon as Miles had completed his first, hasty sketch of Lillie and given it to her as a memento, he set about making another. This was for sale to a printer for a guinea or two. Reproductions of it showed up in shop windows soon afterwards, price one penny. The face of Lillie was to be impressed on a wider public than she had ever imagined might be susceptible to her visible charms.

While the males among the Sebrights' guests concentrated their attentions on the stranger with the manner of a queen, the ladies by and large dismissed her as an upstart and occupied themselves by exchanging the latest tidbits about the prince and the Aylesford affair.

Lord Randolph's immediate response to the prince's challenge to duel had been to name his second, then send a curt note to the prince to say that no one knew better than the heir to the Throne that the idea of meeting over pistols was absurd. This insult to honour was handed to His Royal Highness by Beresford when *Serapis* put in at Malta. He refused to yield under this fresh pressure. Churchill could do his worst so far as the prince was concerned; he would not intercede with Aylesford. He appealed to his mother, however, to back him. He would delay his homecoming if she wished. An immediate telegram brought her reply: He was perfectly right not to bow to threats.

Disraeli, in whom the prince placed little trust, entered the picture and sent for Churchill. He had no intention whatsoever of apologising, said Randolph.

His brother was proving no easier to manage. After promising not to see Edith for a year, Blandford retreated to Brussels and wrote Randolph from there: "If A. leaves matters as they are between him and Edith I shall only wait until H.R.H. comes back to appear on the scene and then if A. tries to lick me I shall do my damnedest to defend myself and afterwards if I am all right, I shall lick H.R.H. within an inch of life for his conduct generally, and we will have the whole thing up in the Police Court!!"

Only an unprecedented blizzard that covered London with inches of drifting snow on the eve of Good Friday replaced the prince's troubles briefly as the prime topic of conversation. He broke his voyage home to spend three weeks in Spain and Portugal, with yet another insult to mar the pleasures of his six months away. Without a word to him from his family or any Cabinet minister, he had been left to discover from the newspapers that Disraeli had plans to proclaim Victoria Empress of India on May

1, when her son would still be absent from England.

The prince had his paragon of a private secretary, Francis Knollys, express his indignation to Downing Street: "He is certain that in no other country in the world would the next Heir to the Throne have been treated under similar circumstances in such a manner." Disraeli appeased him by relaying a secret: The next list of honours to be awarded on the queen's birthday would recognise several companions of the India expedition, including Suffield, who was to be made a Knight Commander of the Bath.

Prince Louis' reward was his promotion to full lieutenant. In the matter of social precedence within the shipboard group, he came second only to the Prince of Wales. This was reflected in the seating arrangements in the officers' mess and his constant presence at the side of the man he called "Uncle Bertie." Louis, born in Austria in 1854, was a Serene, not a Royal, Highness by virtue of his birth, and "really a remarkably nice boy," in his uncle's opinion. Some women called him the best-looking man they knew. Louis' father, Prince Alexander of Hesse, had committed the genealogical blunder of entering into a morganatic marriage with a girl he loved, Julie, Countess of Hauke, daughter of a general in the Russian army. Louis and his brothers therefore had no claim to their father's title or property. The Battenbergs could not be regarded as one of Europe's great royal dynasties.

Uncle Bertie wanted Louis to go on half pay and join the entourage at Marlborough House. The young man had endeared himself to the royals by taking on British citizenship to join the queen's navy. The queen, moreover, had permitted his cousin, also named Louis and another Prince of Hesse, to marry her second daughter, Alice. Family ties were close, but Lieutenant Battenberg's only home remained an unassuming little palace in the sleepy town of Darmstadt, capital of the pocket-sized principality of Hesse, in west-central Germany.

Though his uncle promised him a permanent room in Marlborough House as an added inducement, Louis was intent on his naval career. Idleness on half pay held no attraction for this sprightly junior officer, who had been happy to offer his services as an amateur artist to the *Illustrated London News* when that magazine's staff illustrator, Mr. Simpson, was hurried off to China on a new assignment as *Serapis* anchored in Bombay.

"I made quite a lot of money," Louis reported proudly, "and Simpson had me elected an Honorary Member of the Institute of Painters in Water Colours."

Instead of spending his time with Uncle Bertie, he elected to go to sea again in HMS *Sultan*. Under the Duke of Edinburgh's command, the new warship was armed with the latest-model eight-inch guns, and was capable of making fourteen knots with steam up or under sail. As a Serene Highness, Louis would again rank next to the commander. Uncle Bertie was disappointed by his young cousin's choice, but he kept the room waiting for him in Marlborough House.

Disraeli had not long to wait for his own share in the postscript to glory after the Indian excursion. In August, Her Majesty was delighted to elevate her favourite flatterer from a commoner to an earl. Henceforth, he was Lord Beaconsfield, as wily in the Upper House of Parliament as he had ever been in the Lower.

Sentiment and expediency usually combined in the prince's thinking. Alexandra received "a very dear letter from my Bertie," asking her to meet him *"first and alone"* as soon as *Serapis* entered home waters. She rode out in an admiralty yacht, *Enchantress,* to meet the glistening white troopship with a menagerie on its decks when it dropped anchor. Her husband climbed down into a barge, and a crew of bluejackets rowed him off to collect her. She noticed how the trials of his trip had thinned him.

After a few minutes together, man and wife were returned to *Serapis.* The ship's band, assembled on the main deck, welcomed them aboard. The anchor was winched up, and Serapis led a triumphant procession into Portsmouth Harbour. Another band there blared out "God Save the Queen." The rifles and swords of an honour guard whipped into a salute. With their children and attendant nursemaids, with his brothers Affie and Arthur, Duke of Connaught, the prince and princess rode in a royal train to London. Inquisitive crowds collected at every station along the way for a glimpse of their faces.

A line of carriages, with the prince's at its head, wove its way from the railway station to Marlborough House. Less than an hour after entering its doors, the prince and princess set out to face the public. There might be hostile demonstrations over the Aylesford scandals as there had been for weeks following the Mordaunt trial. They had been hissed on the streets then, and a near-riot erupted when they visited a theatre. He was booed on the course at Ascot, but a lucky winner in the last race turned the mob's catcalls to cheers. "You seem to be in a better temper now than you were this morning, damn you!" muttered the prince, with a cigar in one hand and his raised hat in the other.

The test he set for himself and Alexandra tonight was an appearance in the royal box at Covent Garden Opera House, where a gala performance of Giuseppe Verdi's *Un Ballo in Maschera* was being staged. For good measure, he took along their two sons, Prince Eddy, twelve last January, and Prince George, one month short of his eleventh birthday. The gamble worked. The audience rose in applause the moment the group appeared and repeated its ovation before and after every succeeding act. The soprano and chorus led the singing of his personal anthem, "God Bless the Prince of Wales," followed by the similar standard wishes for his mother.

The next morning, Sporting Joe passed the word to Marlborough House that he would not file suit to divorce Edith. A deed of separation would serve the purpose. Lady Blandford followed the same course against her husband, then divorced him two years after Edith bore him a son. By that time, Lady Aylesford had been excluded from Court circles for so long that she might never have existed. Ostracism was as deadly in its effects as slow poisoning.

The prince, for once, stayed away from the Derby that spring—it was understood that his varicose veins were bothering him—but he did go to Ascot races two weeks later. Alexandra seemed outwardly unaffected by the events of the past months. She had brought herself to accept her husband on the terms he set for their manufactured marriage. But those who were close fancied that they detected a new sadness in her.

Lord Randolph felt the power of ostracism. Since the prince held that his former friend had permanently lost the right to be called a gentlemen, the Marlborough House set accepted that judgement. Churchill suppressed his pride to send the prince a letter of apology for his behaviour to the princess. He received no acknowledgement. With the doors of the great twin houses closed to him, he had little choice but to leave the country. In July, he took his American wife, Jennie, to stay in the United States with his father-in-law, Leonard Jerome.

For the sake of Randolph's long-suffering parents, the Duke and Duchess of Marlborough, who were old friends of hers, the queen wished to see peace restored between her son and theirs. Under pressure, the prince agreed to accept a formal apology from Randolph, but only on condition that its language be strictly legal, phrased by the Lord Chancellor, Earl Cairns, and approved in advance by Disraeli and Harty-tarty. The resulting paragraphs were read by the queen herself and Marlborough before the wounding document was despatched to Randolph.

He elected to sign it in Saratoga, New York. There it was that General John Burgoyne, soldier and dramatist, was forced to hand over his British army to the Americans on October 17, 1777, a turning point in the Revolutionary War. Churchill, rebellious to the last, added a postscript: "as a gentleman," he felt compelled to accept the Lord Chancellor's phraseology, abject as it was. He returned his signed surrender by way of his father.

The prince acknowledged its receipt to the Duke of Marlborough, though the postscript had infuriated him. He refused to communicate with Randolph. The prince's personal involvements, said Disraeli, were "almost as troublesome" as the mounting crisis in the Balkans, where the Turks had let loose a horde of Bashi-Bazouks, their heavily armed irregulars, to slaughter twelve thousand Christian Bulgars.

Aesthetes in general were less concerned with Turkish atrocities than with the summer's exhibition at the Royal Academy. Public opinion might be outraged by news of the massacre. Disraeli might be discredited for having favoured the Turks, like the heads of Jewish communities in Europe with whom he kept valuable contact. Gladstone might be appalled by Turkish misrule of Christians—he pounded out a pamphlet, *The Bulgarian Horrors and the Question in the East,* which would help win the Liberals the next election. Aesthetic London had been led to expect great things at the Academy show, but it was sadly disappointed.

Millais' "Over the Hills and Far Away"—a brooding moor, pools, reeds, and heather—was acclaimed as the landscape of the year, yet the critics found something wanting in the canvas. They concluded that it "lacked feeling." Edward Poynter was exhibiting the first of four enormous panels he had been commissioned to paint for the Great Hall of Wharncliffe House. The earl's country seat at Wortley, Yorkshire, was happily situated on lands that covered a seemingly inexhaustible fortune in coal to be mined. Wharncliffe's tastes ran to the classical. The painter gave his patron his money's worth in "Atlanta." The legendary, swift-footed maiden was depicted, hair and drapery flying, as she stooped to gather up the golden apples dropped in her path by Hippomenes as he raced against her, with death the penalty if he lost and marriage to her the prize for winning.

The critics found fault with this canvas, too. Poyn-

ter, they sniffed, showed "disregard of proportions
. . . unless we are to assume the lady to have been
a giantess." They calculated that if Atalanta stood
up, she would tower over Hippomenes, who was "all
too compressed in look and limb." Clearly, the artist
needed better judgement and better models.

Millais congratulated himself on finding Lillie at the
Sebrights. He claimed the right to take her in on his
arm when supper was announced. If Edward complained on the way home about how she and everyone else except Whistler had neglected him, she
dismissed his comments out of hand. "Whatever my
husband said and felt, I absolutely revelled in the
novelty of it all," she remembered nearly fifty years
later.

The landlady of the Eaton Place apartments let Lillie know how upset she was the following day. She
and her only maid spent far too much time, she said,
in answering the front-door bell. A series of footmen
presented invitations from their masters for the Langtrys to come to dine or take tea, to attend a reception,
an at-home or a ball. There were enough requests to
keep them in London for another six months. Lillie
accepted all of them. Bitterly aware that he was no
more than an appendage, Edward retreated into sul-
lenness, too weak in character to challenge her, too
hidebound by the code of a gentleman to consider
letting her go alone.

The first dinner party of the new era took them
to Curzon Street and the Wharncliffes. Artists gathered at the Wharncliffes, the literary set—Tennyson, Browning, Matthew Arnold, and the rest—at
Mrs. Jeune's. The earl's wife, Susan Lascelles, was
also an earl's daughter, Lord Harewood's. This
middle-aged *grande dame* with the suspiciously golden
hair had a fondness for out-of-season flowers on the
table to complement her coloring. The embroidery on
which she constantly worked marked her as another
arts-and-crafts aesthete. The cigarettes she smoked
endlessly in closed company disturbed most of her
friends as a habit indulged in only by actresses and

other loose women. Lillie was tempted to try a puff or two herself in keeping with her emancipation.

Lady Wharnecliffe came forward with a splendid idea. She would help overcome Poynter's problem with models by posing herself for a future panel. Her friend Violet Lindsay's cameolike beauty should be featured in the canvas, too. Violet, who dabbled with pencil sketching herself besides playing the violin, agreed. Perhaps Mrs. Langtry might also consent to sit for Poynter? She could not be more pleased. The painter's feelings about the frolic were strictly his own, but when the time came to work on "Nausicäa," he included his wife, Burne-Jones' sister, among the handmaidens of King Alcinous' daughter, caught in the act of discovering the shipwrecked Ulysses.

The circle of distant admirers of the face of Lillie Langtry could be counted in the thousands after Frank Miles' sketch went on sale. It qualified her as what Society ironically referred to as a "professional beauty." The printing press and the camera had combined to create a new audience for cheap reproductions, sold like picture-postcards in the corner shops. A photograph album, covered in red plush or tooled leather, was kept in most parlours, perhaps as a token of yearning for something of beauty in the ugliness of the age. Sepia prints of lovely ladies encircled in decorative borders of flowers filled album pages or stood in rococo frames among the crowded ranks of relatives on the sideboard. Other *demoiselles,* unframed, with their underwear coyly disarrayed to expose bulbous buttocks and tantalising breasts, were locked up in desk drawers in the library or secreted in a gentleman's wallet.

Professional beauties, by definition, were those who displayed their faces and demurely clad figures to a commercial photographer, sometimes for a secret fee. The settings in which they appeared and the dusty props employed were limited only by his imagination and their endurance in keeping still long enough for the image to be registered on the sensitized glass plate. They gazed forlornly at vases of paper flowers against painted backdrops of Mediterranean sunsets. They toyed with quill pens at lamplit desks and braved blizzards of artificial snow in their best furs. They languished in hammocks and dangled from swings. When Lillie was enrolled as an apprentice member of the corps, she showed herself willing to pose in any suitably refined *mise-en-scène,* but she jeered at a fellow "P.B." who was coaxed into being pictured holding a dead fish. Lillie's standards were set higher than that.

The little world to which she aspired classified beautiful women in two clearly delineated sets. One was royal and aristocratic, headed by Alexandra, as slim and pretty as a girl, in spite of being thirty-two in December and having borne six children. So far as looks and breeding were concerned, her only rival was the Empress Elizabeth of the dual monarchy of Austria-Hungary, which embraced more than a quarter-million square miles of Europe.

Connoisseurs on the subject, who devoted daily hours to debating the question, added to the roll of honour the names of the Ladies Dudley, Lonsdale, Breadalbane, Granville, Londonderry, Tavistock, and a dozen others. Bewitching Jennie Jerome was automatically excluded from the list because of Randolph's caddishness. When Jennie returned with him that winter, the queen felt that, after his apology, the Churchills could not be barred completely from Court activities. The prince replied that he would bow but not speak to Randolph if their paths crossed. He and Alexandra would boycott any house the Churchills entered, and he proposed to excommunicate any family that entertained or was entertained by Randolph and Jennie. Not for eight more years did he address a word to the princess' tormentor.

The other set of beauties were the professionals, less glorious but more celebrated because of their availability in pictorial form as a product on sale in the shops. Lillie's popularity among customers with a quick response to a beautiful face and a few pennies to buy a picture of her was growing when a telegram arrived from St. Helier. Reggie, out hunting with the Jersey draghounds, had been thrown and crushed by the young mare he was riding. His life was despaired of. She had not seen him since the morning of her wedding day.

The journey to St. Helier could be accomplished within twenty-four hours. The nine o'clock evening train from Waterloo reached Southampton in good time for passengers to catch the eleven forty-five overnight steamer. For some unknown reason, she delayed her départure. Her brother lingered on for three more days. When Lillie reached his bedside, he was dead. She wept from grief and from guilt, which was uncommon in her, and went on weeping through the mid-December night. Her sorrow was small compared with her mother's at the loss of the last child in her household.

The iron tyres of the funeral carriages, black plumes bobbing at each corner of their roofs, rumbled over the granite setts of the streets, accompanied by the ring of iron-shod hooves. The sound softened as the black horses strained to pull the procession up the gravel of St. Saviour's Hill to the old churchyard. Le Bretons as distant as fourth cousins were there, as the custom of the island demanded, women in black bonnets, men with crepe bands circling their top hats, all wearing black gloves, available on request from the undertaker.

Little in the town had changed since Lillie's last visit. The butchers' stalls in the market were hung with Christmas turkeys, geese, chickens and whole pigs, mouths stuffed with holly. The roast-chestnut barrows were out again, selling a dozen for a penny. The town crier with his handbell still bellowed out the day's news and announcements in the Market Square. Incandescent gas lamps had replaced the sooty, old fishtail burners there. After a dozen years of renovations, the courthouse on its south side was still uncompleted. Breton peasants still clattered along in sabots, and the fleas still performed under the magnifying glass in a tobacconist's shop window on King

Street. The dean, too, clung to his old pursuits, more openly now than before. She felt hat her life was over. The mood lasted throughout the weeks she stayed on to comfort her mother. Lillie wore the black dress ordered from Madame Nicolle as a constant reminder that the man she cared for most would never be seen again. Another fetter was broken. In the New Year, she sailed for home with the black dress in her luggage, accompanied by a new Italian maid, Dominique.

"I returned to London," Lillie remembered, "in a state of deep depression, caring little for anything."

II
The First Gentleman in the Country

✤ IV ✤

The prince invariably awoke in a good humour, confident that no matter what ordeals of boredom the day might bring, he would find some pleasure in it, even if only in a satisfactory meal or a decent glass of wine. The early mornings were the only time that he had the upper hand of his appetite. He rarely woke up hungry. If hunger attacked him in the night, there was always a cold bird and a bottle waiting beside his bed.

On this Monday morning his valet could rely on escaping the shouts of abuse which his master was pleased to din in his ears. The least hint of familiarity was intolerable either from a servant or a friend. The prince set exacting standards.

His plump cheeks must be lathered and shaved with respect for his brown moustache and beard, whose style he had experimented with over the past year until he settled on their present shapely dignity to cover his receding Hanoverian chin. The clothes laid out for him must be correct for the occasion down to the last buttonhole, or the radiant cheerfulness would swiftly vanish from his hooded blue eyes. He had been no more than seventeen when his father complained, "Unfortunately, he takes no interest in anything but clothes, and again clothes. Even when out shooting he is more occupied with his trousers than with the game!"

Now, one month past his thirty-sixth birthday, the matter of dress still occupied him. He was well pleased with his tailor, Henry Poole of Savile Row, whom Suffield had recommended, but he liked innovations of his own devising. Aboard *Serapis*, for example, he introduced a short navy-blue jacket as required dinner wear by his entourage and all ship's officers, instead of tail coats and mess uniforms. When he appeared in London sporting tan gloves with black stitching, the young bucks were quick to emulate him. Some of his friends took their cue from him. Lord Hardwicke, for instance, otherwise noted for his bawdy songs, inspired his hatmaker to produce what the Marlborough House set acclaimed as the perfect topper.

The prince's eye for sartorial detail took in the cut of a collar and the design of a uniform's button. Dinner was ruined for him if he detected that any man at table had neglected some nicety essential to proper attire. At any social ceremony he attended, he made an exacting guest. Before setting off for one friend's marriage, a ceremony which always bored him, he chided an equerry who was to accompany him. "My dear fellow, where is your white waistcoat? Is it possible you are thinking of going to a *wedding* in a black one?"

On this January morning, as he submitted to the soothing ritual of being primped and groomed for another day, he was content. He had spent the usual Christmas at Sandringham. In accordance with his habit, he was staying on with his family amid the twenty thousand acres of bleak Norfolk landscape that he regarded as home. For the first time since Albert's death, his mother had gone to Windsor Castle for the holidays. An outbreak of fever on the Isle of Wight had driven her to retreat from Osborne, her customary choice for this holiday season.

The promised pleasures of the Sandringham estate had appealed to him more than the house itself at first sight thirteen years ago, when he picked it up for 220,000 pounds as a home for himself and the slender Danish princess he had undertaken to marry. He might have bought nearby Gunton Hall, Suffield's place, had it been up for sale. As it was, he could count himself fortunate. Sandringham was the only suitable property on the market. Its owner, the Honourable C. S. Cowper, had thought it expedient to go abroad with his new wife, Lady Harriet d'Orsay, who had been his mistress.

The prince considered an additional 80,000 pounds of inherited capital well spent in tearing down the original eighteenth-century building and replacing it with a Victorian-Tudor-Jacobean establishment of red brick and liberal applications of brown local stone, with a multitude of gables and two huge cupolas. The result was more opulent than imposing, an oversized facsimile of a self-made ironmaster's mansion rather than a palace. It enjoyed the distinction of having almost enough bathrooms for everyone, a point on which the prince set great store. Its walls supposedly contained a room for each day of the year, though he had not personally undertaken to count them, and neither had Alexandra, who had not a particle of interest in housekeeping. The sleeping quarters for Prince Eddy and Prince George were little bigger than closets.

He made his way to breakfast with no expectation that Alexandra would join him. He had long since reconciled himself to the fact that she would be late, sometimes by an hour and more, for everything. He was extraordinarily patient about it, though the drumming of his fingers gave away his impatience. She remained in her bedroom, whose every foot of space was cluttered with ornaments, photographs, sentimental mementos, and holy pictures. Over her bed, between the divided curtains draping the carved headboard, hung a crucifix surmounted by a gilded cherub. A statue of Christ stood on her bedside table. She could not be expected to appear until eleven o'clock at the earliest.

Usually he ate a frugal breakfast—nothing more than toast and coffee, with a newspaper propped against the pot. A day's shooting called for a heartier start—poached eggs and bacon, followed by smoked haddock or woodcock. The rest of the day's meals would be more robust: a substantial luncheon; possibly a lobster salad at teatime; an enormous dinner at which ten courses would be rated skimpy. The dining room was equipped for equal appetites in his guests, who ate at small round tables set only for

101

breakfast. Silver chafing dishes covered the sideboard, filled with bacon, eggs, sausages, kidneys, steaks, and chops.

Only personal friends acceptable to Alexandra as well as to the prince were invited to Sandringham. They came down in a special coach of the train from St. Pancras Station to the nearest stop at Wolverton. His carriages with a corps of footmen in red livery met them there, together with horsedrawn vans to transport the huge, roofed leather trunks, suitably identified with coronets, that covered the platform from one end to the other. Every guest needed to have at least three changes of clothes for every occasion. A platoon of ladies' maids, clutching their mistresses' jewel boxes, and gentlemen's gentlemen made up the contingent.

The file of carriages turned in through the massive "Norwich" gates of ornate ironwork, given by the county gentry as a wedding present, then through the glade of rhododendrons to the front steps of the house. The host and hostess made a habit of standing to greet their visitors in the oak-panelled hall. A stuffed baboon extending a tray for calling cards, a grand piano, easy chairs, a pet cockatoo, desks and tables holding an assortment of newspapers and trashy books completed the decor there.

Every clock in the house was set thirty minutes fast. Guests were advised to advance their watches accordingly, since the prince expected punctuality in everyone except his wife. Toying with time was a notion he adopted from a Norfolk neighbour, Lord Leicester, with the happy thought of squeezing in an extra half hour's light for the sake of more shooting, the principal daytime occupation at Sandringham.

An invitation to visit evoked mixed feelings in many of his guests. It was sought as an accolade because it showed the world that the prince accepted them as intimates. But the east wind off the North Sea blew bitterly cold in winter. Keeping up with their host's conversation, which alternated between English, German and French, was taxing. Living up to his rules for always doing the right thing grew wearying after a day or two. He went to bed abominably late, and nobody was permitted to retire before he did.

With breakfast over, at ten thirty Sandringham time, the prince in heavy tweeds and a jaunty Norfolk hat led his male guests and a squad of loaders out to the coverts. An army of beaters, recruited from the tenant farms, waited to flush the birds. The women, who could dress for breakfast in outdoor skirts or elaborate day gowns as they pleased, were left to their own devices to fill another empty day. A handful of "darlings" would help in passing the time, nonsporting men deliberately invited for the purpose. The distant thudding of the guns began to sound through the house.

Pheasant and partridge abounded on the estate. Under the prince's husbandry, the annual bag of game rose from seven thousand to thirty thousand, yet he was never satisfied. With the instincts of a businessman, he demanded better figures every year, and never mind the cost. It was not that he considered himself a first-class shot. He let difficult targets go rocketing by without bothering to aim. But he wanted to afford his friends the same zest that he felt from the bracing air and robust exercise.

The superb shots among them avoided places next to him, if they could. He had a habit of claiming all birds on the ground around him as his own. His dogs were well trained to collect them to add to his total. On the other hand, he was usually tolerant of any blunders made by tyros at the sport. It was they who blenched, not he, if an unlucky shot whistled uncomfortably close.

Some of his tenants, infected by the radical traditions of the country, complained in private that their master cared more about his precious birds than about themselves or their trampled crops. He rewarded his keepers generously when the game count was high. He accepted without question their reports that a tenant was guilty of damaging the preserves and punished him in consequence.

The whispering extended among the ranks of the household servants who staffed the kitchens, the stores, the lodge, the gun room, the tapissier's office, the butchery, the pastry room, and the cold-meat larders, which could hold seven thousand head of game. It centred on him, not on Alexandra, whom one otherwise disgruntled farmer's wife described as "some exquisite little being wafted straight from fairyland to say and do the kindest and prettiest things all her life and never, never grow old or ugly."

The servants were well fed but paid in reverse ratio to the prestige incurred by working for the prince. When he was in residence, they were kept on the run from before dawn until after midnight, harassed by the demands of the hard-pressed maids and valets of the guests as they scurried up and down the backstairs and through the halls of the staff quarters on missions for their lords and ladies.

The cost to his reputation in maintaining Sandringham was matched by the cost to his pocket. Rents from the farms brought in no more than seven thousand pounds a year, a pittance compared with the income amassed from their tenants by some of the twenty-one other nonroyal dukes of the land. Buccleuch, for instance, who occasionally played host to the prince at Dalkeith Palace outside Edinburgh, drew 217,000 pounds from his 460,000 acres. Sutherland, a close friend in spite of the queen's objections to his wild way with cards and women, took in 141,000 pounds every twelve months, but then his 1,358,000 acres, the largest landholding in the kingdom, made Sandringham seem no bigger than a paddock.

Mixing with men of this wealth and striving to outshine them in style and hospitality led the prince to spend at least 20,000 pounds a year more than the 110,000 pounds or so that came to him from his own holdings and from the Exchequer. That included 10,-000 pounds earmarked as pin money for Alexandra, who had nothing of her own.

The morning's shooting ended with an elaborate luncheon of hot and cold dishes transported in hampers and heated metal boxes, served with vintage wines in a large marquee set up away from the house. Carriages brought out any ladies who cared to join the guns for the meal before shooting resumed for the afternoon. That involved the women in the first obligatory costume of the day, a suit of sturdy tweed and accompanying hat and topcoat. Not every lady chose to attend; some were not quite awake by then. After the meal, the ladies watched the first drive of the afternoon for half an hour, then returned to the house. Alexandra drove out in a dashing little trap, drawn by two ponies. To her mother-in-law's dismay, she had relished riding in the past, before shooting replaced hunting as Sandringham's primary sport. Now a permanently stiff knee, the legacy of rheumatic fever, made following hounds impossible except when she drove herself in a chaise and impressed everyone as a reckless whip. The prince, on the other hand, was not at all a good whip and found no joy in handling reins.

The whole house stirred with the approach of dusk. Every ironing room was occupied as fresh clothes were laid out for the day's next rite. Out in the coverts, an equerry went the rounds of the party, recording their scores in the game book. The prince and his weary guests made their way home—some with splitting headaches from the nonstop thunder of the breechloaders, three or four to every man—in time to bathe and change for tea. A wagon or two followed with the kill, a thousand and more birds on a good day. In the brushing room, the ladies' and gentlemen's tweeds were restored to immaculate glory for the next day's sortie.

Tea was a full-dress meal. The prince appeared in a short black jacket and black tie, a model the males were encouraged to follow. The ladies tried hard to outdo each other in flowing chiffon gowns in rainbow colours, adorned with embroidery and seed pearls, sometimes hemmed with fur. Gloves were required for every lady. A string orchestra played the prince's favorite Strauss and Offenbach for an hour in the hall. Then there was more time to fill again before dinner. Bridge tables in the card room helped relieve the tedium. The billiard room, one of the first details to be settled on in the architect's reconstruction plans, was always available. Or, where the old conservatory stood, there was the bowling alley, furnished in Turkish fashion, with water-pipes ready for anyone willing to try them. The prince was fond of bowling, a game which once prompted a joke from him, typical in its bite.

On a formal visit to Coventry, he was accompanied by Harty-tarty and the notorious Duchess of Manchester, whose hold on Hartington did not deter him from a short-lived affair with the demimondaine Catherine Walters, born in a Liverpool slum, fondly called "Skittles" by her host of lovers as well as the Duke of Devonshire, who permanently maintained her. Through an equerry, the prince passed a message to the mayor of Coventry. Could a bowling alley be included in their itinerary, and would the mayor let Hartington know that this was done at the prince's specific request. When the royal party reached the alley, Harty-tarty seemed unimpressed until their host innocently remarked, "His Royal Highness asked especially for its inclusion, in tribute to your lordship's love of skittles."

The pace of the house quickened two hours before dinner. Maids and their mistresses fussed together over the choice of gowns, jewels and coiffures. The ladies took their turn in the bathtubs. Footmen tapped on guestroom doors with news of what waistcoats would be *de rigueur* this evening. Curling irons glowed warm for ladies and some gentlemen alike.

Guests assembled in the drawing room, the most formal setting in a house that for the most part was furnished more for comfort than style, to await the entrance of their host and hostess. Tiaras glittered on nests of curls, medals tinkled on black tailcoats if the occasion was formal. Alexandra glided in with the smooth, rustling walk in which she had trained herself to hide her limp. The inevitable jewelled band around her slim throat covered the scar of a childhood tracheotomy. In a floating Doucet gown, she exuded charm as light as a butterfly's wings.

Every lady wore gloves buttoned up to her elbows. An equerry told every man whom his partner was to be at dinner and where he was to sit. Nothing was left to chance. Details preoccupied the prince, who personally allocated the bedroom in which each guest would be accommodated.

At nine o'clock precisely, the prince took the arm of his chosen partner and the stately processon into the dining room was under way. On the walls hung Goya tapestries, the only outstanding treasure of art in the house. The table gleamed with silver, bone china, crystal glasses, greenhouse flowers, and epergnes of fruit and sweetmeats, every item placed with millimetric preciseness under the butler's finical scrutiny.

The master chef and his assistants had toiled all day to perfect the appearance as well as the taste of the food. The prince's palate as a gourmet as well as a gourmand was kept keen by the visits to Paris which were essential to his well-being. *Haute cuisine,* with the finest wines for every course, was the rule here, reflected in the handwritten menus standing upright in silver holders on the tablecloth. Not plain roast turkey but *dindon rôti aux truffles à l'Espagnole;* no barely warmed grouse but engraved silver platters bearing pheasant *à la Flamande.* The prince's guttural voice, instantly identifiable by its rolling Germanic *r,* led the soaring conversation. The princess, increasingly deaf, covered her difficulty by turning a radiant smile on everyone.

Hock, claret, burgundy and madeira flowed as one dish succeeded another: turtle soup, two kinds of fish, game and roast meats, sherbets and desserts almost too magnificent to be divided. Windsor was not at all like this. There, at the queen's round table, the fare was less elaborate and the talk more subdued by her tiny, overwhelming presence.

She objected strongly to smoking. She vowed that the tobacco odor of any letter written while her correspondent had a cigar at hand offended her sensitivities. At Windsor, smoking was permitted only in the billiard room, which was so distant from the main quarters that a page was stationed there to make sure that nicotine addicts found their way safely to their bedrooms. At Sandringham, the prince could scarcely wait for the last course to be served before he lit a cigarette at table. The clocks would then be striking ten.

Footmen brought in cigars the moment the ladies had withdrawn to the drawing room. The prince was impatient to rejoin the ladies. No more than half an hour later, the gentlemen went back to the drawing room and the frivolities of the evening began. Cards were the unvarying pastime, played for stakes as high as the prince thought reasonable. Whist was a favourite game until he learned bridge one rainy day in Cannes and decided that he had been wrong in concluding that "It does not appear to be particularly interesting, and I do not think it will be popular." Baccarat, infallible for escalating the scale of bets, had become something of a rarity in the house. It was too explosive except for profligate tastes.

His heavier gambling days lay in the recent past, when the rumour mills of London scattered the word that he was enlisting young men into hands of whist for stakes they could not afford. In those days, he had lost as much as 400 pounds in a night at White's Club, to his mother's dismay, but he had learned better, and White's saw him no more. He resigned in a huff the day after a steward spotted him with a cigar in a room where smoking was forbidden and reminded him of the club rules. Now the prince reigned unchallenged over his own premises, the Marlborough Club at 52 Pall Mall, a few steps from his Marlborough House. He persuaded a handful of his wealthier acquaintances to put up the capital. He gave his closest friends no choice but to desert White's and join the Marlborough, where his word was law.

Cards filled the rest of the night unless the group was convivial enough for Alexandra to draw her guests into simple party games. She was not above slipping out of her shoes to take part in a rollicking round of "General Post" or to skip up and down the up-stairs halls, while a spoiled dog to which she was currently devoted—a pug, spaniel or Pekinese—barked at her heels. The horseplay, especially at Christmastime, might develop into a giggling battle fought with syphons of soda water, mother versus her two sons, who were taught to address her fondly as "Motherdear."

The princess retired earlier than the prince, who could survive on little sleep. Until she had murmured her good nights and received the ladies' curtsies, no man was allowed to leave the company. When old Major General Sir Dighton Probyn disappeared ahead of the time prescribed by protocol to nod in a library chair, the prince counted the heads of the company, then sent a page to find him, shake him awake and bring him back.

After Alexandra had gone up, perhaps to enjoy a final girlish romp in the corridors with her ladies, there were more rubbers of whist before one o'clock chimed and the host reached the end of one more day. If baccarat was the game in hand, it might be four or five before he decided to take himself to his suite.

The day before this had been quieter. The breakfast gong did not sound until ten on Sundays. The prince lived up to his own precept—"Wherever you may be, always remember to go to church on Sunday"—but with personal modifications to suit his nature. He lacked the patience to sit through more than half the service. With the male guests in tow, the prince timed his arrival at the church in his two-hundred-acre park to coincide with the start of the sermon, which by his order was to last no more than ten minutes. As he was ushered to the royal pew, the bells must peal for a second time. His wife's religion differed from his. She was High Church, given to three solid hours of devotion, which horrified the queen.

If weather permitted, a conducted stroll in the garden preceded luncheon at one thirty. Afterwards, the ladies were encouraged to change into walking skirts and sturdy shoes so that the whole party might follow the prince and princess on a tour of the stables, kennels, model farm, the stud, and finally the arts and crafts school set up by Alexandra for the instruction of local boys. She loved every corner, every nook, every stone of the estate.

On Sabbath evenings, playing cards were kept out of sight. There were only innocent parlor games to beguile the household. On Tuesday morning the week-end party broke up. Carriages and wagons took guests and luggage back to Wolverton Station. In pursuit of better shooting, the prince departed for his brother Affie's place, Eastwell Park, in Kent, leaving Alexandra and their children to the placid pleasures of Sandringham.

The two brothers had much in common, including the happiness of bagging game and their mother's poor opinion of the manner in which both her Bertie and her Affie conducted themselves. Bertie, she felt, was more to blame for leading Affie, three years his junior, down the paths of unrighteousness. The coarse-tongued young Duke of Edinburgh was an habitué of the prince's late-night parties at Marlborough House lasting until the following morning. "Come to a *baccy*" was Bertie's form of invitation, short for baccarat.

They might on occasion set out in hansom cabs with Louisa Manchester, whom the queen had barred from the Court, with Lady Filmer or others to sample the night joys of the city, winding up at Evans's Music Hall in Covent Garden, ripe with the odor of vegetables from the market outside. Francis Knollys, an accomplice in some escapades, was once commissioned to ask a special favour of young Lord Rosebery, a future Prime Minister who was currently devoting himself to horseracing. Would he be willing, Knollys asked, to make his little house at 2 Berkeley Square available as a rendezvous for the prince and the duke to entertain their "actress friends"?

Rosebery begged off. The place was too small for such revelry, he said. But he did go with them and an assortment of girls to 2 Brook Street for a night of drinking, cockfighting, and lechery, organized by the tenant there, Frank Lawley of the *Daily Telegraph*. To cleanse his soul, Rosebery was out of bed early the next morning. At the City Tabernacle, he heard Charles Spurgeon, who preceded Moody and Sankey in preaching fire and brimstone to the middle classes. Other friends were happy to oblige the two royal brothers by supplying them with the more permanent accomodations they needed for their amusements.

For the prince to travel from Sandringham to East-well Park demanded as much planning as a minor military expedition. A few days' stay meant taking a dozen or two suits and half that many pairs of boots and shoes. He would travel with two equerries, a valet, a footman, two coachmen, and a young brusher, whose job was confined to sprucing up the royal trousers after a muddy day outdoors. A shooting party necessitated adding two loaders for himself and possibly one apiece for his two aides. Had he asked Alexandra to go with him, that would have added the indispensable Charlotte Knollys; another lady-in-waiting; her hairdresser; and probably three maids.

The prince returned from visiting his brother in time to celebrate the thirteenth birthday of Prince Eddy, in line after him for the throne. The boy was a problem from the moment of his birth, two months premature, weighing less than four pounds. A few hours before, his mother had been gaily whirled over the ice of Virginia Water in a sled-chair. She had fussed over him since the days when she put a flannel apron on over her evening gown to give his his daily bath and invited her guests to help her.

He grew into a backward, sullen child, a constant irritant to his father. Suffield, who saw a lot of his neighbours, thought Eddy was "so nice and more like Alexandra than any of the others." The tutors found otherwise. On the other hand, the younger boy, Prince George, was a bright, good-looking lad, and the only member of the family who could stir Eddy into a semblance of interest in anything. Their three sisters—Louise, ten; Victoria, nine; and Maud, eight—

were still too small to join in their brothers' work or play.

The personality of their father would always bear the wounds of his own appalling upbringing. He had no intention of submitting his own sons to the pains he had suffered. With the best will in the world, the prince consort had effectively guaranteed that Bertie could never become a wholly adult being. In Albert's opinion, the heir to the throne must be "the first gentleman in the country." He set down in writing the criteria to be applied for his son:

> A gentleman does not indulge in careless self-indulgent lounging ways, such as lolling in armchairs or on sofas, slouching in his gait, or placing himself in unbecoming attitudes with his hands in his pockets. . . . The manners and conduct of a gentleman towards others are founded on the basis of kindness, consideration and the absence of selfishness. . . .

He must

> devote some of his leisure time to music, to the fine arts, either drawing or looking over drawings, engravings, etc., to hearing poetry, amusing books or good plays read aloud; in short to anything that whilst it amuses may gently exercise the mind. . . .

At the age of seven Bertie was delivered into the hands of a team of tutors commissioned to turn him into a human paragon. On Albert's orders, he was worked six days a week for as long as seven hours a day, crammed with arithmetic, geography, English, religion, German, French, handwriting, drawing, and music. Riding, gymnastics, and military exercises to a drill sergeant's orders completed the curriculum. Beyond that, his father had a miniature cottage built on the grounds of Osborne House so that his eldest son might be taught elementary housekeeping and bricklaying. A phrenologist was called in periodically to examine the bumps of Bertie's skull to assess his intellectual and moral progress.

He was isolated from other boys except Affie in his parent's conviction that a prince must have no friends. His first tutor, Henry Birch, had Albert's permission to box the boy's ears or cane him whenever his frustrations got the better of him. At ten he was "extremely disobedient, impertinent to his masters and unwilling to submit to discipline," according to his teacher's report to Albert. The little prince could not "play at any game for five minutes, or attempt anything new or difficult, without losing his temper." The prescribed penalty for that was "severe punishment." Brutality bred brutality. By the time he was twelve Bertie "had a pleasure in giving pain to others," his latest, detested tutor, Frederick Gibbs, reported. It was concluded that the insanity of his Hanoverian great-grandfather, George III, was reappearing in Bertie.

He grew up afraid of the aloof, inflexible father mother, however, Albert could do no wrong. "None of you can ever be proud enough of being the child of such a Father who has not his equal in this world—so great, so good, so faultless," she told her son, who was left in no doubt that Albert's favourite among the eight children was the first-born, Toria, the princess royal. His sister was a year older than he, precocious and fond of putting him down. Their mother's affection for her family stopped with Albert. "I find no especial pleasure or compensation in the company of the elder children," she confessed.

Much the same was true of Bertie in his own role as parent. Family life for more than a few days on end bored him. His solution to the challenge of how to educate a prince was to give the problem no more than perfunctory attention. So long as his sons escaped the severities of his childhood, he was content to leave the day-to-day business of child-rearing to his wife. The unforgotten anguish he had suffered as a boy showed in some lines he wrote to the queen, explaining his creed as a father: "If children are too strictly or perhaps, too severely treated, they get shy and only fear those whom they ought to love."

Alexandra's thoughts for disciplining her children were nonexistent. She came from a happy-go-lucky family, permanently short of money, where fun, which cost nothing, had to substitute for pomp and fine clothes. Motherdear, who rarely opened a book, set little store on her sons' formal education. What she asked for was their unquestioning love, and peace within the household. "Above all *don't ever quarrel* with your brother" was one of the pieces of motherly advice she gave Georgie, whom she encouraged to brush her long hair as she dressed for dinner.

The queen found her daughter-in-law's attitude quite inexplicable and deplored its effect on her grandsons, "wild as hawks," as she described them. "They are such ill-bred ill-trained children I can't fancy them at all," she confessed when Eddy was eight. Motherdear seldom let any one of her sons or daughters leave her side except to visit their Danish grandparents or the queen, whose welcome for her grandchildren was likely to be cool.

Now, five years later, even Alexandra saw faults in her sons. She wondered whether all the excitement she treated them to at home had not spoilt them for schoolwork. She warned their latest tutor, the Reverend John Neale Dalton, that they were "perpetually quarrelling and using strong language to each other." Given the run of the house, "they always break into everybody's conversation and it becomes impossible to speak to anyone before them."

The greatest ambition of her husband's life had been to be a professional soldier, like his Uncle George, the Duke of Cambridge, commander in chief of the British army. The queen refused to sanction that. The next best thing, so far as the prince could see, was to give his heir the chance he had been denied. Eddy must go to Wellington College, which trained boys of his age for a military career, and learn how to mix with them as equals. Georgie, like Louis Battenberg, would enter the Royal Navy as a cadet.

The Reverend Mr. Dalton questioned the wisdom of that idea. Hopes of making a man of Eddy depended on Georgie's companionship, he thought. The brothers should not be separated. The prince, always a good listener, accepted the tutor's advice. Dalton must prepare both boys to sit the entrance examinations at the Royal Navy College, Greenwich, in the coming May. Alexandra shuddered at the prospect of losing them. For a while, it looked as though fate in the form of typhoid would result in the permanent loss of Eddy several weeks later, but he recovered in time to take the dreaded test.

After Eddy's birthday party, the prince stayed on at Sandringham for a few days, shrugging off domestic problems, cheered by the news that the Duke of Marlborough, discountenanced by his sons' conduct, had entered Dublin in state as the new Lord Lieutenant of Ireland, taking Randolph and Jennie with him. The decision to accept the appointment as the queen's viceroy in the trouble-torn country had been expensive to the old duke. His salary would be 20,000 pounds, but it took twice that amount to live in the regal style that the post demanded. The only way to make up the difference was to sell off some of the artistic treasures of Blenheim Palace. The prince joked that a better solution would have been to exile Randolph and Blandford on some desert island, but he was satisfied to see Churchill out of England.

Bertie had a day's fox hunting with Suffield and the West Norfolk hounds, then took Alexandra off for a week-long house party at Kimbolton Castle, Huntingdonshire, as guests of "Kim" and Louisa Manchester. Meantime, reports on health conditions on the Isle of Wight were sufficiently reassuring for the queen to leave Windsor for Osborne, where she ordered a consignment of pheasants shot on the royal estates to be sent to tempt the appetites of patients in London hospitals.

After enjoying the Manchesters' free and easy hospitality, the prince sent his wife home to Sandringham. He squeezed in some more shooting with Affie at Eastwell Park before spending the weekend as a bachelor in Marlborough House, with a Saturday night out at the Folly Theatre. A lively play was one of the things he could sit through with no inclination to start drumming his fingers. Theatre-going was probably the one unadulterated pleasure of his boyhood. His father felt that some knowledge of the drama was important in the education of a prince, so he enlisted Charles John Kean, an old Etonian and second son of the more celebrated Edmund, to stage productions of Shakespeare at Windsor for Bertie's edification.

In February the burden of official duties descended once more on the prince's thick shoulders. He spent most of his time in Marlborough House with Alexandra to help with the formal chores, notably that of sitting in state at the levees at St. James's Palace. They went with the queen when she formally opened another year's work by Parliament. Then she took off again for Osborne, adding one more task for her underemployed heir to perform in her absences. "It is Her Majesty's pleasure," said the palace announcement, "that presentations to His Royal Highness at the levee shall be considered as equal to presentations to Her Majesty."

It was a constant source of aggravation that she saddled him with the rituals of royalty but pointedly excluded him from matters of state. In her opinion, her eldest son could not be trusted with any secret. He was too likely, she thought, to blab confidential information out of the desire to impress his intimate friends. The son in whom she had complete confidence was Leopold, twelve years younger than Bertie. The difference in her treatment of his brother was galling to her heir.

The two men could scarcely be less like each other. White-faced Leopold, with his gentle eyes and scanty hair, was a hemophiliac. His mother was a carrier of the disease, which strikes only males but is transmitted by their mothers. The patterns of genetic inheritance

116

were unknown to the medical profession of the day, but the symptoms were clear enough: a sufferer's blood was slow to clot. Leopold lived in fear of even grazing his skin lest he die from uncontrollable hemorrhaging. As a child, he came close to that when a pen he was sucking on scratched the roof of his mouth. A doctor had to press a finger over the scarcely visible wound for hours before the bleeding stopped.

Leopold was too delicate to ride or join in outdoor sports, where a brambles scrape against a shin might kill him. His mother employed her virtually housebound son as her confidential secretary. He made a gay and amusing companion for her, with his deep love of art and music. Alexandra and Leopold had idolised each other from the day she was summoned from Copenhagen to Osborne on approval, for examination by the queen as a prospective bride for Bertie. The slim, smiling princess clutched the nine-year-old boy in her arms and kissed him at first sight. "A gleam of satisfaction for a moment shone into my heart," Victoria confided to her journal that day.

Now Leopold stayed at the side of his mother and the locked, black despatch boxes holding the day's Cabinet papers that went with her wherever she travelled. He was encouraged by her to share in her decision-making as queen and empress. She was on the point of obtaining for him his own personal key to the boxes, a privilege always denied Bertie, who was barred from seeing secret papers of any sort. He suffered this new slur without protest, as no more than his usual treatment at his mother's hands.

For once, on a question of foreign policy, she and her heir held similar views. They were both ready to minimise the importance of what he described as "the so-called Bulgarian atrocities," the massacre of Christians by the Bashi-Bazouks which enraged Gladstone. The prince's reasoning was imperialistically simple, as always. The Russians, in their greed for expanded frontiers, were plotting to drive the Turks out of Europe. The outcry against the slaughter of twelve thousand Bulgars played into Russian hands. What Britain must persist in was Disraeli's policy of support for the Turks as a bulwark against the forces of Czar Alexander II, whose government backed the Bulgars. War between Britain and Russia was probably inevitable, the prince decided. In one more effort to make himself a soldier, he was busy canvassing the possibilities of obtaining a military command. Gladstone and the czar both made his blood "boil with indignation," he told his mother.

This was another subject on which he and Alexandra found themselves at odds. Her knowledge of international politics was as limited as any real interest in the arts or the emerging trade union movement, which was creating a wave of strikes and lockouts in British industry. Because her heart ruled her head, she sided with the czar. Her sister, Dagmar, had been married to his bashful heir, the Czarevitch Alexander, ten years ago at the Winter Palace in St. Petersburg. Alexandra was five months pregnant and forced, therefore, to let Bertie attend the wedding without her. The reports that came back were disturbing. The prince, it was murmured, paid far too much attention to young Russian ladies. The news could only have pained her. At that point in her married life, Alexandra had not reconciled herself to his compulsive infidelities.

Besides being the czarevitch's sister-in-law, she had a stronger reason for family loyalty to his father. She looked on the czar as the principal guarantor of her brother Willi's tenure on the throne of Greece, which he had held for fourteen years. As an impoverished young naval cadet, he had been chosen almost offhandedly by agreement between Britain, Russia, and France. The job was open because dissatisfaction among the Greek people compelled the abdication of his predecessor, Otto of Bavaria, who had been implanted in Athens as king in somewhat similar fashion after Greece threw off almost four centuries of Turkish rule in 1827. Willi, who elected to be known as George I to his new subjects, was initially asked whether he would like to be nominated as monarch one night in Marlborough House soon after his sister was married to Bertie. Nepotism weighed heavily with the great powers of Europe in the making of puppet kings and the establishment of dependable dynasties.

In this early spring of 1877, there were no obvious signs of tension between Alexandra and her husband. They took their children to theatre matinees and went together to the Opéra Comique. He had a day's hunting with the Royal Staghounds near Maidenhead and another with the Royal Buckhounds near Slough. She attended a Sunday concert at St. James's Hall. They listened to a debate in the House of Lords, opened a new ward in Charing Cross Hospital, and gave another spectacular ball in Marlborough House.

The prince took his customary morning rides with his entourage in Hyde Park. There Lillie, still in mourning for Reggie, caught her first glimpse of him as she strolled out from Eaton Place. "He is a very large man," she wrote to her mother, "but appeared to ride well for one of his bulk." She had never before seen a royalty, but she was not overwhelmed by the experience. Objectivity seldom deserted her.

At the end of March it seemed that any hopes she had of spotting him again must be postponed. The official announcement said: "The Prince and Princess will leave Marlborough House today (Saturday, March 24) for a cruise in the Mediterranean in the royal yacht *Osborne*, during which the Prince will visit the Duke and Duchess of Edinburgh at Malta and the Princess will visit the King and Queen of the Hellenes at Athens. Their Royal Highnesses are expected to be absent about six weeks."

Alexandra's health had broken down. Her outward gaiety was a mask. The Aylesford scandal had left deep wounds. The prospect of giving up Eddy and Georgie to the Navy was more than her possessive nature could bear. She cracked under the added stress of what appeared to be imminent war between Britain and Russia, which her husband contemplated so eagerly. She must have a holiday, her doctors said. She chose to go to Greece, to find early sunshine and see her endangered brother Willi; his Russian wife, Queen Olga; and their son "Tino," otherwise Prince Constantine.

Bertie grudgingly agreed to sail with her, but he drew the line at calling on Willi. Family visits with any of the Denmarks could reduce him to a state of profound ennui. His sentiments about the rights and wrongs of the Bulgarian situation might be misinterpreted, too, if he appeared beside the King of the Hellenes, who was no favourite of the Turks. Bertie would find his own pleasures with his brother Affie at Sant Antonio Palace, overlooking Valetta Harbour, Malta, even though Affie was tainted as pro-Russian by the fact of being married to the czar's daughter, the Grand Duchess Marie.

The Mediterranean cruise was postponed at the last minute. "A slight indisposition on the part of the Prince" was the excuse made. But he was well enough to sit for another portrait of himself in oils and go with the princess to the Fulham Road studio of J. E. Boehm, who was completing a glorified statue of the prince astride a horse to be erected in Bombay as a memento of the Indian tour.

Two weeks later Alexandra left for Athens without Bertie. This time the explanation given was that he was "suffering from an abscess attributed to a hunting injury." Eddy and Georgie were sent off to Sandringham. The prince remained in Marlborough House. The official word was that he expected to be well enough to leave for his postponed journey in a matter of days. That did not still the rumours of estrangement between prince and princess that went the rounds of the fashionable drawing rooms.

Another seemingly unconnected story circulated, too. Leopold had caught a spring cold when he came back to London from Osborne in mid-March with the queen and her youngest child, twenty-year-old Princess Beatrice. To brighten up the walls of his bedroom in Buckingham Palace, he had hung up a silver-framed sketch by Frank Miles of Lillie. Like his older sister Louise, Leopold occasionally visited the effete young portraitist's apartments on a corner of Salisbury Street.

The queen stopped short, so the story went, as she bustled into her invalid son's room at the customary trotting pace that marked her as perennially busy. Who was the woman portrayed in the pencil sketch? "Mrs. Langtry," said Leopold. His mother pulled a chair to the wall and climbed up for closer inspection. Her own tastes were sentimentally vulgar. She had a fondness for massive white marble statuary that required a small crane to be hoisted into place along the echoing, mosaic-tiled corridors of Osborne. Yet in her early married years, she and Albert had solemnly presented each other with paintings of coyly draped nudes.

The face of a professional beauty had no place in her palace. She carefully removed the picture from its hook for later disposal by a footman. Leopold had another sickbed visitor in Bertie. There was no telling whether that preceded or followed the queen's invasion. In any event, the call on his brother gave Bertie either his first sight or else his first news of the woman from Jersey whose reputation was starting to grow in the hothouse circles of London society.

By the middle of April all pretence that Bertie intended to join his wife on holiday was abandoned. Willi met Alexandra when *Osborne* anchored at Athens. "The Prince of Wales has recovered from his indisposition," the court circular announced at the close of the month, "and having visited various members of his family, left for France. . . . The Prince of Wales has arrived at Cannes. . . ."

His departure from London coincided with the outbreak of yet another war. His anticipation of conflict with the Russians came one step nearer to reality when the armies of the czar struck across the Turkish frontiers into Romania and from Transcaucasia into Asia. A conference of the Great Powers in Constantinople had failed. Abdul-Hamid II, Grand Signior and Sultan of the Ottoman Empire, regarded its recommendations as an affront to his dignity. The Russians, proclaiming their holy mission to protect the Slavic race, were out to liberate Christians from Muslim rule and simultaneously seize more territory in Europe.

At first it seemed that nothing could stop the Russian invaders. In Asia three columns totalling 150,000 men drove towards Batum, Kars, and Byazid, with savage Cossack horsemen hacking down the fleeing Turks. In Romania, 72,000 of the population rose to join the czar's 310,000 soldiers fighting with his brother, Grand Duke Nicholas, as commander in chief. Only the flooded Danube halted their military promenade. They camped on the north bank of the surging river, facing 247,000 Turks spread thin along five hundred miles of its far side.

The prince was later than usual in arriving on the French Riviera this year. In general his annual bachelor outing began early in March and lasted for five or six weeks. Whenever possible, he liked to send *Osborne* ahead of him, to serve as his headquarters. He firmly believed that he went unidentified under one incognito or another, often as "Le Duc du Lancastre." He laid down a similar rule in his London clubs, where fellow members must remember not to recognise him. Since he deviated not an inch from his autocratic habits under any pseudonym, considerable efforts were needed on both sides of the channel to indulge him in his whims. If a dining room maître d'hôtel forgot himself and addressed him as "Your Royal Highness" when the prince was engaged in his practice of ordering what all his guests would eat and drink, le Duc was apt to stump out in a huff.

His social calendar was arranged to mesh with his mother's only twice a year. In August he yachted at Cowes, while she was at Osborne House. In October he shot grouse and deer at Abergeldie, a cosy, comfortable place not far from Balmoral, where Alexandra was doomed to rustic boredom.

The prince and Affie managed to fit in a few days of fun together in Nice that spring. Affie steamed down in style from Malta with his wife, their two young daughters and Louis, who was pressed into service as a seagoing nursemaid when the professional nannies

122

were bedridden with *mal de mer*. Young Battenberg, generally known as "PL" to his friends and messmates, acted as an informal equerry, chamberlain, and playmate of Uncle Affie's. The holiday stayed vivid in his memory after he went with the two older men to the new casino at Monte Carlo for an evening of *rouge et noir*. PL put two old louis on red and let it ride nine times. Being necessarily careful with money, he carried off his winnings to a bank the following morning in a bag he cut and sewed from an hotel towel.

According to his unvaried routine, Bertie had a few days in Paris after he left Affie and Louis and before he returned to Marlborough House. From there he went to spend an hour or two with his mother in Windsor Castle. His two sons sat for their examinations at the Royal Navy College, and the outlook for Eddy could only depress their father, though the standards would certainly be engineered to give the sluggish young prince a passing mark.

One May morning Bertie had his valet lay out the short coat, striped trousers, top hat, and cane which he ruled were the only fitting attire in which to inspect an art exhibition. He was off to the Marsden galleries on King Street, close by Christie's auction house, to see a new painting by Millais which was being acclaimed as a masterpiece. The prince knew exactly what he liked in all the arts. In music, anything heavier than Sousa and Offenbach was intolerable, except Italian opera and the thunder of Richard Wagner. In painting he shared the prevailing fancy for pictures that told a story. With a flourish of his cane, he dismissed as "daubs" such work as the Impressionists were creating in France and the impossible James Whistler in Chelsea.

What he saw at the King Street galleries was exactly the kind of picture to appeal to the prince, as well as to the middle-class market, where the new Millais was selling famously as an engraving. "Effie Dean" was a high-class illustration of a scene from one of Sir Walter Scott's Waverley novels, *The Heart of Midlothian*. It portrayed the eager Effie keeping tryst with Geordie Robertson, the outlaw who betrayed her.

The critics, who had betrayed Millais in the past for the chalkiness of some of his models and complained that he "used dentifrice instead of paint," were charmed by this latest canvas. "Her sweet lips are parted," wrote one of them, "and there seems to linger on them the trace of the last quivering sob which made the blue, upturned eyes glisten. It is in this sorrow-laden mouth, in the azure depths of tenderness in her appealing eyes that the rare art of Mr. Millais is exemplified to a marked degree."

In point of fact, "Effie Dean" was Lillie, sitting as a model for her first full-scale portrait by the painter who had singled her out in the crowd at the Sebrights. The prince's interest in Mrs. Langtry was piqued again.

V

Little resemblance remained between the Langtrys' first lustreless year in London and life at present. The Eaton Place apartments were still their home. Edward's presence continued to give Lillie the respectability required of a married woman. Otherwise, the transformation was complete. The flurry of invitations that began to arrive again as soon as she reappeared on the scene put an end to her brooding over the loss of Reggie. The glimpse of sadness in her eyes only added to the paradoxes evident in this woman.

First the reproductions of Frank Miles' sketches and now "Effie Dean" qualified her as the latest and accordingly the most sought-after recruit to the corps of professional beauties, who were as necessary to decorate a *salon* as fresh-cut flowers. "*Do* come," the hostesses would scribble on the invitation cards delivered to their best friends, "the P.B.s will be here." The requirements placed on a beauty were not demanding. All she was expected to do was display herself in her glory at the prescribed hour in a suitable gown with her husband, should he exist, at her side, accept the admiration of her fellow guests, then go home or on to another homage.

Between dusk and dawn, Lillie sometimes made two and three appearances a night, to the intense dislike of Edward, chained to her by his sense of propriety and the implicit threat that if he refused her in this, she would set out alone. She could browbeat him into submission by the simple exercise of her will against his. Domestic peace counted for little with her, though she waspishly accused him later of "sometimes losing his temper and blaming *me!*"

When she made an entrance into a drawing room, there was a latent abandon in her manner that distinguished her from tamer members of the corps. In the words of one woman who watched her, she walked like "a beautiful hound set upon its feet." She had never encased her statuesque body in the tightly laced whalebone corsets that fashion called for, and she was not inclined to start now. Hours spent with curling irons and tissue paper struck her as being time wasted. She wore her long hair brushed to a gleam and loose or caught up in an artless knot. Since she could not afford clothes from Renfrew or Worth in Paris, she turned the shortcomings of her wardrobe into a form of distinction. The black dress she had bought as mourning for her brother appeared at party after party as a deliberate flouting of a convention that compelled less adventuresome women to support their egotism by dressing themselves in a new gown for every occasion. Lillie found different means to impress her image as a new breed of woman on such competitive society.

The acclaim she was finding resulted in a new working partnership. The Cornwallis-Wests were neighbours of the Langtrys on Eaton Place, living in a dingy, dark house at Number 49. The former Mary Adelaide Virginia Thomasina Eupatoria Fitzpatrick, daughter of the Marquess of Headfort, had been married in high style in St. Patrick's Cathedral, Dublin, at the age of seventeen. Five years later, this "beautiful Irish savage," as one of her circle described her, was the mother of three children and highly regarded as probably the most stimulating of the already established beauties.

Instead of carrying a well-curried spaniel on her lap for ornamentation on a carriage ride around the Park as so many ladies did, she displayed her young son or one of her two daughters. She was careful to air them one at a time to avoid giving her admirers the impression of undue fecundity. Little, shining-eyed, golden-haired Patsy, the name by which her retiring husband and close friends knew her, looked for admiration as plainer women might collect trinkets for a charm bracelet.

Lord Randolph Churchill considered it "difficult to find a fault in her bright, sparkling face, as full of animation as her brown eyes were full of Irish wit and fun." She took pride in a hat made of ptarmigan feathers, a gift from the Earl of Fife, a rich Scots friend of the Prince of Wales and one of the few of his companions who met with the queen's approval; she raised Fife to a dukedom after he married her granddaughter Louise.

Gladstone called at Number 49 to be entertained by Patsy, as colourful as a lovebird. Hearing her sing "The Wearing of the Green" was a particular treat for him. Charlie Beresford came to the house, handing out odd shillings and half-crowns to the Cornwallis-West children. Millais and Leighton stopped by the studio in the ground-floor rear, which William Cornwallis-West, an amateur in the arts, liked to make a gathering point for such distinguished Bohemians.

The supreme visitor at number 49 was the prince himself, who was fascinated by Patsy. He would arrive to listen to her prattle by the hour, usually with some small gift for each child, or seek her out at country-house parties whenever she was a guest. She was an inveterate matchmaker, for herself, her friends, and then, as it turned out, for her children. She married off her younger daughter, Shelagh, to the next Duke of Westminster, possibly the wealthiest man in England, and her elder daughter, Daisy, to the richest prince in Europe, Henry of Pless. Only her son George kicked against the traces by taking Jennie Churchill as his wife after Lord Randolph had died of the effects of syphilis.

Though Patsy was in the same category as herself, with their shop-window photographs on sale side by side, Lillie looked on her as a friend, not a rival. She had other feelings about another professional beauty, Mrs. Luke Wheeler. This doe-eyed competitor for attention, with her delicately formed head set on seductively slender shoulders, looked as fragile as porcelain by comparison with Lillie. A rumour went the rounds that she fainted away from mortification one evening when the crowd gathered to gaze on Mrs. Langtry instead of on herself.

Like Patsy, however, Mrs. Wheeler so far had one enormous advantage over Lillie. She had been introduced to the prince, who was noticeably taken by her charms. Mr. Wheeler, in fact, resented the attention the prince paid to her at one shooting party on the Scottish moors. In spite of the dazzle Lillie was creating, she had as yet been no closer to His Royal Highness than on the morning she saw him on horseback in his tall hat, tight blue trousers, and Wellington boots, cantering past in the tanbark of Rotten Row. If she analysed the mysterious workings of the bijou world she was entering, it was clear that he was responsible for the very existence of the professional beauties. He responded to the sight of a pretty woman like a trout rising to a deftly cast hackle. To attract the prince to a gathering under her roof, a hostess had to offer him something more stimulating than superb food, which he took for granted, or the companionship of people whose paths crossed his as a matter of routine. The guarantee that he would meet a beautiful woman, no matter whether her face was new or familiar, was lure he seldom refused.

He was an incorrigible flirt. Within minutes of

making her first curtsey to him, a pretty girl could expect to feel his arm and probing fingers around her waist and hear his practised words of flattery growled in her ears. He took it as a seigneurial right to court any woman, single or married, who impressed him as attractive. Eligible young women fluttered with the knowledge that, on meeting him, he might make explicit overtures to them as soon as the opportunity arose. That was accepted as a standard in his circle in much the same way as the soup could be counted on to precede the fish at dinner. How did one deny him, assuming that a rebuff had been decided on in advance? The best advice that experienced women offered in discreet conversation was to pretend to be ignorant of what his words and actions implied. He accepted such innocence philosophically. Ladies who set a higher value on virtue than on gratifying the prince could testify to that.

He had been philandering since the summer before his sixteenth birthday, when his father sent him to further his language studies at Königswinter on the German Rhine. The first night after he arrived, Bertie drank too much wine and grabbed a pretty girl for a kiss, exhilarated by his temporary release from the treadmill of his education as "the first gentleman." Gladstone, who was Chancellor of the Exchequer at the time, heard about the incident and dismissed it as "this little squalid debauch . . . a paltry affair . . . this sort of unworthy little indulgence." In spite of his priggishness, Gladstone detected the causes of the outburst. "Kept in childhood beyond his time," he wrote to his wife, Mary, "he is allowed to make that childhood what it should never be in a Prince, or anyone else, namely wanton."

The following year, Bertie, "so idle and weak," as his mother lamented, was sent to live with the hated tutor Gibbs at White Lodge in Richmond Park. He was to be kept "away from the world," according to his father's instruction. His restlessness there was occasionally eased by letters from one of the queen's ladies-in-waiting, Lady Churchill, aunt of Lord Randolph, who felt strong compassion for him. The queen swiftly put an end to that correspondence.

"Bertie," his mother once declared, "is my caricature." His father thought that "Bertie's propensity is indescribable laziness. I never in my life met such a thorough and cunning lazybones." Under Albert's pressure, the adolescent prince had developed a polished veneer that enabled him to handle himself well in any group with which he came in contact. He took out his repressions on his valet, pouring candle-fat on his livery, dousing his shirts with water, and now and then punching him in the nose.

At nineteen Bertie had already been scolded by his mother for being addicted to cigars. He had spent four terms as an undergraduate at Oxford, where he was tutored in seclusion and his fellow students rose to their feet on the infrequent occasion that he walked into a lecture room. Now he was entered at Trinity College, Cambridge, to avoid showing favouritism to one university over the other.

That summer, Albert ordered that his son should spend ten weeks in training with the Grenadier Guards at Curragh Camp near Dublin. He was to wear a colonel's uniform but be taught to "learn the duties of every grade from ensign upwards." At least one man alert to the prince's weaknesses was alarmed at the probable effect of his keeping close company with young officers notorious for wenching and wine.

The queen and her consort had decided that only an early marriage could improve his unmanageable nature. He was guache enough to insist to them that he would marry only for love. Albert methodically began drawing up lists of suitable brides, with reference to the *Almanach de Gotha,* which was as indispensable for the task at hand as stock books to a horse-breeder.

The necessary qualifications for the girl were intimidating. She must be royal, since there could be no thought of the heir to the mightiest kingdom in the universe marrying a commoner. She must be a Protestant, or at least show willingness to be converted, because the British would not tolerate a Catholic as their future queen. She must come of sound breeding stock; it would be her duty to bear children to secure the inheritance. Above all, she must be young and physically attractive for Bertie even to consider her. Whether she would prove to be intelligent was a matter of indifference to him, though his mother itemized her requirements for a prospective daughter-in-law as "good looks, health, education, character, intellect, and a good disposition."

On the face of it, there was no dearth of dynasties to provide an eligible wife for Bertie. Every great power of Europe was a monarchy, and every monarch gave due thanks to God for ordaining it so. Napolean III still ruled France; William I was Emperor of Germany and King of Prussia. The Russians revered Czar Alexander II as their holy father, as previous generations of them had honoured the House of Romanov since 1613. Francis Joseph occupied the throne of the sprawling Austro-Hungarian Empire. Bavaria, Belgium, Denmark, Italy, the Netherlands, Portugal, Saxony, Sweden and Norway, Württemberg —there were kings galore, and Queen Isabella II reigned in Madrid. If Bertie did not object to looking farther afield, the families of grand dukes could be combed in Baden, Brunswick and Luneburg, Hesse-Darmstadt, Mecklenburg, and Saxe-Weimar. Lesser principalities and fiefdoms filled in every last square mile on the map.

Yet the restrictions were so limiting that Albert found no more than a few names to put to his son. The most promising candidate appeared to be Elizabeth of Wied, nineteen years old and developing forceful dowdy maturity. Bertie had not met her on his early travels, so a selection of photographs was sent over for his approval. One look at them was enough to convince him that Elizabeth was not the wife he wanted.

His older sister Vicky, a special bane of his childhood, was enlisted in the search. It was two years now since Prince Frederick of Prussia had taken her as his wife. She was as strong-minded as ever and strategically placed to cast around for a bride for Bertie, who would be sure to play the tyrant over any girl less forceful than Vicky and their mother.

Mother and daughter went over the lists together, striking out names left and right. The Weimar girls? "Delicate and not pretty." The princess of Sweden? "Much too young." Alexandrine of Prussia? *"Not* clever or pretty." Marie of Altenberg? "Shockingly dressed and always with her most disagreeable mother." The gorgeous Marie of Hohenzollern-Sigmaringen? A Catholic. Princess Alexandra Caroline Marie Charlotte Louise Julie of Schleswig-Holstein-Sonderborg-Glücksburg? Bertie was not to be told that she even existed.

The Queen had ruled her out from the start, though Alexandra's father, Prince Christian, was designated by the congeries of Great Powers to be the next King of Denmark. Christian, who lived on the 2,000 pounds a year he drew in pay as a Guards officer, had the foresight to marry a first cousin of the reigning Danish king, Frederick VII, impotent, a drunkard, twice divorced, and the last of his line. The queen felt certain that any relative of Frederick's must be tainted by his debauchery. "The mother's family are bad, the father's foolish," in her considered opinion.

The brand-new craft of photography, which was to establish Lillie as a regnant beauty, was responsible for Bertie's choice of a wife. Vicky sent their mother a photograph of Prince Christian's "lovely daughter . . . just the style Bertie admires," as she wrote in her covering letter; Christian had no money to spend on painted portraits or miniatures. "Lovely," agreed Victoria after she had inspected Alexandra's picture. "From the photograph, I would marry her at once," said Albert. Alexandra was then sixteen.

With her three brothers and two sisters, she had been brought up in the house where she was born in 1844. Only the name of the Yellow Palace was pretentious. It was an unassuming home on a quiet Copenhagen street, with the pavement immediately outside its front door and no yard of any description to prevent strollers from staring in through the first-floor windows. "Alix," her family's pet name for her, was mercurial in temperament, athletic in her pastimes; an excellent dancer and horsewoman, a gay illiterate who never lost her thick Danish accent. She was born deaf from otosclerosis, inherited from her mother, which she was in turn to pass on to her eldest son, Eddy. The only visible blemish in the strikingly beautiful princess with skin like a ripe peach was the scar on her throat.

Vicky had not personally seen this unsuspecting treasure. As soon as that could be arranged and she reported glowingly to the queen about the "indescribably charming" girl, Bertie had to be urged into an early marriage before she was borne off by a suitor from some other royal family. Dynastic rivalries ran high in the matrimonial stakes. The Queen of Holland was known to be angling for Alix as a bride for her son, the Prince of Orange, which magnified the need for urgency, in Victoria's reckoning.

Bertie was not to be hurried. It was well enough for his parents to choose a wife for him, but he wanted time to think about it. "In these days," he told his mother, "if a person rashly proposes and then repents, the relations, if not the lady herself, do not let him off so easily." He had not set eyes on Alix, and he could only resent his parents' latest importunity when he went off to camp with the Grenadiers in June, "sallow, dull, heavy, blase," in his mother's despondent words. "May he only be worthy of such a jewel!"

He was ripe for mischief, which his fellow officers were only too willing to provide. One night they smuggled into his quarters a girl well known to and often used by several of them. Nellie Clifden called herself an actress, but her performances were not confined to any theatre. Bertie claimed ingenuously afterwards that at first he resisted her tempting, but clearly not for long. She added the nineteen-year-old prince to the score of men she served and would go on serving.

No word of the continuing affair had reached his

parents by late September when Bertie, travelling incognito, made his way in accordance with their careful plan to the Cathedral of Speyer in the Rhineland. He waited there in the Chapel of St. Bernard with Vicky and her husband, Fritz. Another trio of tourists wandered in—Prince Christian, his wife, Louisa, and their lively daughter, Alix, wearing her best clothes, as her mother had ordered. Vicky introduced her brother to the girl, then eavesdropped shamelessly while she pretended to look at the frescoes with the bishop as her guide. Matchmaking was in full swing.

Alix started a desultory conversation. Bertie's responses were stodgy during the fifteen minutes of their talk. Vicky imagined that he was impressed, but afterwards he commented that Alix's nose was too long and her forehead too low. When he reported back to his mother in Balmoral, she was nonplussed by his lack of interest. "Bertie is extremely pleased with her," she found, "but as for being in love, I don't think he can be, or that he is capable of enthusiasm about anything in the world." He seemed afraid of the very idea of being married and fathering children, of losing the people described as his friends.

Judging his son to be "a little confused," Albert composed a lengthy memorandum to clear Bertie's mind. Vicky, he wrote, had gone to a great deal of trouble to indulge her brother in his desire to meet Alexandra before he proposed to her. Albert was willing to go further now and concur with Bertie's wish that the princess and her parents should be invited to stay at Windsor before his reluctant son came to a final decision. However, *"We must be quite sure, and you must thoroughly understand* that the interview is obtained in order that you may propose to the young lady. . . ."

The liaison with Nellie Clifden remained a secret until she began to boast that the prince was her lover. His twentieth birthday on November 9 was four days past before Albert heard the story that flew around the Beefsteak, White's, the Turf, and the other London clubs. He asked his son to confide the

133

truth, "even the most trifling circumstances," but only to an aide. Albert personally was far too distressed to hear out the sorry tale, "which has caused me the greatest pain I have yet felt in this life." To live up to his father's hopes for him as the first gentleman in the country, Bertie should have been a virgin bridegroom.

The prince vowed that the affair with Nellie was over. In fact, by the following spring, she had planted herself in the bed of his university friend Charles Carrington, later the Marquess of Lincolnshire. Though Bertie's remorse was transparently sincere, he drew the line at naming the officers who had caused his fall from grace. An early marriage to Alexandra was essential to save him from further sinning. "You *must* not, you *dare* not be lost," his father told him. "The consequences for this country, and for the world, would be too dreadful!"

On November 25 Albert travelled to Cambridge to talk with his son and tell him that his transgressions were forgiven. They met in Madingley Hall, a country house four miles out of town, where Bertie was compelled to live. Albert would not allow him to share accommodations with other students. In the course of a long walk together to thrash out the state of Bertie's soul, the prince lost their way back. Albert returned to Windsor Castle the next day physically and mentally exhausted.

A week later he collapsed with symptoms of typhoid. The queen, close to hysteria, blamed only Bertie. For ten days she refused to send for him, while his father slipped nearer to death. Their daughter Alice finally sent a telegram to Cambridge that brought her brother to his father at three in the morning of the day he died.

The queen poured out her bitterness in an incoherent letter to Vicky:

". . . Bertie (oh, that Boy—much as I pity, I never can or shall look at him without a shudder, as you may imagine) does not know that I know all—Beloved

Papa told him that I could not be told all the disgusting details. . . ."

Contact with her son was unbearable to the queen. Nothing else would serve but to remove him from her sight. He was packed off on a five months' tour of the Near East, while a woman courtier was commissioned to confide to Alexandra's mother, Princess Christian, the sordid facts concerning Nellie Clifden. In spite of it all, Alix must become Bertie's wife. "The marriage is the thing," the queen wrote to Vicky, "and beloved Papa was most anxious for it. I feel it is a sacred duty he, our darling angel, left us to perform." But mourning for Albert, which draped the Court in black, forbade an engagement for the time being.

The black pall that covered England like a sea-coal fog did not extend over the prince's travels. In Vienna, home of twenty-seven archdukes, Johann Strauss, and the white Lippizaner horses of the Imperial stables, he was entertained by Emperor Francis Joseph. In Venice the Empress Elizabeth was his hostess. He shot wild boar in Albania and sent off a note to his friend Carrington advising him to abandon Nellie Clifden and "occasionally look at a book." The prince sported his first full beard when he broke his journey home from Constantinople to spend a few days in France.

At Fontainebleau, the Empress Eugénie, renowned for her almost embarrassing beauty, gathered together the most attractive young bluebloods within call to surround him at an informal soirée. "You are going to enjoy yourself for once," she told him, "and don't worry about your keeper."

He danced in turn with the women that Eugénie had so thoughtfully provided to give him "one evening that is all pleasure and no duty." None of them had reached the age of thirty or remained unmarried; there could be no matchmaking here. But one of them, Anna, Duchesse de Mouchy, and her husband became so highly regarded by Bertie that they would often stay with him at Marlborough House and

135

Sandringham, while he used their château as a base in Paris. Another guest at the Empress' party, Princesse Jeanne de Sagan, fascinated him more than that. She was happy to take him regularly to bed with her in the early years of his marriage.

But as he resumed his journey home to Windsor, Bertie gave no sign of wishing to disobey his mother. He, Alix, and her parents were equally submissive to the widow's will. Before he left France, he went shopping for jewellery for his prospective bride. The emotional battering he was undergoing brought tears to his eyes when the queen received him, welcoming him like a brand saved from the burning.

He followed her wishes to the letter by going to Laeken, outside Brussels, where Alix had arrived beforehand with her mother and father. In the gardens of the Palace of Laeken, owned by Victoria's Uncle Leopold, King of the Belgians, Bertie asked Alexandra to be his wife. He sat down that evening to report every last detail of what happened to his mother. "She immediately said *Yes,*" said the key passage the queen was waiting to read. "I then kissed her hand and she kissed me."

Victoria's haste to see her son safe from fresh enticements drove her to set March 10, a day in the middle of Lenten fasting, for the marriage. She overrode the shock that this produced among the prelates of the church of which she was the temporal head. Albert had lain in the new marble mausoleum at Frogmore in the Little Park, half a mile from Windsor Castle, for three months, but mourning was not to be interrupted, no matter how the British as a whole yearned for some cause for rejoicing. *She* would wear jet black to the wedding in St. George's Chapel; all her immediate family must appear in white and grey or lilac; Alexandra's dress must be English-made. Yet her irrepressible British subjects, eager for a royal show, swamped so densely around the carriage of the eighteen-year-old princess when she arrived in London from Copenhagen that Life Guards with drawn sabres were commanded to ride their horses into the cheering crowd.

Archbishop Longley, whose soldier son was to court Lillie in vain four years later, conducted the service. The jostling that followed among the distinguished guests was not unlike the riot that marked the wedding of William Le Breton to Lizzie Price. Rowdies ripped the diamond star from the uniform of one foreign count. The Duchess of Westminster risked losing a fortune in jewels when she was jammed into a third-class railway carriage of a train so overcrowded that Disraeli had no choice but to sit on his wife's lap all the way back to London.

The queen was far from satisfied that Bertie, by the act of marriage, had atoned for the death of his father. The four or five hundred people who constituted Society at the pinnacle looked to the young prince and his captivating wife to restore gaiety and glitter to the London scene. Paris was gay, Vienna was enchanting, but the British capital had been as dull as a Sunday sermon since George IV downed his final goblet of brandy in 1830.

Albert the Good disapproved of carnal appetites and the pleasures to be found in satisfying them. The pursuit of those pleasures was a preoccupation of the handful of men and women with fortunes big enough to foot every bill incurred. They were frustrated by Albert's high-minded standards of morality, which his widow clearly intended to perpetuate as a monument to her dear departed.

Society expected the prince and princess to light up London. Bertie hungered so for approval from any source that he was anxious to oblige, even if it did bring him into head-on conflict with his mother. With money to burn on new dresses for the first time in her life, Alexandra was delighted to help him force the pace. When the doors of the freshly painted town mansions, with daffodils and hyacinths blooming in the window boxes on either side, were reopened on May 1, that first season after their marriage, the ballrooms and salons of the city glowed more brightly than in living memory. The Marlborough House clique was beginning to take shape.

The queen was appalled. Bertie and Alix, she complained to Vicky, were becoming "nothing but puppets, running about for show all day and all night." She bemoaned the fate of her kingdom if she should die. "I foresee, if Bertie succeeds, nothing but misery, and he would do anything he was asked and spend his life in one whirl of amusements, as he does now."

She saw the profligate habits of the aristocracy as a clear threat to the country's future. Instead of setting an example for the lower orders to follow, pleasure-loving peers and peeresses were, she believed, setting the seeds of revolution along the lines of the French march to the guillotine. "And in this lies the real danger of the present time," she warned Bertie at a later date. Her sharp mind foresaw that "in the twinkling of an eye, the highest may find themselves at the feet of the poorest."

Three months after her wedding day, Alix was pregnant. Her mother-in-law's alarm over the paths Alexandra was following so happily with the prince increased. "For although Bertie says he is so anxious to take care of her, he goes on going out every night till she will become a skeleton, and hopes there cannot be." Another spectre besides a miscarriage for Alexandra haunted the queen, whose residual state of anxiety was heightened by the onset of menopause. Affie had taken to spending far too much time at Marlborough House. If Bertie had not married Alexandra, Affie would have been more than willing to. He "has not the strength of mind or rather of principle and character to resist the temptation," his mother fretted, "and it is like playing with fire."

The queen had no reason to fear. Alix went through an easy pregnancy. Baby Eddy was born healthy in spite of being two months premature. The princess was certainly too virtuous and perhaps too cool-blooded to dream of having her head turned by the calf eyes of her husband's young brother.

Victoria, who had borne nine children in seventeen

years of marriage, was satisfied with her daughter-in-law's performance in childbearing. A second son, Georgie, also premature, was born fifteen months after Eddy. Unless the country fell into the clutch of anarchists and the monarchy were swept away, the line of succession was secure—or it would be if only Bertie could be depended on.

Marriage was doing nothing to improve his nature, so far as she could judge. On the contrary, it was building a new self-confidence in him, which led him to talk back to her as he would never have dared to do in the past. Typically, she rebuked him for crossing her by calling on Garibaldi when the Italian revolutionist came to stay in London as a guest of the dreadful Sutherlands. She placed equal blame on old General Knollys of Eaton Square, the prince's "Comptroller and Treasurer" for permitting her son to flout her wishes. Bertie made a tart "I have now been of age for some time and am *alone* responsible, and am only too happy to bear *any* blame on my shoulders . . . as I know you like my confiding in you and letting you openly into my thoughts, I have done so now."

He ignored her warnings about his friends' evil influence and persisted in visiting their houses. He was an idler, a gambler, and, worst of all, he consorted with loose women. Bertie, his mother concluded, had become "quite unmanageable."

He had found no lasting sexual satisfaction with Alix. His physical needs were more demanding than those of the guileless young woman who had been brought up to expect no joy in intercourse and presumably found none, only a sense of duty performed. For his part he took it as an obligation to be attentive to her, to cater to her extravagance, to keep her supplied with expensive gifts, but the idea of fidelity seemed alien to him from their wedding day onwards. If either of them dreamed of discovering mature love for and from the other, she disappointed him as much as he failed her. Possibly, that was no more than each had anticipated.

The queen's attitudes towards Alix fluctuated between petulance over lack of attention paid by her daughter-in-law to grudging admiration for her acceptance of Bertie's obvious failings. "I often think her lot is no easy one," Victoria said, "but she is very fond of Bertie, though not blind."

Neither was the prince unaware of his wife's short comings. His detached appraisal of her character, expressed later to his mother was accurate enough: "None of us are perfect, and she may have her faults; but she certainly is not selfish and her whole life is wrapped up in her children."

Bored with domesticity, he flirted with high-born ladies, courtesans, and shopgirls alike, craving affection from any woman. Wherever he travelled—Copenhagen, Stockholm, St. Petersburg, Moscow, Paris—rumours of his affairs filtered back to London. Up to now he was discreet in observing the rule not to muddy his own doorstep. Alix did not appear to be unduly neglected.

The pretense wore thin at the birth of her third child. Bertie came home from St. Petersburg in February, 1867, when Alix was approaching the end of a difficult pregnancy and complaining of unaccustomed pain. He went through with a plan to go steeplechasing at Windsor, however, and ignored three telegrams urging him to return to her side. He showed up at Marlborough House for luncheon the next day, after her doctors had decided that she had rheumatic fever. After five days of suffering, unrelieved by chloroform in spite of her pleas, she bore their first daughter, Louise.

Alix's fever lingered on, together with constant pain in a leg and hip, which drew her tears. One month later she was still confined to bed, unable to move. Not until July could she at last sit up in a wheelchair for a breath of air in the garden. One knee was stiffened for the remainder of her days.

The prince concealed any anxiety he felt for her by going out night after night on his usual excursions. She refused sleeping medicine so that she would be awake when he came home, even if it was three o'clock or later. As soon as the baby was christened on May 10, he left for Paris and the opening of the exhibition there. General Knollys grumbled about the prince taking to supper "some of the female Paris notorieties, etc. etc."

Alix grew increasingly deaf, but vanity barred the use of an ear-trumpet. More and more she turned to her children as the focus of her life. The gap between prince and princess stretched wider. By the close of the year, she could walk on two canes, and she was expecting another baby. Whatever happiness the prospect brought her was dimmed by the unprecedented paragraphs that *The Times* and other London newspapers were printing about the prince's amorous relationship with another "actress," Hortense Schneider. Gossip around the Court went further than that in avowing that he had a whole "troop of fine ladies."

Alexandra continued in her part as the dutiful princess. She was adored by her household, which included Cecilia Suffield as a lady-of-the-bedchamber and most especially Charlotte Knollys, a bedchamber woman. The inevitable Charlotte held the less exalted rank, but Alix treated her as a more intimate friend.

Alexandra bore "my Bertie," as she called him, two more daughters—Victoria on July 6, 1868, and Maud on November 26 the following year. Before she reached her twenty-sixth birthday in December, 1870, she was beginning the most trying of all her six pregnancies. She tired easily and had moods of fitful depression, but she carried out every social obligation, almost as though she were afraid to leave her husband's side.

At Sandringham on April 6, 1871, she was delivered of her last child. Like the others, the baby was premature. She was attended not by Dr. Faure, the physician accoucheur of her household, but by a hastily summoned general practitioner. There was no nurse waiting, no layette ready. The baby was christened with desperate speed: Alexander John Charles Albert. He lived for a single day. Tears welled from his father's eyes as he settled the body into the coffin, pulled up the white satin pall, and spread the white lilies.

Only Alexandra was changed by the loss. Bertie promised to take better care of her from now on, yet "I am sure a sedentary life would not suit her," he said. The memory of the baby she remembered as "John" remained painfully sharp. There could be little doubt that his death marked the end of her physical role as a wife to Bertie. The sweetness of her expression increased over the years.

To meet Lillie in the spring of 1877 was to realize that there was more to Mrs. Langtry than a calm face and a body like Galatea's, of living marble. Here was the most exciting of the professional beauties, investing all her skills in the task of making a place for herself in Society and finding satisfaction as a woman.

She cultivated any friendship that promised to be rewarding, starting with John Millais. She reported faithfully to sit for him in his studio in the double-fronted house at 7 Cromwell Place, Kensington, a few minutes' walk from Hyde Park. She had many calls to go to him. After "Effie Dean," he wanted to portray her simply as herself, in the black dress she wore for Reggie. He would stand, wearing the belted, homespun jacket he worked in, staring at her in silence for fifteen minutes on end, smoke curling from his pipe. Then he would pick up his palette for a similar length of time, converting the controlled passion into paint on canvas, before he turned to study her again. He needed the glow of her presence to stir him. Unless she was in the room, the portrait was put aside.

He found her, as he said, the "most exasperating" subject he had ever attempted. "You look beautiful for fifty-five minutes of an hour, but for the other five, you are amazing," he told her. She had never heard such praise. Edward kept the habit of brushing aside compliments paid to her with, "Oh, you should have seen my first wife."

Lillie's emancipation from him had progressed to a further stage. She went alone to sit for Millais or walk with him around the streets of Kensington. He postponed other commissions to concentrate on her portrait, to Lillie's delight, which she concealed in pretended embarrassment. One subject whose sittings were rearranged was Mr. Gladstone, who was squeezing in yet another Millais portrait as he stirred the nation with his denouncements of Disraeli's pandering to the Turks in their mounting quarrel with Russia.

The aging statesman, with the curl of his sideburns matching the curl of his long grey hair at his neck, arrived at the studio from his Harley Street house. The windows there had been smashed by a mob of rabid patriots a few days earlier. His attacks on Disraeli convinced the queen, who shared her Prime Minister's regard for Turkey, that Gladstone was deranged. Her Court seethed with lying stories that on his nightly walks through the London streets he sought out prostitutes to entertain him. In fact, he deluded himself that they could be saved from themselves by his lectures.

After being introduced by Millais, Gladstone was as much impressed with Lillie as the painter had been at first sight. "When was it we conquered Jersey?" he asked, opening a bantering conversation.

"You did not, sir," Lillie answered sedately. "We conquered you, and England belongs to us."

That was a private joke between the Jersey woman and the painter, whose interest in his island ancestors had suddenly been reawakened. The same response turned up again at a dinner party in the Millais house when another guest repeated Gladstone's question. "You mean when did we Normans conquer England," roared Millais, whose tenor voice sounded strangely boyish in his thick-set frame. "And when did *we* subjugate London, Mrs. Langtry?"

The portrait took shape slowly. It was a somber, loving exercise in charcoal blacks and greys, picturing Lillie as a shy young matron standing, with one awkward hand across her skirt, the other at her side. Millais decided a single extra patch of colour was needed to complete its impact. He had the solution, he thought, in having her hold a flower. What could be more appropriate than a Jersey lily? She sent to St. Helier for a few specimens to serve him as models.

"A Jersey Lily" was the title he gave the painting when it was finished and varnished, ready to be hung in the next year's Royal Academy exhibition. But the flower in her hand was the sedate *Nerine sarniensis,* which was special to Guernsey. The true Jersey lily was the belladonna, fragrant and rose-coloured, synonymous with beauty and the relief of pain.

Of the dozens of portraits painted of her, this stood first in Lillie's affection. She felt a matching warmth for the man who painted it, an invader who had used his talents to make a national reputation. He was old enough to be the father she rejected, robust enough to be her lover if she chose one. She was not ready yet for that. She valued friendship with his wife too much. Both the Langtrys spent a holiday with Effie and John Millais when he rented a shooting box near Birnam Wood in Scotland from the Duke of Rutland, who married Violet Lindsay. Millais took Edward salmon fishing, while Lillie and Effie waited tea for them on the lawn. The following year Lillie went alone, in a clinging red dress, to the wedding of the Millais' daughter to an army captain and danced afterwards at the bridal ball.

Frank Miles had to bide his time until "A Jersey Lily" was completed, though his commercial instincts urged him to outpace Millais and have his portrait of her on display first. But she knew that he was not in the same class as the master painter, in ability or distinction. She could not afford to spare him the hour or two he asked of her every day, she said. Miles filled the interval by making hundreds of India-ink sketches of her for sale as originals or reproduced as postcards, earning more than he ever made from his best-paid commissions, a pioneer in the exploitation of Lillie.

Her feelings about the fey young man were ambiguous. She was impressed by his popularity with royalty—the day came when he painted a portrait of Princess Alexandra. He fascinated her with his hobby of cultivating fresh varieties of lilies and narcissi in an era when the middle classes were emulating their superiors and planting flower gardens around their suburban homes. But her solid common sense led her to take his adoration with a grain of scepticism. Her association with him ended before he was arrested for his preoccupation with little girls.

She used him as he used her. The Salisbury Street house was the best place she knew for meeting informally the people she wanted to cultivate. Even the frivolous young undergraduates from Oxford who lingered around the twisting corridors were as often as not sons of the aristocracy. She could come across Rossetti, Swinburne, and prosy Walter Pater there. Most important, she could be introduced to the men and women who composed the only universe she recognized, London Society.

She was aware now that it was divided into two parts, as distinct as the North and South poles. The queen and her Court made up one hemisphere, the prince and the Marlborough House set the other. The two halves overlapped to some extent. The prince's intimates often occupied court appointments, as in the case of Suffield. The queen, besides thirsting for gossip from every source, found that reprobates were often much more amusing than the virtuous. She kept some ladies around her who would have failed to meet Mrs. Grundy's approval. In the process of educating herself, Lillie felt it advisable to know how both halves lived.

It was a particular pleasure to meet a dear friend of both the queen and Disraeli when Frank Miles introduced him. The Scottish Lord Rosslyn, gazing loftily through his eyeglasses, had brought his stepdaughter, Frances Maynard, to the studio for her last sitting for a portrait. The girl thought Lillie was the loveliest woman she had seen in all her fifteen years of life. Half a century afterwards, Frances wrote, "She had dewy violet eyes, a complexion like a peach. How can words convey the vitality, the glow, the amazing charm that made this fascinating woman the centre of any group she entered?" Rosslyn had similar ideas. His stepdaughter saw that he "lost his heart" on the spot. "My dear Mrs. Langtry," he said, "you must come and dine with us at Grafton Street tomorrow."

She arrived at the house in the same dowdy black dress trimmed with a toby frill of white lace in which she had been modelling for Miles. The only change she made was to open the top buttons to bare her throat. Edward was with her—"an uninteresting fat man," in the eyes of Frances, who was worth 20,000 pounds a year in her own right under the terms of her grandfather's will. Lillie's dress had become almost a uniform. Lord Randolph had remarked on it when he dined at the Wharncliffes one night during one of his frequent visits from Dublin to attend to his parliamentary business as the Member for Woodstock. In a letter he told Jennie that he "took in to dinner a Mrs. Langtry, a most beautiful creature, quite unknown, very poor, and they say has but one black dress."

Her evening with the Earl and Countess of Rosslyn was another victory. Their friends, Frances noted, "were as willingly magnetised by her unique personality as we were." Before Lillie left, she had been asked to spend her next free weekend with them at Easton Lodge, set in a thousand acres of Essex, with deer roaming in its park.

Politically, she constituted a party of one, concerned only with her personal future, accepting admiration from any man, Tory or Liberal. Hartington, the Liberal Party's leader in Parliament so long as Gladstone chose to be a voice of conscience, paid her as handsome a compliment as she had received to date. As a change from the round of dinner parties, the patrician Irishman asked her to a political reception at Devonshire House, his family home. As soon as she had made her way up the receiving line, he left his place at the head of the staircase to take her on a conducted tour of the place, ending with the indoor lily pool. Always careless about his clothes, he plunged his arms into the water to haul out handfuls of the flowers, then flung them into the arms of two liveried footmen as a gift for her.

She was immensely impressed by his gesture towards "a country girl like me," as she remembered, "who had not been allowed by my band of brothers to think much of myself in any way." But the "country girl" had already disappeared. She no longer identified herself as the dean's daughter yearning for acceptance. If a Le Breton from Jersey was not high-born by English standards, she was finding a different kind of glory, which was taking her fast along the way to becoming a monumental snob.

"There was a simplicity about the people which one finds only in those born to greatness or who have achieved it," she said years later. "Probably the security of their station enabled them to be charming and gracious." She would mould her ways on theirs.

She discerned no such qualities in her husband. When they left Devonshire House together in a brougham provided by Hartington, its floorboards were covered with dripping water lilies. Edward threw them out of the window one after the other on the way home.

In the clubs, where seductive women were discussed and sometimes traded like horseflesh at a fair, the talk turned increasingly to Lillie. Suffield, a member of the Marlborough and the Royal Yacht Squadron, recalled in old age that, "All but the upper classes of women were treated as little more than beasts of burden."

Convention called for a wife to be guarded like a private treasure, kept locked up at home. Her husband was free to travel farther afield and vary the monotony. A rebellious spirit like Lillie, who went where she pleased, raised a standard question in a man's mind: Could she be coaxed into adultery?

The clubmen revelled in the gossip that grew more tantalising in the relating. She wore no corsets, with their telltale creak. If a man got close enough, he could see the three *plis de Venus* in her neck. If he followed her up a staircase, he would glimpse ankles as pretty as any thoroughbred's. She was a cunning young witch, too, who in the seclusion of her little drawing room would swoon at the sight of a handsome man, irresistibly tempting him to take her in his arms.

Stories about her came to the prince from several segments of the circle that surrounded him—Suffield, Hartington, and the Dudleys among them, and now from Captain Allen Young. "Alleno," as he was known to all his friends, had been knighted by the queen half a year ago, after *Pandora* sailed into Portsmouth, battered by the ice of the Arctic seas. Captain Young, a newcomer to the Marlborough House set, was just the man to arrange the prince's first sight of Lillie before any more time was wasted.

❧ VI ❧

Alleno belonged to the long line of adventurers who had been flaunting England's flag across the farthest reaches of the world since the days of Sir Francis Drake. Their mission in this generation was to extend the frontiers of Victoria's empire, and she gave them her blessing in their task. She ruled in accordance with an elementary formula: Prosperity at home depended on expansion overseas. Men like Alleno were essential to the system that turned primitive lands into colonies under the Union Jack. First the explorers, then the soldiers, and finally the traders—the prescription was foolproof.

It had made Britain the mightiest power on earth. The cost in lives lost in the wars that flared sporadically throughout her reign was scarcely to be reckoned. British dead lay buried where they fell in

Egypt, India, and Africa, but the officers for the most part counted it an honour to face any enemy for the queen, and there was an endless supply of men from the jails, the slums, and the workhouses who were willing to accept a recruiting sergeant's shilling in exchange for a red tunic and more food on their plates than they had seen before.

Imperial policy in Europe was equally simple. Rival empires like the czar's must be held in check, if not by rivalry between themselves, then by intervention by land and sea to maintain the balance of power with Britain standing at the fulcrum. The Crimean War, which ended Russian dominance of southeastern Europe with the loss of 50,000 of Britain's soldiers, was intended as proof of British determination. The prince, whose memory seldom faltered, had keen recollections of those battles. As a boy of fifteen, he drew a sketch of an armoured knight, which sold for fifty-five guineas at a charity auction for the relief of the families of men fighting there.

Alleno's particular ambition in serving the queen was to discover—and possibly claim rights for her in—the Northwest Passage, sought for centuries past as a shortcut to India at the top of the world between the Atlantic and Pacific oceans. Thirty years had passed since Sir John Franklin and his company perished on the ice floes within a few miles of their goal; the elusive sea route was still a legend to beckon men of valour.

Alleno's latest expedition had failed again to find the Northwest Passage. *Alert* and *Discovery,* which set sail almost simultaneously with him, had been no more successful. But the taciturn merchant captain with the remote grey eyes was greeted as a hero when he brought *Pandora* home, scarred by icebergs. Some crewmen were missing after a hurricane swept them from her decks. Others were crippled by the twin hazards of polar exploration, frostbite and scurvy. The prince admired the courage of Allen's kind and envied him a life of action, which was barred to the heir to the Throne.

Bertie disliked doing anything by halves or by chance if it could possibly be avoided. The plan for meeting Lillie was carefully prepared. Alleno, a bachelor, would invite the Langtrys and half a dozen other guests to supper at his house on Stratford Place. She was not to be told that the prince would arrive as soon as he could leave a formal dinner party that he had promised to attend. Alexandra was still in Greece, recuperating in the sun, amused by the frugal ways of her brother Willi, who made a practice of personally gathering male guests' cigar and cigarette butts to be converted into tobacco for free distribution to the poor of Athens.

Family affairs weighed heavily on the prince in the week before his supper engagement at Alleno's. His sister Helena and her husband, Christian of Schleswig-Holstein-Augustenborg, another German princeling, arrived in England. The queen had them to dinner at Windsor, and Bertie was left to do them the normal courtesies. On the preceding Thursday, May 17, Christian talked at some length with Bertie in Marlborough House. That same day the prince treated Eddy and Georgie to a visit to the Royal Aquarium, to see the crocodile that had been added to the collection and watch Zazel fired from a cannon, before packing them off with their grandmother on an overnight train to Scotland. No one was less surprised than their father to learn that they had both been accepted as Royal Navy cadets.

He dined that evening with the Suffields, who could be relied on to supply any background information he asked for about Lillie, then went on with them to the theatre. The following night he was the guest of the Marquess and Marchioness of Hamilton, whose pastimes included baccarat, played in their house in Belgrave Square.

The queen had arrived that afternoon at Balmoral Castle after a journey marked by the usual ceremonies. She took breakfast at Perth, with the city's dignitaries lined up on the station platform. Telegrams and a despatch from the Foreign Office were handed to her at Aberdeen. An honour guard of the 79th Queen's Own Cameronian Highlanders waited in the chilly wind at the end of the journey at Ballater. Carriages took the royal party from there along a road bordered by snow-covered hills to Balmoral Castle, where she would spend her fifty-eighth birthday.

Affie's wife, the Duchess of Edinburgh, was staying at Buckingham Palace on her way to their German home in Coburg. Bertie had her to a Saturday luncheon in Marlborough House together with his sister Louise and her husband. The duchess stayed for dinner before she went with Bertie to the Italian opera. She gave a return luncheon for him and all three of his sisters at the palace on Sunday.

The following morning the main thoroughfares of the city were uncannily empty, the shops shuttered, offices and factories closed. Most of the population, except the million and a half on servants' pay, was enjoying a rare weekday's break from labor. Whit Monday, the fifty-first day after Good Friday, was still a novelty, sanctioned by Parliament as a holiday as part of the creeping movement to sweeten the lot of the common people.

The parks were packed with picnic groups in spite of a brisk east wind. On the breezy heights of Hampstead Heath, children in their Sunday-best skipped and danced and played kiss-in-the-ring. Tens of thousands left their row houses in the clerks' suburbs to take cut-price excursion trains to the nearest seaside resorts or ride the Thames riverboats. Thousands more watched a balloon ascent at the Crystal Palace or trailed in awe through the gloomy state apartments of Windsor Castle.

At Madame Tussaud's waxworks museum, lines waited patiently to inspect the latest additions, effigies of the czar and the Sultan of Turkey, whose armies battled half a world away. In the Turf Club, odds were laid that England would be at war with Russia within a year. On London commons and in country fields, army volunteers in freshly pressed uniforms and studded boots marched and countermarched. The crack of rifles sounded on every practice range in evidence of their readiness to fight any foe that the queen was prepared to name.

The prince's keenest personal pleasure lay ahead, three days away. Whit Monday for him brought another dutiful luncheon for the Duchess of Edinburgh at Marlborough House, with the same hospitality repeated on the Tuesday. He had rarely been so taken up with his female relatives. For a man bored to distraction by domesticity, the temporary bachelor was showing extraordinary patience in having his hours filled by them.

At Balmoral, preparations were under way to celebrate the queen's birthday in traditional fashion, beginning with choral singing and winding up a few days later with another bacchanalian gillies ball for the tenants on the estate. Good malt whisky flowed in the castle every day. The coachman who drove her carriage kept a bottle handy under his seat. She had a fresh bottle given to each guest before he set out for stag, with drinks all round poured unwatered after breakfast. At dusk the stalkers swallowed whatever was left, which could bring them stumbling back from the hills as tipsy as most of the visitors.

A ball, which the Highlanders attended in unaccustomed top hats, started with the swirl of bagpipes and ended with half the tenants and staff drunk on the floor. Anything was excusable on those nights, in the queen's tolerant view. She could not understand why Bertie came so seldom to Balmoral. This year, as always, his absence irritated her.

He escaped from the attentions of his sisters and sister-in-law after luncheon on Tuesday to involve himself in what was essentially only more family business. For the sake of his sons' futures, he was taking a keen interest in the Navy. He rode in an afternoon train to Portsmouth for a two-day visit to the dockyards there. Britain's imperial strength would vanish if she lost command of the seas. New armour-plated battleships and the perfected Whitehead torpedoes would guarantee supremacy in a war at sea. The prince watched the thin steel tubes of the steel fish glide through the water in an exhibition firing. He clambered aboard half a dozen warships and enjoyed two good dinners.

Before he embarked in the London train on Thursday morning, he promised that one month from now he would bring his sons with him when he presided at the inauguration of the new training ship, *Warspite*.

Lillie could not understand why Alleno's butler was so slow in announcing supper. When he entered the drawing room, where she stood by the fire, he was walking as fast as dignity allowed. A whispered word in his master's ear sent Alleno hurrying out. She heard a guttural baritone voice booming in the hall—"I am afraid I am a little bit late"—and the prince appeared in the doorway. For a moment she stood as straight and still as everyone else in the room, but she was too nervous to imitate their smiles.

He was as cheerful as a lark and plump as a partridge in his black evening clothes, whose tailcoat was studded with the glitter of jewelled orders worn for formal dining. He had a passion for wearing decorations. His heavy blue eyes passed slowly over the company. His cheeks glowed with a look of the outdoors, but he was not as tall as she had expected—only an inch or two more than her height. As he circled the room at Alleno's side, shaking hands with bobbing women and bowing men, he carried with him an aura of cologne and cigar smoke.

She and Edward were the only newcomers, and they were the last to be introduced. The prince and Alleno advanced across the carpet towards the fireplace. "For various reasons, I was panic-stricken," she remembered. The insane thought of climbing the chimney to escape flickered through her head. The "various reasons" were not difficult to assess. She had been feted often enough to know that she was an acknowledged beauty. Everything she had been told about the prince convinced her that he courted women like herself. She could sense that she had been invited here for his

153

inspection. She had to make up her mind how she would respond if he wanted her.

She touched his right hand for a second and swept down in a deep curtsey. Instead of feeling overawed, she had a curious detachment, almost an acceptance in advance of what she believed, and hoped, was bound to happen. She watched her red-faced husband stammer through the ordeal of bowing. She enjoyed the abject spectacle he made of himself. Edward knew as much as she did about the tastes of the prince.

Alleno sat her next to Bertie at the supper table. When he opened the conversation, she responded only in monosyllables, feeling her way, too wise to attempt to impress him. He showed all the graces she had expected—dignity, good humour, consideration for his host, even compliments for the cook. The waspish delight in Edward's embarrassment flickered again as she saw that her husband was "even more dumb than I was."

The prince left, well satisfied with his evening. He would make certain of seeing Mrs. Langtry again. She was a woman worth pursuing. In Balmoral, his mother celebrated her birthday. In Athens, Alexandra arranged to leave for home after four more days.

He would have to leave London to meet her in Paris in little more than a week's time, and he was still beset with family duties. The following morning he set off to see his in-laws, who were being put up at Cumberland Lodge in Windsor Park. Christian came as a guest to Marlborough House soon afterwards, to go racing with Bertie at Epsom. On Saturday the prince kept a promise to take his three daughters to a band concert in the Royal Albert Hall. In the middle of the coming week, Eddy and Georgie would be back from their visit to their grandmother. But somehow the prince squeezed in an afternoon call on Lillie.

Holding hands on a sofa while the tea cooled in its silver pot was a recognised step in the process of courting a married woman. After she had deposited the tray, Dominique, like any other obedient servant, would not reenter the drawing room until Lillie rang the little bell. The ceremony called for the gentleman's hat, cane, and gloves to be left on a nearby chair or table, never in the hall, to give the impression that he had dropped by for only a few minutes and was about to depart. Edward's behaviour infringed the rules. A husband was supposed to take tea elsewhere —at his club or with some other available lady. But Edward belonged to no club and had no other woman to squire. Stretched out on the dining-room settee, he dozed off the aftereffects of some lunchtime bottles of beer.

He had no training for handling the situation in which he found himself. Edward was provincial middle-class, confused by the morals of his betters. They would seldom question the right of a husband to keep a mistress or of a wife to take a lover if it were done discreetly. A young man would claim that he preferred death to dishonouring a virgin of his own level in Society. A well-bred girl was given not a hint about the physical facts of intercourse. Discovery of the shape and purpose of the secret parts of a man's body was left for her wedding night.

A different set of rules prevailed if a man's desires turned to a woman already married or known to be someone else's paramour. Then she was regarded as game for any gentleman of a sporting fancy, and a working-class girl was natural prey for lechery, with a possible half-crown pressed into her hand to compensate her for her pain. It was an uncommon bridegroom who had no mistress either to maintain in a flat somewhere for the pleasures he did not expect from a wife or to pension off, according to his conscience.

A kept woman lived in a shadowy world of her own, invisible to more estimable ladies. A young girl of good family was cautioned by her mother, or more probably her governess, to look the other way if she happened to notice one of the fashionable *demimonde* out walking or passing in a carriage. Society women were careful to give no sign of recognition if they encountered even a brother of theirs arm in arm with his mistress or with one of the constantly growing regiment of girls referred to as actresses, since no coarser term could decently escape a lady's lips.

Prostitutes must be secluded from gentlewomen like the nymphs of Muslim paradise in a sultan's harem. Skittles herself unwillingly proved that when she appeared with Charlie Beresford's brother Bill at the New Club in Soho. Until that night, married men had often brought in their wives to mix with leading actors and other Bohemians, who could not be invited into a respectable home. Skittles might hunt with the Quorn and live in a Mayfair house with a carriage, servants and 2,000 pounds a year provided by Harrington, but she was not considered fit company for ladies. Her pair of thoroughbred chestnut horses had to be led from their stableyard and exercised by night so that no scandal would be stirred.

Any liaison, any habit, any vice was sanctioned so long as the partners involved were discreet. "A scandal was a romance until it was found out," said Frances Maynard in her old age, long after she had become the Countess of Warwick and survived more than her share of empassioned entanglements. The code allowed a husband to do as he liked to find sexual satisfaction with the wife of a friend, a housemaid, or sometimes with a stable boy. If he was broad-minded enough to offer his own wife similar freedom, that was entirely his concern.

The unpardonable sin was to expose the secrets of a fellow member of the group sharing the same social stratum. Suing for divorce came under that heading. Class loyalty also ruled the servants' halls. From butlers down to under-footmen, housekeepers to scullery maids, they would all join the conspiracy of silence as a matter of course for the sake of the master and lady of the house whose standards they aped.

Generations of the aristocracy had obeyed the code before the prince came on the scene. Older members of his circle welcomed him as a traditionalist more than an innovator. His value to them lay in his willingness to restore the lusty values that his father had driven underground. The prince was privileged, too, to stretch the rules to please himself. A young married woman was customarily left free of enticements until she had done her marital duty and borne her husband an heir. At twenty-three Lillie was childless, but neither she nor Bertie let that stand in their way.

Edward was caught like grain between a miller's grindstones. His Ulsterman's sense of decency was outraged, but his patriotic loyalty told him that a prince could do no wrong. Better-class husbands in the same circumstances looked for consolation in mistresses of their own or played the pander's part and were duly rewarded at the prince's behest with a medal, a title, or an appointment at court. Edward had to accept that he was in process of being cuckolded. He was powerless to avert it. His recourse was to hunch his shoulders and shrink deeper into obscurity, with a bottle to ease the way.

The prince brought Alexandra home with him from Paris early in June. Lillie's range of social appearances broadened almost immediately. Sales of her postcard portraits soared. She could afford now to be disdainful of what she derided as "the curious whim of the public which eventually led to my being treated like a lion at the Zoo." Society lionised her, since gossip travelled fast.

General Ulysses Grant landed at Liverpool with his dowdy wife on the first stage of a trip around the world shortly after the March inauguration of his successor, Rutherford B. Hayes, in Washington, D.C. The grizzled commander in chief of the victorious Northern armies against the Confederates a dozen years earlier was a houseguest of the outgoing American minister in London, Edwards Pierrepont, at 17 Arlington Street. The prince wanted his new favourite to meet Grant, so arrangements were made for her to be his partner at one of the round of dinners and receptions that were held for him.

She had been given good cause to overcome her watchfulness over herself. She was ready to take a lead in conversation. As Grant escorted her in to dine,

157

she asked, "What have you done since your Civil War, General?"

Grant, whose reputation was to lay in ruin after disclosures of White House corruption, turned to her with a grim smile. "Well, I've served two terms as Presidest of the United States, Mrs. Langtry," he said. Lillie was unabashed. She was cultivating a coolness of manner that nothing could penetrate.

It was time, she decided, to display herself in the Park, where she had never been more than a strolling spectator. So far as the fashionables were concerned, there was only one park in London. St. James's and Green Park were no more than a shortcut to the House of Lords. Regent's Park was where the animals were to be seen in the zoo. But "the Park" meant Hyde Park, or more particularly the corner of it that lay between the Albert and Grosvenor Gates, taking in the mile and a half of Rotten Row.

The Park was the envy of foreign visitors of all ranks whose capital cities offered only faint copies of it. The Prater, the Pincio, Unter den Linden, the Allée des Accacias could not stand comparison with this as a setting for grandiose display. During the season, from May to July, the show was staged every day along the walks, on the painted wrought-iron chairs, and over the trimmed grass. Not more than a few dozen yards across the lawns, however, because only engaged couples or illicit lovers ventured as far as the banks of the Serpentine, where common people from suburban Bayswater, on the far side of the six hundred acres of greenery, munched sandwiches under the trees and rented rowboats at sixpence an hour.

It was safer to drink straight from the weedy waters of the Serpentine than to take a glassful tapped from the Thames. The health authorities gave warning that the river was "more or less turbid and unfit for dietic purposes." Sewage swirled up and down the river with the tide. Contamination had its part in the current weekly tally of seventy deaths from smallpox and almost as many from measles. Scarlet fever and whooping cough each accounted for upwards of another score. That summer mad dogs roamed the streets, and there was alarm over hydrophobia. Poverty continued to spiral. More than eighty thousand Londoners were counted officially as paupers, which amounted to a fraction of the full total. The workhouses held thirty-seven thousand men, women, and children, and forty-three thousand more lined up for free gruel and loaves of bread.

In the early morning, on a horse identifiable by its brow band of royal red, the prince came riding into the Park with his equerries, friends, and officers from his preferred regiments, the Blues, and the 10th Royal Hussars. From noon to two o'clock ladies in faultlessly tailored habits congregated to canter their thoroughbred hacks or stroll in chiffon gowns under silk parasols. A flourish of top hats greeted them from admiring gentlemen in their frock coats, pearl-grey trousers, and varnished boots. Between tea and dinner, the performance was repeated like a garden party that refused to end or the grand finale in some preternatural outdoor theatre.

Carriages jingled around the gravelled drives throughout the day, coachwork freshly lacquered, harness brasses polished, horses curried until they gleamed. The variety of carriages seemed infinite, from staid four-in-hands to sleek racing turnouts, from barouches with a bewigged coachman on the box to the hooded two-wheelers pulled by a single horse that some old buck relished driving, with a stunted, raucous boy in boots and breeches, the "tiger," clinging on the rear step.

The preeminent attraction was Alexandra. On most afternoons a mounted policeman signalled the approach of the princess. The chattering of the spectators that gathered to admire her faded into silence. Her carriage rides were one of the sights of London, an institution like the changing of the palace guard or the trooping of the colours on the queen's birthday. A pair of high-stepping bays drew the swaying deep-claret barouche with its panels lined in red. The coachman and footman sported brocade frogcoats, dark-blue plush breeches, white silk stockings, and cockaded hats with narrow gold braid. Alix's smiles embraced the crowd as she bowed left and right, acknowledging the curtseys of the ladies and the raised hats of the gentlemen. Only the malicious believed the tale that on occasion, she was known to give a lady-in-waiting a petulant whack with an umbrella.

Lillie would not be satisfied unless she rode in the Park, too. At this point she had received little in the way of material favours from the prince. His custom in the past had been to reward his women with pieces of jewellery, nothing more. There had been no known complaints. They found his physical presence, and the esteem it created, compensation enough. Lillie had no reason to buy a horse. She already owned a magnificent show-hack, Redskin, who, in his previous owner's estimation, "had the nuances and devotion of your favourite dog."

Moreton Frewen, six months older than Lillie, was the younger son of one of England's biggest landowners with estates in Sussex and Lincolnshire. Hunting and buying horses had been the principal occupations of this muscular young man, six feet two inches tall, until he came to London to take a nibble at Society. By and large the taste repelled him. He found "vast numbers of rich, well-dressed absolutely idle people," he said. "Coal and wood barons were entering the smart clubs and regiments, all in frank pursuit of pleasure, all idlers."

Lillie's energy in pursuit of her goals struck him as forcibly as her beauty when he met her at Lady Manners' dinner table. He came in late and was humbly apologetic. After he had been introduced and seated next to Lillie, she tried out one of her new conversational gambits. "What are your spiritual beliefs?" she asked him intently. He was dumbstruck. "I felt that I required direction," he told a friend the following day.

He preceded the prince as a teatime visitor at the Langtrys' apartments. As a gentleman of no earned income, Frewen had run through half his inherited capital. He felt an uncommon urge to make something more of himself, and the arena he chose for the test was a cattle ranch in Wyoming. Before he finally committed himself, he made Lillie a farewell gift of Redskin.

She rode regularly on Rotten Row in a black habit cut like a glove to her body. Who had paid for it was a matter of speculation. The style had not changed since Skittles made her debut in the Park almost a generation earlier, wearing a similar costume in the saddle of a livery-stable owner's hack. The ladies had been fascinated to see Skittles progress towards finer mounts, but when Lillie's turn came to dazzle London, they went so far as to stand on their little chairs for a better look at her as she passed by. Skittles had a piquant turn of phrase that seldom failed her. She was thrown one day by one of her chestnuts, and a gentleman hurried into the Row to ask if she was hurt.

"Hurt be damned," said Skittles, dusting the tanbark from her skirt. "Wait till I get my arse on that damned saddle. I'll teach the bastard to go."

In her demeanour, her tone of voice and language, Lillie was more regal than most of her audience, with the exception of Alexandra. At first, her morning rides drew a regular escort of followers on horseback, "Langtry's Lancers," as they were scoffed at in the clubs.

When she first took to Rotten Row, she was still identified as Mrs. Langtry. Not until the Millais portrait was shown next summer at the Royal Academy, behind velvet ropes to control the throng, was she pinned with the sobriquet which persisted throughout her life: The Jersey Lily. In the spring of 1887 the newspapers printed nothing about her. "The Tottering Lily" was the focus of their attention—Madame Kuo ta jen, wife of the new Chinese ambassador and a woman less emancipated than Mrs. Langtry. She was coaxed into showing her bound feet, the toes doubled under the arches and swathed in bands of blue silk, to interviewers, who reported that they were "just the size of a lady's doubled fist."

161

"The Jersey Lily" had not yet become a household name like Pears' soap, a familiar standby, and Captain Webb matches, which had recently arrived in the tobacco shops. But a number of artists were sufficiently excited by her to want to paint her portrait. It was hard to spare enough daylight hours to sit for them all. In her eagerness for the immortality that a painting promised, she rarely disappointed any of them. She was pleased to pose in whatever clothes they suggested. The black dress had outlived its usefulness.

She modelled for Edward Poynter soon after "A Jersey Lily" was completed. The manner of this new member of the Royal Academy, a principal of art schools in Kensington, was as conventional as his style with a sable brush; Frederick Leighton was his idol. Poynter saw an entirely different woman from the soulful governess that Millais had captured on canvas. The contrast was as dramatic as the transformation of Cinderella into the heroine of the royal ball.

Poynter had her wear a gaudy dress of patterned silk whose low-cut neckline hinted at the fullness of her breasts. A string of pearls circled her throat, and in her right hand she held a crumpled white rose. On that hand, she wore a ruby ring, but, like Millais, Poynter painted no wedding band on the left. Parted lips, amber skin, and inviting eyes contributed a look of sensuality, not sadness.

When the satin-smooth portrait was put on display in Burlington House, the staid academician was seen to have pictured Lillie as an enchantress, a man's dream of unsatisfied desire. When the exhibition closed, he made her a present of the picture, but she felt none of the same warmth for him as for Millais. "It didn't catch my colouring," she said matter-of-factly.

Poynter's brother-in-law, Edward Burne-Jones, made a better impression. She tried to put him off when he originally asked her to pose for him. He taunted her into agreement by standing one night under her bedroom window, singing and shouting in turn that she was a pitiless tyrant who trampled on the arts—wild words from a man of forty-four.

She admitted to spending "a good deal of time" at his studio after that. Nobody knew whether he or any of the other artists who employed her paid her the current seven shillings a day plus two meals that models expected. The men who painted her portraits kept that secret. Extravagance of any kind, in words or deeds, had a powerful appeal for her. When she analysed what it was in her that attracted Burne-Jones as a painter and a man, she concluded that it was her sturdy good health, which served as a tonic for him after the usual run of pallid girls that Pre-Raphaelites like himself idealized.

Lillie approved the way he depicted her in "The Golden Stair." Burne-Jones, she decided, was a sweet, simple dreamer—in those days traces of the romantic survived in her. She changed her mind when he proceeded to paint her as "Dame Fortune." An attenuated figure in grey draperies, with a face that knew no compassion, turned a wheel on which kings and princes, millionaires and statesmen revolved, certain to be crushed by destiny. Young Arthur Balfour, who would be Prime Minister one day, bought it to hang over the mantelpiece in his London home on Carlton House Terrace. "I always disliked it," said Lillie.

She posed for George Frederic Watts, another poet-painter; this could have been the prince's doing. Bertie, too, was giving sittings to him at the same time for an official portrait commissioned for the Middle Temple. After Watts' divorce from Ellen Terry, whom he married when she was seventeen, he lived as a hermit in a Queen Anne house off Holland Park. A private income enabled him to give away rather than sell many of his pictures. He firmly believed that he had a divine mission to light human minds with the themes he set down in his painting.

In appearance as well as technique, he emulated his chosen master, Titian. Lillie, who had some original thoughts but no ability to express them, let it be known that she found him "quite as interesting as Millais."

She was living in a state of nervous tension that demanded tight control, but she felt relaxed in Watts' studio. At some sessions, he did not pick up his palette. They could talk by the hour until his maid brought in the tea.

He had met no one quite like her. She flattered this white-bearded moralist with the flowing robe and little black skullcap. "How simple are the great!" she would sigh as he lectured her on the niceties of Italian painting. He accepted her words as a reference to himself. "He had an extremely sympathetic nature," she remembered, "and interested himself in the smallest details of my life."

She had a facility for appearing to be whatever a man expected to find. To Watts, she was not Jezebel but "The Dean's Daughter," the title he gave his first portrait of her, prim and virginal in another black dress and a poke bonnet. When she bought it to pose in, it was topped by an elegant ostrich plume. He tore it off. He could not finish a second painting of her after it was begun. He called her back time and again to sit for him, but it was useless. The new vision he had of her could not be captured in paint. After forty sittings he acknowledged defeat.

Her relations with Jimmy Whistler were less platonic. The debonair little egotist joined in the chorus of flattery. "You are the loveliest thing that ever was," he told her in his nasal Massachusetts accent that grated on most art critics who met him as much as his painting. He was "oddly arresting," she decided.

The critics conceded that he could turn out superb etchings, but they derided almost everything else he produced. She saw him rage at what one of them had to say in print: "Mr. Whistler has deliberately chosen to affect these monstrous eccentricities, secure of admiration from a clique which prides itself upon possessing artistic perceptions too fine for common understanding. And as long as misguided people can be found to go into ecstasies over 'Harmonies in Smudge,' so long, we suppose, will Mr. Whistler go on producing them." The anger fired by such abuse was flaring in him when Lillie posed in a yellow robe.

She spent whole days in his "White House" on Tite Street, Chelsea, a jumble of narrow rooms with mustard-yellow walls, hung with the Japanese prints that inspired his approach as a painter, absorbed with simplicity and harmony of colours. The atmosphere was Oriental, from the low tables to the delicately patterned porcelain. It made a whimsical setting for the Sunday breakfasts she liked to eat there, when Whistler served his followers American-style buckwheat cakes, corn muffins, and popovers.

She would still be there by nightfall. Sitting for him was "enjoyed by us both," she said guardedly. They shared a similar disregard for convention. Hers was tempered by her hunger for fame, and there were few other places besides this house where she could confess to that. He kept a mistress, but Lillie found her own way of intimating that she was one of the painter's other loves. She saved an article written by the New York *Tribune's* art critic, George Smalley, after he found her sitting alone in the parlour of the White House one evening, with firelight flickering on her impassive face. He wrote of her and Jimmy Whistler:

"He, too, like Mrs. Langtry, passed private Acts of Parliament for his private use. The Acts of Parliament of these two were for our use, too; we were to obey them. None of us minded, only it was sometimes difficult to know when they were passed and what they were, and when they were repealed and when a new act came into force."

The Eaton Place apartments were not at all suitable for her new circumstances. Before long she and Edward moved into a ten-room red-brick house at 17 Norfolk Street, off Park Lane, a much more elegant address, with stables in the mews behind, a butler, a housemaid, and white-haired Dominique. On the ceiling of the drawing room, Whistler painted his housewarming present, a fresco of white cranes soaring across an azure sky. Together he and Lillie daubed gilt paint on fans of palm leaves to tack on to the walls. The effect was exotic. It concealed the poverty of the spurious antique furniture, which was all she could afford to buy.

She took time to return in style to Jersey. News of the impact she was making on London preceded her there. Lieutenant Governor Sir William Norcott was quick to ask her to dine at Government House. She disembarked from the steampacket at St. Helier with a trunkful of clothes, intending to let no one doubt that she had established herself in Society.

All the islanders were familiar now with the looks and habits of wealthy strangers. Close to twenty thousand visitors landed from the steamers every year, drawn by the climate, the new pleasure grounds, boat rides, and wooden bathing machines that were trundled across the sand to the water's edge, where the brave could take a splash in privacy. Rows of new stuccoed houses were stretching the borders of St. Helier outwards over the surrounding hills. The first railway track had been restored and another line opened. The dearth of accommodation for travellers had been remedied with fresh building, and the old establishments like the British Hotel, the Clarendon, the Royal, and Bree's Boarding House were struggling to hold on in the face of more comfortable competition. The waterfront was changing, too. Shipbuilding and oyster dredging were dead or dying fast. The fishing fleet that sailed out from the harbour for Newfoundland cod had all but vanished.

Lillie chose a dress of white corded silk with a low, tight bodice for dining with the lieutenant governor. Jersey style called for ladies to wear their hair in a chignon at the back of the neck. To denote herself as a woman of independent frame of mind, she dispensed with that. She was no longer impressed by the stiff formality of an evening at Government House, with the inevitable toast to "the Duke of Normandy," or bothered about whether or not to remove her gloves. As she left her cloak in an upstairs room, she heard giggling under the pink calico skirt of the dressing table. Ada Norcott was hiding there with the two young Kennedy girls, Elinor and Lucy, who were staying with her while their parents were in England. Lillie joked with them and promised not to tell Sir William about their mischief.

She would talk about the incident in her old age, when the younger Kennedy girl had made her name as the novelist Elinor Glyn. By then Lillie had trained herself to remember only what she chose to. Lucy became Lady Duff Gordon, but to Lillie she was always "Lucile."

Jerseymen split into two factions when they saw and heard what the dean's daughter had made of herself, with her fancy clothes and imperious ways. Those who approved were in a small minority. Islanders were ambivalent in their opinions of fancy women. It was plain as a pikestaff that its remoteness from London made the island a popular retreat for romancing. The swells brought their mistresses here. Since the money they spent found its way into Jerseymen's pockets, there were few complaints about that.

Sterner judgements were made of local girls. A harsh, puritanical code governed their behaviour. Eager hands threw the first stone at a woman caught in adultery. She was likely to be punished by banishment from the island. If she bore a bastard child, it might be taken from her and raised in the poorhouse. As the child grew, it would never be allowed to forget its mother's sins.

Lillie's visit set off a chain of events that ultimately was to break up the marriage of the dean and her mother. Only the three of them could know all the circumstances. Perhaps Lillie confided to them the truth of her life in London. Inevitably, her father picked up what the islanders were saying about his daughter. The effect was to impel him to prove to his own satisfaction that, in his sixties, he was still a virile male, and he was less and less discreet about it. Where he had been regarded as no more than flighty in his approaches to women, he was flagrant now. The behaviour of the dean grew intolerable to the church elders over the next two years. The islanders had something else to turn their tongues to in the affairs of the Le Breton family. His wife, according to the whisperers, had taken to finding consolation with his curate, the Reverend Mr. Rey.

Bertie made sure that his calendar gave him opportunities to enjoy Lillie. Suffield continued to share his confidences as a friend, a Norfolk neighbour, and a fellow Freemason. He was one of the handful of men who spoke bluntly to the prince, and he was fond of Lillie. He was ideally placed to help them both. Whenever she came to him for advice, he was delighted to give it, though she did not always follow his suggestions. She was too much an individualist for that. Suffield sympathised with his master's position. "It is difficult," he once reflected, "to escape the vigilance of our neighbour's eyes."

Above all, he took an urbane view of any man's sexual desires. "Virtue, after all," he said, "is not so much a question of morals as of environment and circumstances."

The prince, like his mother, had little sense of humour. He was no more amused when the first newspaper paragraphs appeared about Lillie than the queen was when she learned that Charlie Beresford entertained his friends with irreverent imitations of Her Majesty. But Suffield smiled when hostesses started to ask Lillie and willowy Mrs. Luke Wheeler to the same entertainments with the idea of watching the two foremost professional beauties compete with each other for attention. He was happy to see that Lillie, the born winner, was seldom outshone.

Earlier in the year, the prince had added the Four-in-Hand Club to the endless list of organisations of which he was a member. Personally handling the reins of a coach was no pleasure of his, but he liked the raffish company. On one club run in the park, a waggish fellow-member arranged for the prince to be given a seat on the roof between Lillie and Mrs. Wheeler.

A story in the next day's newspaper identified his seat-mates as "Mrs. Langer" and "Mrs. Wheeltry." Lillie resented that, though Suffield failed to see why. "She had no need to be jealous of other beauties," he said, "for, like a second Madame Récamier, wherever she went she was greeted with ovations and public enthusiasm."

Knowing readers of the cryptic announcements from the palace concerning the day-to-day activities of all the queen's family played a game of guessing which events gave the prince his chance to include the young woman who fascinated him. In June he held a week-long party to celebrate the Ascot races. So long as her husband was with her, she could be one of the guests. In July the prince spent some bachelor days with Henry Chaplin at Rutland Lodge, Newmarket, on the Berkshire Downs, a focus of breeding and racing horses, and went again to the Suffields on Upper Grosvenor Street.

In August he left Alix to stay with Eddy, who had been ill again, in Marlborough House, while he took their younger children to Cowes for the yacht racing. Towards the end of the month, he had his yacht out for a jaunt to Ostend and back. He made a brief sortie to London to see his brother-in-law, Prince Christian, whose father was now King of Denmark in accordance with the plans of the Great Powers. Then Bertie took off again for Cowes, and Alix remained with her brother for the rest of his visit to London.

When she arrived at Cowes towards the end of the yachting season, the prince departed for the Riviera and a suite of rooms in the Hôtel des Roches Noires, Trouville. Once more there were vague intimations of unrest in Alix. "The princess," said the official pronouncements, "is expected to visit her parents in Copenhagen soon, but it is uncertain how long her visit will last."

On his return from France, Bertie avoided seeing

her. Instead he went straight back to London for a round of theatre-going, followed by a few days' shooting, then a stay with a trustworthy friend, the Earl of Feversham. It was the end of September before Alexandra was home again from the Isle of Wight with their children. Less than a week later, the family went together to Abergeldie Castle, where the prince looked forward to his annual bagging of deer and his wife anticipated only boredom and melancholy. The queen had been installed nearby at Balmoral for the past month in accordance with her ordained calendar.

At Abergeldie a stroke of chance gave the prince a span of freedom that he had not counted on. Alix's boon companion, the inevitable Charlotte Knollys, fell ill with typhoid fever. Alexandra undertook the task of nursing her back to health. Her sense of obligation to the gaunt woman who seldom left her side allowed her no other choice. The plan to leave for an indefinite holiday in Copenhagen was abandoned.

The prince let nothing interfere with his shooting until, two weeks later, it was time to escort Eddy and Georgie to the training-ship *Britannia* at Dartmouth. The sight of his apathetic elder son tearful in uniform irritated his father. Eddy received a chilling send-off.

November was almost over before Charlotte was convalescing and Alexandra consented to travel south to rejoin her husband. The prince had made the most of his month of freedom by spending days on end with understanding friends—once with Henry and Lady Florence Chaplin at Newmarket, twice with the Londesboroughs at Londesborough Lodge, Yorkshire, the house in which he had caught typhoid six years earlier. With no more than hearsay to guide them, knowledgeable members of Society speculated that Lillie was with him much of the time.

He set a completely new precedent in their relationship. Though he had conducted a dozen affairs with English ladies of his choice, he had never openly flaunted his mistress until now. He had confined his undisguised romances to his excursions abroad, where

170

he was known to honour an attractive partner with a kiss in the middle of a ballroom floor. He made Lillie his first public love, and the Marlborough House set was compelled to acknowledge her as such. Alexandra would have to accept the fact, no matter what her feelings might be.

He had a number of methods of keeping in touch with Lillie. He had learned the lesson of the Mordaunt trial and was reluctant at present to write any more letters to his loves. Alexander Graham Bell's telephone was still a novelty. It had been exhibited for the first time in England that July to a marvelling audience in the Queen's Theatre, when a pianist played "Home, Sweet Home" and "The Blue Bells of Scotland" over two thousand yards of wire. For the sake of discretion, the prince had messages delivered through the good offices of his tailor, who was also a useful man to arrange for money to be passed from hand to hand when the need was paramount.

Lillie had no rich husband to maintain her, in the hope of some princely favour as a reward for his cooperation. So the prince willingly broke another of his long-standing rules for the treatment of women important to him. In the past he had given brooches and necklaces, but he had a house built for Lillie as a permanent rendezvous whenever he wanted it. The site, bought through an intermediary, could only have delighted her. From the top of sandstone cliffs rising sheer from a sandy beach, the view south stretched unbroken to the sea's horizon. Somewhere beyond lay Jersey.

In her lifetime, Bournemouth, in the county of Hampshire, had grown from a village of fewer than a thousand people into a fashionable watering place, thanks largely to the new railway that whisked passengers down from London, a hundred or so miles away. Groves of pine trees, covered gardens, and seafront promenades gave the town its reputation for being decorous but dull. The first wooden pier had been torn down after damage by winter storms, but plans were being drawn for a replacement in steel. The

Winter Gardens, a miniature Crystal Palace, had lost money from the day it was opened two years ago.

The sands were sprinkled with children's Punch and Judy shows, and sedate families buttoned up against the sunshine. It was an offense under the byelaws to swim closer than twenty yards away from a member of the opposite sex. The regulations called merely for men's swimming costumes to cover them from neck to knees, and women must wear a similar "tunic or blouse . . . with belt and knickerbocker drawers." Concerts and dances were frowned upon. Charity bazaars represented the height of permissible entertainment.

It was an inauspicious time for building any house. The prospect of imminent war with Russia brought panic to the London Stock Exchange. The armies of the czar had crossed the flooded Danube and captured the Bulgarian capital of Tirnova with a squadron of guards and two hundred Cossacks, then gone on to lose sixteen thousand men, killed or wounded, to the counterattacking Turks. A victory in battle for either side was followed by the rape of women and mutilation of prisoners. Cossacks and Turkish irregulars were equally guilty, but the Bulgars who rose to join the Russians excelled them both in savagery. They had been degraded by slavery, and they had scores to settle. By Christmas Day, the official count of the dead exceeded eighty thousand, and the Russians stood close to the walls of Constantinople.

Disraeli, crippled with gout, decided it was time to intervene. Gladstone denounced the move as an incitement to war, but the queen enthusiastically approved her Prime Minister's proposal for sending her Mediterranean fleet steaming through the narrow straits of the Dardanelles towards the Turkish capital as a warning to the czar that his troops must advance no farther.

The war had divided one princely family as neatly as the conflict between North and South in the United States a dozen years earlier. One Battenberg brother,

Alexander, known as "Sandro," served with the Russians. Lieutenant Louis, of HMS *Sultan,* took the opportunity to see him when Her Majesty's battleships anchored off Constantinople. War could not be permitted to disrupt courtesies between brother officers and gentlemen. Sandro led Louis to greet the Russian commander, the Grand Duke Nicholas, brother of the czar himself, in the Russian camp and cast an eye on the captured cannon and some of the eighty thousand Turks held in prison stockades.

Building a house ran into further difficulty in the wave of industrial unrest that was sweeping England. Miners were locked out of the pits for refusing to submit to a slash in wages. Workmen in the Clyde shipyards, the linen factories, and the Lancashire cotton mills were all on strike. Accepting a cut of a shilling in the pound, which the owners insisted on, would push many of them below the survival line. The South Wales coal trade had collapsed. In some communities families were at the brink of starvation, turning over garbage in the streets, chewing potato peels and raw cabbage stolen from the fields.

The particular problem in building a house was the stone masons' strike, which had lasted since midsummer. They were after a reduction in working hours from fifty-two and a half to no more than fifty a week and an increase in hourly pay from ninepence to tenpence. The entire civilised world was in distress that year. The masters in the masonry trade beat down the strikers by importing hungry Germans and Canadians willing to sign six-month contracts at sevenpence an hour.

At some point before the year was over, Lillie travelled to Bournemouth to inspect the beginnings of her new house. It had to be clearly identifiable as hers for as long as it stood. She had a local mason prepare a foundation stone, crudely cut in the same lettering style as gravestones in Bournemouth cemeteries. It bore the date, 1877, and "E.L.L." for Emilie Le Breton Langtry.

III
A Place in Society

❧ VII ❧

There was red brick for the ground floor; black beams crisscrossing white plaster above; two chimney stacks and a green tile roof dipping over a multitude of gables. When the place was finished, it was a warm, inviting house, unpretentious and furnished inside for comfort rather than for decorating style, which was a subject that held no interest for either its master or his mistress. According to the town records, the leaseholder was "Emily Charlotte Langton."

All through the rooms, she left her imprint with a touch of welcoming wit and determination to mark this as a home where convention would be ignored. Along a beam in the broad entrance hall, she had a painter inscribe the slogan of the house: "And yours, too, my friend." On a wall in the lofty dining room, whose stained-glass windows contained a pair of entwined swans as a motif, she repeated a phrase that she had perhaps seen carved around some aristocrat's fireplace: "They say—What say they? Let them say." She could have put a similar thought in cruder jerriais: *"Pus nou-s'etiboque la saltai, pus ou pu"*—"The more one stirs up mud, the more it stinks."

Her dining-room fireplace carried no motto, but hidden in the pale oak carving of the mantelpiece there were her inescapable initials, E. L. L. Up close to the ceiling stretched a minstrels' gallery and on the adjoining wall an out-of-sight hatch, through which the prince could inspect the company before coming down to dine.

The size and placement of his own suite of upstairs rooms underlined the social distinction between himself and Lillie. His were the most imposing in the house; hers, on the opposite side of the hall, were not much more impressive than a housekeeper's. He could sit on a deep sofa and admire her as she came down a short flight of steps to meet him after they had dressed, ready for guests.

Her passion for setting down her sentiments about the place and its proprietor extended to the exterior. On an outside west wall of the prince's suite ran a Latin tag, *Stet Fortuna Demesis*—"May fortune attend those who dwell here." On a south wall outside her own quarters, there was lettered a simpler thought: *Dulce Domum*—"A sweet home."

A little balcony opened off her bedroom, where they could take tea in the sunlight on a summer afternoon. She would daydream there about the out-of-sight island, whose smugglers only a hundred years ago had landed on the shelving beaches below her with kegs of brandy, chests of tea, and cases of tobacco, willing to murder any revenue officer who crossed their path. There was a strong streak of Jersey lawlessness in her that could not be suppressed.

She pondered sometimes over her Le Breton ancestry, older than her lover's, and how well it had served her. In a window next to the upper staircase leading to her rooms, she installed two impish coats-of-arms in stained glass, designed in heraldic mockery. "Ye Armes of Ye Britaines" said the inscription on one; "Ye Armes of Ye Romanes" said the other. A similar fancy prompted her to order individual Dutch tiles for the fireplace-surround in the hall up there. Each of them bore a title—"The Kingdom by the Sea" or "Homeward Bound."

She could only marvel at the events that had brought her here, but she was certain enough of her hold on the prince for the time being to tease him with her impiety. Men like Suffield who knew him best tried to analyse just what were the qualities in this young woman that drew Bertie so tightly to her. She had a beautiful face, but she was far from unique in that among the Marlborough House circle. She was willing to give him the delights of her body, but so were any number of others.

What led him to single her out as the woman he chose to let the world recognise as his partner in adultery? His closest companions thought they had the answer: She refused to be subservient. She stood up to him where few others dared. "He was always taken in by dictatorial and cocksure people," concluded one of the men who probed the nature of the prince. No one could say that Lillie dominated him, but neither did she let him dominate her.

In many respects, they were two of a kind, suited for each other's needs, physically and in the patterns of their thinking. Sentimentality was alien to both of them. He showed more warmth in his general attitudes than she, but he admired her disdainfulness. He was businesslike in all his dealings; so was she. "Don't let us fuss" became one of her watchwords. She never complained, explained, or gossiped, which was essential in their relationship; the prince seldom said a word about anyone's personal affairs.

Lillie was punctual where Alexandra dawdled. Like him, Lillie was an early riser, up and about by eight o'clock most mornings after an ice-cold bath for her health's sake and no more makeup than a dusting of powder on her cheeks. They had the same breakfast habits—china tea for her, coffee for him, nothing else but toast and morning newspapers for both of them. He had no long wait while she prepared for the day. She could dress her hair in five minutes after the maid had brushed it.

One of the jokes she told centred on the maid, who supposedly told her, "You've a large 'ead, madam. That means you 'ave a large brain, and a large brain is the most useful thing you can 'ave, for it nourishes the roots of the 'air." Copying Cockney accents was a standard form of humour, popular in the pages of *Punch*.

He made no pretense at being better than he was, and neither did she. "What say they? Let them say" expressed their feelings. "I have always been willing," she said in retrospect, "to take the blame for things I have done."

179

They were ready for each other. She was starved of sexual satisfaction, disdainful of men, driven by ambition. He was bored with idleness, and with a wife unsuited for him. His mother's latest slights and favouritism for Leopold galled him, when he felt certain that war with Russia was a matter of weeks away, and she barred him from knowing what she and her government were doing about the situation.

He believed, as he said, that "Society grows; it is not made." Lillie's self-made place in Society fitted his prescription. For her part, there was perhaps more profound gratification than a woman of her class was expected to find in the act of sex. In her body, she could momentarily carry the seed of a future "Duke of Normandy," the English king.

Before the house was finished, she had to ward off the attentions of another prince who imagined her to be fair game for a man of his distinction. Early in the New Year, Crown Prince Rudolf arrived from Vienna with his mother, Elizabeth, Empress of Austria, to a suite in Claridge's Hotel, London. The heir to the Austro-Hungarian Empire was a callow, nineteen-year-old, more or less in charge of a tutor. In Bertie's opinion, Rudolf was "a very nice young man, but not at all good-looking." He thought the prince was "treated almost like a boy by his parents," which was enough to earn him a measure of sympathy from Bertie.

Rudolf met Lillie at a ball given for him by Ferdinand de Rothschild at his house in Piccadilly. The banker was inordinately proud of his pure-white ballroom, which he wanted to dress up for Rudolf. He had Lillie and some other professional beauties to a preparatory luncheon to announce that he was prepared to buy each of them a pastel-coloured Doucet gown if she would wear it to his party.

Bertie looked on the Rothschild family as good friends, useful in helping him in his perpetually strained finances, from the days when Natty Rothschild was a fellow undergraduate at Cambridge. The Viennese Court was flagrantly anti-Semitic. Bertie may have felt that the time was ripe to instil a touch of tolerance in Rudolf.

He came from Sandringham himself as a guest at Bertie's ball, ceding his claims on Lillie to let Rudolf dance repeatedly with her, amused by the flash of familiar spirit when she discovered that the princeling's moist hands were leaving fingerprints on her pale-pink crepe-de-Chine Doucet dress. "Would you be good enough to put on your gloves?" she asked him in French.

A pained look showed in his deep-set grey eyes. "It is you who are perspiring, madame," he replied with a pout on his Hapsburg lips.

Bertie's forbearance endured a second test. Rudolf escorted the hostess, Ferdie's sister Alice, into supper as protocol required, but he paid no further notice to her. He would not be satisfied until Ferdie had rearranged the seating plan to put Lillie at Rudolf's side.

The next day Rudolf and his tutor paid the first of a series of calls at the house on Norfolk Street. She disliked the spoiled, impulsive young man more than before, but he seemed intent on having his share of her with Bertie, who had returned to Sandringham. Day after day, Rudolf arrived with his escort to coax her, with little else on his brain except the duty visit he must pay to Osborne, where the queen was graciously permitting Professor Alexander Graham Bell to give her a personal demonstration of his telephone. At last, Rudolf rang the doorbell alone one evening, pale with excitement. The tutor, he said, had been left behind when their cab overturned on the way.

Knowledge of Lillie's liaison with the Prince of Wales only heightened Rudolf's hopes of conquering her. It was not uncommon for a gentleman, as a gesture of hospitality, to offer a friend his mistress for the night. Bertie had often been entertained in this fashion in Paris. Rudolf could see no reason why he should not have the same privilege in London. English girls were in demand in the brothels of Europe, whose keepers were glad to pay the current fee of twelve pounds a head and more to the London procurers, including, if required, a false birth certificate in some other woman's name obtained from the records office in Somerset House.

The capital of the Empire overshadowed other European cities in catering to the sexual desires and fantasies of any man. In other countries, a woman's chastity was more or less protected by law until her twenty-first birthday. In England, thirteen was the legal age of consent. Child prostitutes in the thousands prowled the streets and the theatre entrances to supply a vicious demand. The night houses in the side streets off the Haymarket were full of them.

A "fresh girl," as a virgin was known in the trade, was especially prized, worth as much as forty pounds to a customer. Finding them was an organized business, as it had to be when some clients wanted one or more a week and could well afford to pay. Ten-pounds-a-year nursemaids, shop assistants, and newcomers in from the countryside seeking work in the city were the most likely recruits. "The easiest age to pick them up is fourteen or fifteen," one procuress told a newspaper investigator, W. T. Stead. "They begin to want clothes and things which money can buy, and they do not understand the value of what they are parting with in order to get it."

The women who hunted them patrolled the parks and railway stations every day, striking up conversations with likely-looking candidates. They were prepared to cultivate the acquaintanceship for weeks if necessary in view of the ultimate purchase price. Once they had gained the girl's confidence, they would suggest how easy it was to earn a few pounds by meeting a man. "Thus we have always a crop of maids ripening, and at any time we can undertake to deliver a maid if we get due notice," said the procuress who told her business secrets.

The girl would be delivered to a so-called "introducing house" or to the home of the customer, if he wished. Some men wanted her to be certified as "fresh" before they accepted her. There were midwives available for that, just as there were specialists in the craft of producing artificial virgins. In either case, the routine of seduction was much the same. The women in charge plied the girl with gin or what the trade called a "drowse"—snuff added to beer, tincture of opium sold as "laudanum," or chloroform, all of which could readily be bought in any chemist's shop.

Often, the child was unconscious by the time she was violated. If she was not, then all the struggling and screaming in the world would not help her. The procuress would not tolerate being made a fool of or the customer being disappointed. She would hold the girl while she was raped and pay her nothing afterwards. "If a girl makes too much trouble," the telltale in the trade confided, "she loses her maidenhead for nothing instead of losing it for money."

Half the houses in some East End streets were run as brothels. The neighbours paid no attention to cries in the night. A policeman on his beat had no right to break in, assuming he was urged to. A girl taken to a man's home knew neither his name nor the address. After she was clothed again, she was whisked off in a cab and never saw her attacker again.

A girl from a respectable family knew only that loss of virginity under any circumstances before her wedding night branded her as a sinner. That was what had been instilled in her by her parents and teachers long before she had the least idea of the meaning of the words. If she was in need of patching after her introduction to the life, there were places where such hasty surgery was performed, together with abortions, too. Her hopes of anyone listening to her if she complained of rape were infinitesimal. A violated girl was automatically discredited as a witness. The keeper of the brothel and its tenants would swear on oath that she was a willing volunteer. Her accusation would be dismissed as attempted blackmail.

Not all the children were terrified strangers. Some were motivated by want for money. Drunken parents sometimes sold their daughters to the procurers. Some prostitutes brought up their own children to follow them in the life. Once she grew used to it, it was easier on a girl and better paid, after all, than working as a chain-maker for seven shillings a week, for instance, or in a factory enamelling advertisement signs at the risk of poisoning from the lead in the paint, which left her too weak to take any other job.

Some gay women made good marriages, some set up their own houses, others were discarded when their years of usefulness were over. The last stop on the road down was the "Dusthole" of Woolwich, where army cannon were made beside the Thames. Whores waited at the pierhead there to sell themselves for a few swallows of gin before they slept in the streets until morning. Soldiers and sailors had no need to resort to these drabs. The law allowed registered prostitutes at some military and naval stations under police supervision. If periodical medical inspections showed them to be diseased, they were kept in hospitals under compulsory detention.

Boys were available, too, for gentlemen with a taste for them. The male brothel, at 19 Cleveland Street, near the Tottenham Court Road, included a young messenger boy from the Marlborough Club among its offerings. A good friend of the Prince of Wales, Lord Arthur Somerset of the Royal Horse Guards, the so-called Blues, was found there in a police raid a dozen years later. "Podge," as the prince and his circle called him, was a son of the Duke of Beaufort of Coaching Club fame and the prince's superintendent of stables. At first, Bertie stood by Podge. "I won't believe it," he said, "any more than I should if they had accused the Archbishop of Canterbury." But the evidence against Somerset was overwhelming. The "unfortunate lunatic," in the prince's term, was allowed to escape trial on condition that he leave the country. There were suspicions then that Eddy had been a visitor to Cleveland Street, too.

Listening to complaints from anyone about the behaviour of royal guests to the country was nothing the prince enjoyed, so Lillie made none about the attentions Rudolf was paying her. Bertie, in fact, took Alix and Rudolf to Frederick Leighton's studio, where

John Everett Millais' famous *A Jersey Lily* was Lillie's
favourite portrait of herself, though the flower she holds
is, in fact, a Guernsey lily.
The States of Jersey

Above, the old rectory of Saint Saviours, Jersey, where Lillie was born and grew up (*Lynn Photographers Ltd.*); below, her father, Dean Le Breton, who came close to being a paragon among men in Lillie's judgment, and her mother, Emilie.

Edward and Lillie Langtry in Jersey shortly after their wedding. Lillie later admitted she fell in love with *Red Gauntlet*, not Edward: "To become the mistress of the yacht, I married the owner. . . ."
Raymond Mander and Joe Mitchenson Theatre Collection

Lillie with her parents and one of her six brothers about 1864.

Queen Victoria and
Prince Albert, c.
1860.
*Victoria and Albert
Museum*

Alfred, Duke of
Edinburgh, "Affie,"
the second son and
a frequent visitor to
M a r l b o r o u g h
House.
*Raymond Mander
and Joe Mitchenson
Theatre Collection*

Prince Leopold, the hemophiliac youngest son, who was the queen's confidential secretary, and his eldest sister, Princess Louise.
Radio Times Hulton Picture Library

Victoria, "Toria", the princess royal, a year older than Bertie and the bane of his childhood.
Radio Times Hulton Picture Library

Princess Alexandra, who "exuded charm as light as a butterfly's wings," with the inevitable jewelled band around her slim throat covering the scar of a childhood tracheotomy.
Raymond Mander and Joe Mitchenson Theatre Collection

Edward, Prince of Wales, "Bertie," as a young man.
The Raymond Mander and Joe Mitchenson Theatre Collection

Queen Victoria surrounded by two generations of royal children.
Radio Times Hulton Picture Library

The prince taking his sons, Prince Eddy and Prince
George, on board the naval cadet's training ship *Bri-
tannia* at Dartmouth.
The Illustrated London News

Lord Charles Beres-
ford who was Prince
Edward's interme-
diary in the Ayles-
ford scandal.
*Radio Times Hulton
Picture Library*

Lord Randolph Churchill, who incurred the wrath of Prince Edward by threatening Princess Alexandra with blackmail over the Aylesford letters. *Radio Times Hulton Picture Library*

Jennie Jerome, Lord Randolph Churchill's lovely American wife, felt the power of ostracism, excluded from the Marlborough House set and London Society as a result of her husband's involvement in the Aylesford scandal. *Radio Times Hulton Picture Library*

The London social scene, which Lillie had longed to be part of; above, a garden party at Marlborough House; below, a day at the races.
Drawings courtesy of The Illustrated London News

Charlotte Knollys, "the inevitable Charlotte," Princess Alexandra's indispensable companion.
Radio Times Hulton Picture Library

Princess Alexandra, a keen horsewoman, sat her saddle to the right owing to a stiff knee, the legacy of rheumatic fever in childbirth.
Radio Times Hulton Picture Library

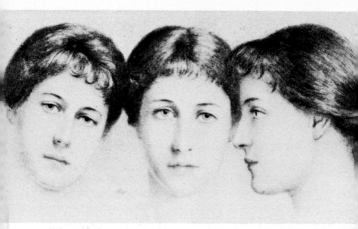

Frank Miles' drawings of Lillie (above and below) launched her as a "professional beauty," and the circle of admirers of the face of Lillie Langtry could be counted in the thousands after inexpensive reproductions of his sketch went on sale. *Peter Oliver*

Raymond Mander and Joe Mitchenson Theatre Collection

Edward Poynter's portrait of Lillie which, she complained, "didn't catch my colouring."
Société Jersiaise

"This was no languid, consumptive maiden, but a sensuous woman. The hint of melancholy in her face was as
tantalizing as the promise of passion in her body."
Raymond Mander and Joe Mitchenson Theatre Collection

"The most exciting of the professional beauties, Lillie invested all her skills in the task of making a place for herself in Society and finding satisfaction as a woman."

"Here was Guenevere incarnate, an unknown face, an air of innocence, seemingly unravaged by the pressures of competing for attention in the *salons* of the city."
Raymond Mander and Joe Mitchenson Theatre Collection

The Prince of Wales in 1876, the year Lillie Langtry
made her entry into London Society.
Radio Times Hulton Picture Library

They say_ What say they? Let them say.

The house the prince built for Lillie was warm and inviting, unpretentious, and furnished for comfort rather than decorating style. Above, the motto in the dining room; right, the discreet hatch near the ceiling through which the prince could inspect the company before coming down to dine; below, the inescapable initials, E.L.L., scratched in the window glass of a small drawing room.
Photographs courtesy of Peter Oliver

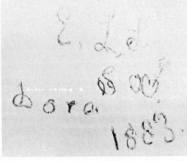

Above, the prince arrives for a Four-in-Hand Club meeting at the Alexandra Palace; below, "In the wigwam of the Savages"—the prince at the Savage Club.
Drawings courtesy of The Illustrated London News

Lillie wrote of Sarah Bernhardt: "This great and overwhelming artist was almost too individual, too exotic to be completely understood or properly estimated *all at once*. Only two words could do her justice, 'transcendent genius.'
Victoria and Albert Museum

Oscar Wilde, a long-time friend of Lillie Langtry, said of her, "I would rather have discovered Mrs. Langtry than to have discovered America. She is the most beautiful woman in the world."
The Bettmann Archive

Prince Louis of Battenberg, Bertie's favourite nephew, an habitué of Marlborough House and the father of Lillie's daughter, Jeanne-Marie.
Radio Times Hulton Picture Library

Two views of the Imperial Theatre in London. Below, Bertie, now Edward VII, and Queen Alexandra attend a performance of *The Crossways* written by Lillie and Hartley Manners, to be included in the repertory on her forthcoming American tour.

Views courtesy of the Raymond Mander and Joe Mitchenson Theatre Collection

A photograph of Lillie, after she had embarked on her career as an actress, an idea which had tantalized her since she saw Sarah Bernhardt's triumphs with Londoners and with Bertie.
The Bettmann Archive

Lillie in *Mademoiselle Mars* at the Imperial, 1902 (*Raymond Mander and Joe Mitchenson Theatre Collection*); below, in costume as Cleopatra at the Princess, 1890 (*The Bettmann Archive*).

Lillie in two other Shakespearean roles: above, as Rosalind at the Imperial, 1882, and left, as Lady Macbeth in New York, 1889. *Photographs courtesy of the Raymond Mander and Joe Mitchenson Theatre Collection*

Lillie as the bar-
maid, Kate Hard-
castle, in *She Stoops
to Conquer*.

As Marie Antoinette
in *A Royal Neck-
lace*.
*The Raymond Man-
der and Joe Mitch-
enson Theatre
Collection*

Lillie was news when, even in America, it was considered vulgar to make news. Above, one of the Americans she impressed, "Judge" Roy Bean, shown trying a horse thief on the porch of his saloon under its sign, "The Jersey Lily" (*The Bettmann Archive*); below, Lillie in a fashionable pose (*The Bettmann Archive*).

Prince Louis Battenberg at the time of his wedding to Queen Victoria's granddaughter, Princess Victoria of Hesse.
The Illustrated London News

"London Society was not surprised to learn that Lillie had found another means of turning her renown to commercial advantage. . . . She had agreed to sell her name—and flout every precept for how a lady should behave. . . ."
The Raymond Mander and Joe Mitchenson Theatre Collection

Above, Lillie in New York in her electric brougham; left, Lillie's film debut in *His Neighbor's Wife*. She pleads for her faithless husband's life with the husband of the other woman and stays the wronged husband's hand as he prepares to shoot the guilty pair.

Photographs courtesy of the Raymond Mander and Joe Mitchenson Theatre Collection

Daisy, the Countess of Warwick, Bertie's mistress in his
later years.
Radio Times Hulton Picture Library

Jeanne-Marie, Lillie's daughter, was taught to call Lillie "my aunt" and did not learn the true identity of her father until she was a young woman.
Courtesy of Mrs. Colin McFadyean

Lillie, still lovely at seventy-five, once observed, "In life I have had all that I really wanted very much—a yacht, a racing stable, a theatre of my own, lovely gardens." *The Raymond Mander and Joe Mitchenson Theatre Collection*

the likeness of Lillie was emerging from the marble. Toward the close of the year, he asked his mother for a knighthood for Mr. Leighton. During much of Rudolf's visit Lillie's protector was out of England, going off first to Berlin for the marriages of two daughters of his sister Vicky and her husband Fritz, the Crown Prince of Prussia.

To fend off Rudolf and prevent further damage to her uncertain reputation, Lillie called Edward home from a fishing expedition, to be on hand as a reluctant chaperon, whenever the infatuated Austrian presented himself on Norfolk Street.

Bertie had little time to see her after his return from Berlin. He spent only a few days in London before he left for Paris. Seven years earlier, that city had been besieged, bombarded, and demoralised. Even rats had been served up as food for its two million citizens and the flood of refugees seeking refuge behind its walls. Prussian troops marched into its streets after Napoleon III was deposed and the Communards seized control. The soldiers of Marshal MacMahon had two enemy forces to overcome—Prussians and Communards fighting from barricade to barricade, setting fire to the Tuileries and the Hôtel de Ville, planting kegs of gunpowder ready to blow up the Cathedral of Notre Dame.

Now the prince found Paris seething with excitement as the final preparations were made for opening the spectacular Universal Exhibition, designed to prove to the world that French power and prosperity had returned in the new Republic whose president was the Irish-blooded MacMahon. Bertie was something of a hero with the French, more consistently popular with them than among most of his fellow countrymen. Crowds waited to greet him whether he arrived as Le Duc de Lancastre on private pleasure or now, when he was on official business, preoccupied with meeting the organisers of the British and Indian displays, which included some of his own trophies, at the forthcoming festival.

MacMahon's government was less enthusiastic about

Victoria and Disraeli. The show of force made by British battleships at Constantinople had resulted in an uneasy truce between the warring sides. England promised not to land troops in support of the defeated Turks. Russia, in return, undertook to stay out of Gallipoli, the peninsula of mountains that reached out from the Turkish mainland into the Dardanelles. Russian guns on Gallipoli would threaten the supremacy of Her Majesty's fleet in the Mediterranean. Londoners flocked out to cheer the tottering Prime Minister when he announced that he had secured "peace in our time," but that was a month ago. The Russo-Turkish War was formally ended with the Treaty of San Stefano, but England rated its provisions as being too pro-Russian to be acceptable. The French fretted over what Disraeli was plotting to do next in the Mediterranean, and Bertie was in no position to tell them.

He made one more trip to Paris before the exhibition's grand opening on May 1. He was joined there by Queen Isabella of Spain, princes of Denmark, Italy, and the Netherlands, and a platoon of royal dukes. Half a million Parisians endured drenching thunderstorms to turn out and cheer. *"Vive la République!"* yelled the rain-sodden crowds, and Bertie roared with laughter. Workmen were still putting the finishing touches to most of the new buildings, but a hundred-cannon salute signalled the start of the first public rejoicing the French capital had known for seven years.

If the occasion was not appropriate for showing Lillie the city he liked above all others, there would be other opportunities. He returned, again without Alexandra, in June, putting up as usual in his suite at the Hotel Bristol, which had seen a succession of women guests before Lillie.

The City of Light entranced her. Its houses flourished flags of every nation. Gas jets and coloured lanterns brightened the main boulevards, thronged day and night with visitors wandering from the magnificent new Trocadero to the Champs de Mars, their faces glowing in the glare of the hissing pyramids of gaslight on the freshly furbished buildings.

Napoleon III was dead; his widow, Eugénie, and their only son, the prince imperial, were refugees in England. But the Republic had remade Paris in the vision he had conceived. The impeccable railway stations, the Opéra, the Hôtel Dieu, the completed galleries of the Louvre, the chestnut trees that lined the boulevards that he had ordered built—they all added up to his memorial, in Lillie's dazzled eyes.

They danced together, which was one of her special pleasures, and the prince was as light on his feet as a boy half his weight. They went to the shops and to the theatres, followed always by the same hollow-cheeked chief of police whom the prince stalwartly refused to recognise. They dined at Bertie's favourite restaurants, Paillard's, Voisin, the Café Anglais, and the word reached London that at Maxim's he kissed her on the dance floor.

In the Place de la Concorde, they inspected the inscrutable column of granite, patterned with hieroglyphs and brought from Egypt to be erected there by a previous generation. A companion piece to this obelisk had been unearthed from the desert sand at Alexandria and shipped at last in an iron box towed by a steamer to England. Six crewmen were drowned during the course of the autumn voyage in a seven-hour gale in the Bay of Biscay.

The English obelisk, 816 inches tall and named Cleopatra's Needle, waited in storage to be raised on a plinth on the Thames Embankment during the coming September. When the time came to winch it into place behind a hoarding, it was left hanging overnight until two earthenware jars were hidden in the pedestal beneath it. Possibly a suggestion from the prince ensured that a picture of Lillie went into one of the jars with eleven others to give her a measure of immortality.

The early summer saw a surge of events in Europe, which intrigued the prince, and in England, to which he paid little attention. Domestic politics were one of the subjects that bored him. Foreign affairs, on the other hand, and whatever involved the army and navy could always capture his attention. Lancashire cotton-spinners smashing mill windows in a desperate riot held no interest for him. They had been locked out of the mills because their employers were not satisfied with the workers' promise to accept a fifty percent cut in wages. The militia were called out to quell them, which was precisely what was needed for the maintenance of law and order in most people's opinion.

What disturbed him was the outrage caused in France by Disraeli's tactics at the June conference in Berlin, organised to end the perilous deadlock between England and Russia. The seventy-three-year-old Prime Minister scribbled a note to his "Dearest Prince" when the talks were over. "Turkey is in my pocket," he crowed. The island of Cyprus was to be occupied by the English, with permission from the sultan; Russia was excluded from the Mediterranean; and the frontiers of Greece had been stretched a little for the sake of Alexandra and her brother Willi.

The takeover of Cyprus angered French politicians. They envisaged the island's use as a base for a British invasion of Egypt, which the French regarded as their preserve. In July, Bertie was given official warning to stay away from Paris for the time being or chance being affronted. He ignored it. The *entente cordiale* between England and France, between himself and both categories of friends—social and political—on the opposite side of the channel, was too important to him. His jaunts to Paris as prince or *en garçon* continued without interruption.

A greater danger than the risk of abuse coloured the background of these days with Lillie. Every foreign crowd through which he passed contained a possible assassin. The movement called Nihilism had received its name in Russia some twenty years earlier. Agitators there dreamed of freedom from the tyranny of the czars. Intellectuals in peasant garb incited the serfs to revolution, preaching that only science must govern mankind; the churches must crumble; men and women must be treated as equals under the law; established society must be overthrown as the first necessary step toward remaking the world.

The czarist government had done its worst for the past four years to destroy the movement. Thousands were imprisoned under conditions so harsh that dozens were driven to suicide before they ever appeared in court. A speech made privately to a few workmen or the handing out of a revolutionary text resulted in up to fifteen years of hard labour. Thousands more were exiled to Siberia without trial. But repression only increased the fervour of the Nihilists. Their doctrine spread over Europe, drawing more followers from the professional classes than from the embittered poor.

The International Society was a phrase that spelled death to kings and princes in 1878. Its membership of Nihilists, in the words of one of then, Giovanni Passananti, intended to see "monarchies, ministries, authorities and misery abolished." The method they chose was assassination.

In February a young noblewoman, Vera Zasulish, shot the prefect of St. Petersburg, General Feodor Trepoff—and the jury acquitted her. In May more shots were fired at Emperor William I of Germany as he rode in a carriage down Unter den Linden. Towards the end of the month, alarm echoed down the corridors of Whitehall and Downing Street. Nihilism was infecting England. An attempt on the life of Fritz, the Queen's German son-in-law, was due to be made, it was rumoured, when he arrived in London. Bertie discounted that and went to meet him at Paddington Station, unconcerned. The rumour proved to be false.

In June the Nihilists of Berlin tried again. Emperor William, in the same carriage as before, was taking a drive along the same route, Unter den Linden, when a doctor opened fire with a shotgun from a house window. The eighty-one-year-old monarch, a firm believer in the divine right of kings, was riddled with pellets, severely wounded, but his surgeons saved him. Victoria's indignation over the attack exploded in a flurry of family letters.

King Humbert of Italy was the target selected in November, when he had just succeeded to the throne of his father's death. His royal carriage was entering the Via San Giovanni, Naples, when the would-be assassin lunged at him with a dagger folded in a red flag of revolution. *"Viva la Reppublica!"* cried the internationalist, but Humbert had a soldier's training. With his sheathed ceremonial sword, he knocked the weapon aside. He had twenty-two more years to live before the Nihilists finally slew him.

Bertie disregarded the attempts that were made to improve his security. He would not tolerate such fussing. He was never told that in Paris, at least, the crowd that pressed closest to him were almost always made up of detectives under the direction of the hawk-faced chief of police. The prince refused to let fear interfere with his pleasures, which was another characteristic that Lillie shared. They both had the added ability to endure pain. When a carriage door slammed on his hand, he brushed aside all sympathy. His own turn as a target came in the year Humbert was assassinated.

Then a Belgian student, aged fifteen, fired a revolver at Bertie through the open window of his train compartment in a Brussels railway station. "No harm done," the prince commented, and marvelled at what a poor shot the lad must be to have missed him from four feet away. He asked that the student not be punished too harshly—and was enraged when the only punishment he suffered was to be put under police supervision for six years.

By the summer of '78, most of England suspected that Lillie was the mistress of the prince. The upper classes accepted the fact. No more of them than the stalwarts of Victoria's immediate circle condemned him, though not everybody accepted her. The lower classes envied him. For many of the men, Bertie's was the life they dreamed of leading in their wildest fantasies, replete with beautiful women, high stakes, fast horses, magnums of champagne, and a banquet to work his way through any day he chose. Only the middle classes as a whole took a distinctly critical view. It was sinful to take a mistress, totally out of keeping with what they imagined the moral standards of the queen to be and accordingly tried to emulate. Sympathy was strong for Alexandra.

Publicity was one of the inventions of the new age. It was fashionable to be famous. For the first time, the personal lives of the swells were hashed over as a permanent commercial commodity that helped to sell newspapers and magazines. Lillie had made herself manna from heaven for editors bent on titillating their readers.

Crowds gathered to goggle at her when she appeared on Redskin or in an open carriage or on a street. If she entered a ballroom, dowagers would climb on chairs for a better view, just as they did in the park. Manufacturers hurried to turn the fame of the Jersey Lily to advantage. The prince escorted her to Ascot races on the heath at Berkshire, his landau with four horses leading a line of others, with outriders in scarlet livery, and his equerries on horseback in tall hats and frock coats. The pink dress she wore started the high-class sweatshops in the East End of London producing copies of it. The parasols, cloaks, shoes, and muffs she wore on other outings set off the same surge of imitation.

She protested that she was more embarrassed than pleased. Bertie could chuckle when she told him what happened if she took a stroll in the park: "People ran after me in droves, staring me out of countenance and even lifting my sunshade to satisfy their curiosity."

If she went shopping, she usually had to be let out of a side door to avoid the crowds that gathered outside the entrance. "It became risky for me to indulge in a walk," she recalled, "on account of the crushing that would follow my appearance."

She regaled Bertie with the tale of what befell one young girl who bore some resemblance to her when she was spotted one Sunday afternoon on a park bench. "Someone raised the cry that it was I, people rushed towards her and before the police could interfere, she was mobbed." An ambulance had to be called to take

Lillie's double, suffocating and unconscious, to a hospital.

"London," Lillie assured him, "has gone mad," and she felt she should apologize to him for all the fuss she was creating.

She was seductive, exciting, and, best of all, wicked. Women, rich and poor, tried to reproduce something of her appearance in their own. The Jersey Lily hair style—a single, heavy plait reaching halfway down the neck with bangs covering the forehead—showed up everywhere.

She had the instincts of a businessman, too. As pictures of her filled the shop windows, she struck a bargain with one popular photographer of Society. In return for a commission, he would have exclusive rights to make new portraits of her, and woe betide him if the proofs he submitted did not come up to her expectations. "You have made me pretty," she scolded him then; "I am beautiful." She had learned the value of the commodity which she exemplified.

"If I had lived in the days of the Stuarts," she liked to say, "I would have been a duchess in my own right."

She remembered the phrase from an encounter with Disraeli, whom she met at a reception to celebrate his victories at the Congress of Berlin. She tactfully left him to open the conversation, aware that his tongue could be sharp. One lady who fussed over him at a similar occasion heard him turn to an aide and snap, "Get this little monkey off my back."

"What can I do for you?" asked the Prime Minister.

"A few new gowns for Ascot," she replied.

"You are a sensible young woman," the old man said, with a pat on her shoulder. "Many a woman would have asked to be made a duchess in her own right."

She was encouraged to try a joke. "Mr. Gladstone," she ventured, "tells me he has dizzy spells," which was a play on words for the benefit of the Prime Minister nicknamed "Dizzy." "What will cure them?"

"Nothing, and long may he suffer them." That exchange turned up in the morning newspapers.

For all that, Gladstone was closer to her. Like the prince, she found Disraeli's edge of irony disturbing. Gladstone was intent on cultivating a friendship with her, possibly with a view to improving his own relations with the prince when the queen made no secret of her hostility toward the "mad" Liberal. In the middle of storming the country denouncing Disraeli and all his works as an incitement to war, Gladstone paid an evening call at Norfolk Street, intent on improving Lillie's mind. He brought her an armful of books, with an offer to tutor her in English literature. She won a new ally in her drive for self-improvement when Frank Miles introduced her at his Salisbury Street apartments to a young Irishman who had recently graduated from Magdalen College, Oxford, with the Newdigate prize for a poem he had written, "Ravenna." Oscar Fingal O'Flahertie Wills Wilde rented a floor of the house below Miles, which he proceeded to decorate with flowers, peacock feathers, and old china like the Oxford rooms which fellow undergraduates had wrecked when they simultaneously ducked him into the River Cherwell as a pretentious fop.

Wilde made an unimpressive sight. She noticed dirty fingernails, a pale face filled with freckles, coarse lips and stained, green teeth. He struck her as grotesque in a shabby black frock coat, unbuttoned to display a flowered waistcoat, swinging pale lavender gloves for theatrical effect. On the positive side, she noted the assured presence of the young man, his alluring voice, and his "great, eager eyes," as she commented afterwards.

He seized on Lillie as a precious prop in his mission to publicise himself. At twenty-two he was three years her junior, but she was happy to make him her mentor in the greenery-yallery arts. The Jersey Lily's notoriety could be employed for his own self-advancement. He advertised his attachment to her by sauntering through London streets holding a single, long-stemmed white amaryllis, bought in the Covent

Garden flower markets for a penny or two, which was all he could afford.

She found him "really ingenuous" in the beginning and a natural Irish eccentric in private, not the affected poseur that he became as soon as he made a public reputation for himself. He rehearsed the lines he would trot out when aesthetic Society lionized him as the star performer of the afternoon tea tables: "Nothing succeeds like excess" . . . "Give me the luxuries, and I can dispense with the necessities" . . . "If one had the money to go to America, one would not go."

He capitalized on the Pre-Raphaelites' use of flowers for symbolism to make a passion for botany part of his stock-in-trade. He sported a daisy in his buttonhole, and young men of his colouration picked up the fad. He praised the "adorable" virtues of sunflowers, and suddenly they filled the vases of London salons. He made the lily he carried a badge of fidelity synonymous with Mrs. Langtry. "Art for art's sake" was the text of his preaching in the drawing rooms he frequented. Lillie was a work of art in herself.

They were foils for each other. Students at King's College, London, cheered when they arrived together at Professor Newton's series of lectures on Greek art, and she consented to sit facing the audience as a living exponent of Attic beauty. She studied Latin at Oscar's urging, though she fell behind in her homework when she was away with the prince at someone's country house. On one such excursion, at a mansion near Portsmouth, she wrote to Wilde:

Of course I'm trying to learn more Latin, but we stay here until Wednesday night so I shan't be able to see my kind tutor before Thursday. Do come and see me that afternoon, about six if you can. I called at Salisbury Street about an hour before you left. I wanted to ask you how I should go to a fancy-dress ball there, but I chose a soft black Greek dress with a fringe of silver crescents and stars and diamond ones in my hair

194

and on my neck and called it Queen of Night. I made it myself.

I want to write more but this horrid paper and pen prevent me, so when we meet I will tell you more (only don't tell Frank.)

She was too certain of herself to be deceived by Oscar's self-seeking. "The lily is so tiresome," he complained to a friend. "She *won't* do what I tell her. . . . I assure her that she owes it to herself and to us to drive daily through the Park entirely in black, in a black victoria drawn by black horses, and with 'Venus Annodomini' emblazoned on her black bonnet in dull sapphires, but she won't do it."

She introduced him to some of her newfound friends, and he returned the courtesy. His performance occasionally disappointed her. When he brought John Ruskin to Norfolk Street, she was irked by Oscar's fawning over the shaggy Slade Professor of Art whose judgements could make or break a contemporary painter. She listened attentively as ever while he pontificated about the virtues of the Greeks and the "glorification of ugliness and artificiality" that was all Japanese art meant to him.

She was amused by that. In a magazine he edited, Ruskin had denounced Jimmy Whistler, for whom Japanese art reigned supreme, and in particular a new painting of his, "A Nocturne in Black and Gold." "I have seen and heard much of Cockney impudence," Ruskin wrote, "but never expected to have a coxcomb ask two hundred guineas for flinging a pot of paint in the public's face." That was going too far. She knew Whistler planned to sue for libel. At the October trial he was awarded damages of one farthing, which he wore with pride on his watch-chain. She was one of Whistler's clique as well as a friend of Mr. and Mrs. Millais, and Ruskin was impotent. They held no further interest for each other.

She lent Wilde the portrait of herself that Poynter had given her, so that Oscar could stand it on an easel in a place of honour in the long, panelled drawing room of his Salisbury Street apartments, where such guests as Irving and Ellen Terry were encouraged to scrawl their signatures on the white paint alongside the tapestries on the walls.

Oscar, whose strongest affections were already reserved for other men, had a ready-made poem, "Wasted Lives," that could easily be changed and circulated as a tribute to her. His original version read:

A fair slim boy, not made for this world's pain,
With brown, soft hair close braided by his ears
And longing eyes half veiled by slumbrous tears
Like blue water seen through mists of rain. . . .

Before it was published, he revised the opening line to "A lily-girl, not made for this world's pain." In the course of the next two years, he composed a panegyric explicitly for her, "The New Helen," which was eagerly published in Edmund Yates' magazine, *The World*. Oscar formally presented her with a hand-bound copy of it in white vellum, dedicated by him on the flyleaf, "To Helen, formerly of Troy, now of London." His talents had not yet matured. She did not feel expecially flattered. It was tedious stuff, page after page of it, from its start:

Lily of love, pure and inviolate!
Tower of ivory! Red rose of fire!
Thou hast come down our darkness to illume.

In the changed years ahead, when she saw him for the last time, some quirk of memory brought to her mind not "The New Helen" but the first poem he had doctored to fit her. "You have only wasted your life," she said. She had few illusions about Oscar or anyone else.

By then she had seen him invited to Buckingham Palace, a celebrated playwright, novelist, and audacious wit. The prince had visited Wilde's new quarters at 3 Tite Street, where John Keats once lived, a few steps from Whistler's White House. Frank Miles moved in with Oscar. The Irishman had taken to curling his long hair and tinting it amber.

He had tried to keep up a friendship with Lillie. She was one of the first to hear his news that at last he had found a wife: "I am going to be married to a beautiful girl called Constance Lloyd—a grave, slight, violet-eyed little Artemis, with great coils of heavy brown hair which makes her flower-like head droop like a blossom, and wonderful ivory hands. . . ."

Lillie had a shrewd idea that Oscar was bisexual. It was no surprise when he fell in love with twenty-one-year-old "Bosnie," Lord Alfred Douglas, third son of the Marquess of Queensberry, and was sentenced as a pederast to two years in Reading gaol. Looking back on the days when she and Wilde used each other for their separate purposes, she said with the callousness that had rooted itself in her, "I always found him a terrible bore."

The pleasure of serving the prince took her to Cowes for the August yachting. Bournemouth lay only twenty miles away. A pretense at discretion made it advisable for Edward to go with her and for them both to be ostensible guests of Alleno in his schooner *Helen.* Bertie and his family lived, as always, aboard *Osborne.* Leopold, a regular caller at Norfolk Street, was there, too, in *Alberta,* a less imposing royal yacht. The queen commanded a view of the water from the windows of Osborne House, where a telescope was kept on hand to make sure that she missed nothing in sight.

From the first of August until sails were furled in September, the town was strained at its seams by visitors, with every hotel and boardinghouse booked to capacity. This was of no concern to the wealthy, whose yachts served them as miniature, floating palaces. Lillie's desire sharpened for a seaworthy palace of her own—as she revelled in the routine of the summer days.

The centre of activity ashore was the Royal Yacht Squadron standing like a castle on the waterfront, whose lawns made a green promenade for seeing and being seen. The near-great rubbed shoulders with their superiors, the men jaunty in dark-blue blazers, white ducks, and rakish caps, the women languid under parasols. Less privileged people waited patiently for a glimpse of the queen riding in her carriage along the short seafront roadway. She would inevitably be accompanied by her youngest daughter, Beatrice, whom Louis Battenberg had thought of as a bride four years earlier, when she was seventeen. Victoria made sure nothing came of that by sending word to the First Lord of the Admiralty for Louis to be kept in out-of-the-way foreign stations until his ardour cooled.

There were sailing races every day for all classes of craft. Lillie had a choice of being a spectator or taking a cruise in one of the two-hundred-footers built for comfort rather than speed. They had deck space enough for dancing if the prince was in a mood for *al fresco* entertainment. Otherwise, they could dance every night of the week but Sunday in one of the mansions on the shore, outdoors when the weather was warm, under swaying Chinese lanterns to violins playing Strauss, while they waited for the rockets and Roman candles to be fired as a fillip to the fun.

Alberta, Helen, and a dozen other yachts like Suffield's *Flower of Yarrow* provided the settings for Lillie and the prince to mix with the celebrants of a way of life that seemed theirs by natural right. Aboard *Alberta* she stayed below-decks until the vessel was out of sight of Osborne. Her pale-skinned youngest son was circumspect about the range of Mamma's telescope.

Lillie's self-possession did not desert her. It had been tested earlier in the season in the house that Ferdie de Rothschild rented for the horse-racing at Goodwood. Lillie was preparing for dinner when her maid's dress flared up from the coal fire in the bedroom grate. When their screams went unheard, Lillie doused the flames with water from a pitcher. "Had I not . . . we might have been burned to death," she said calmly after she joined Ferdie and his guests.

In and around the town, Bertie showed off his new plaything. He introduced her with satisfaction to the understanding hostess of his youth, the Empress Eugénie, who was staying at Lord Hardwicke's place, "Egypt," with her son, Louis Napoleon, the Prince Imperial of France and a great favourite of Bertie's. In return, Lillie introduced Bertie to spiritualism in the form of table-turning. She retained her belief in the power of spirits to influence her destiny. She would have it that the Langtrys' Norfolk Street was haunted because it stood close to the site of Tyburn Tree, where criminals had been publicly hanged up to a century ago. Doors burst open without apparent cause, she told him. Her housemaid vowed that a cavalier in long curls barred her way downstairs one morning. The butler, whose room was in the basement, swore that he saw ghosts clutching their heads in their hands.

The seafront cottage, covered with wisteria, of Mrs. Cust was the scene of the dabble in spiritualism. Mrs. Cust's lean-cheeked bachelor son Harry, Lord Brownlow's heir, known variously as "the lady-killer of the century" and "the most notorious lecher of the day," was one of the party, Louis Napoleon another. Bertie took table-turning more seriously than most of the others. Like Lillie, he had no doubt that there was an afterlife "that would bear," as he once said, "some relation to the merits of men." Where his own station in heaven might be, he was not prepared to guess.

The curtains were pulled, and the group sat in darkness around a small table. As a token of affection from the prince, Louis Napoleon was seated next to Lillie to hold her hand. The séance followed the course she expected when she felt his fingers slip away from hers. The table began to rock so forcibly that the group quickly caught on to the trickery. Louis Napoleon was evicted and the door locked behind him.

The lights were turned off, hands linked, and the spirits summoned again. In a matter of minutes the company sensed the almost imperceptible touch of ghostly fingers on heads and faces in the darkness. One sceptic promptly lit a match. The prince imperial was back in the room, sprinkling flour from the bag he had carried with him as he climbed the wisteria and slipped in behind the window curtains. Bertie, white-faced, thought it was a huge joke. On a different day he joined Louis Napoleon in a livelier escapade. Together, they hoisted a donkey through the bedroom window of another guest, who found it there, dressed in a nightgown with a mobcap pulled over its ears.

Bertie did not stop with displaying Lillie to his friends, young and old. When their father introduced her to Eddy and Georgie, they were equally taken by her charm and her attentiveness, without questioning her motives or her sincerity. The following summer she bought Eddy the dullard, a trinket as a going-away present before he set sail with his brother in HMS *Bacchante* on a seven-month cruise to the West Indies as part of their navy training. Eddy had narrowly escaped being removed from the service for failure to keep up in his work. Possibly, gestures of affection were rare from most people except his mother. He attached Lillie's souvenir to his watch-chain, worn with his cadet's jacket with rows of bright brass buttons, narrow trousers, and shiny-peaked cap. "I had to take off grandmother's locket to make room for it," he told her.

With Edward escorting her for appearance's sake, she dined regularly with the prince and Alexandra aboard *Osborne,* where food and wine were served in the same polished style as in Marlborough House. After dinner, if the evenings were fine, the deck served as a dance floor.

Wearing kindness as a badge, Alix treated Lillie with the attentions she showed all her guests. She had long since reconciled herself to Bertie's compulsive appetites, and she gave no signs of resenting the woman he delighted in parading in front of her with all the pretended deference of which he was capable. If her temper was tried, Alexandra kept that a personal secret just as she suppressed any vestige of jealousy. Jealousy, she confided to Louise, her sister-in-law, is the bottom of all mischief and misfortune in the world.

It seemed that perhaps she spent more time in

Copenhagen and that members of her family came more often to England than before. But the legion of her admirers, close to her or far removed, took their cue from her. They did not stigmatise Lillie.

The closest of the men around Alexandra was Colonel the Honourable Oliver Montagu, commander of the Blues and an equerry to the prince for the past ten years. In their tall, plumed headdresses, blue jackets trimmed with lace, and skin-tight breeches striped with white, officers of the Royal Horse Guards were counted among the elite of Society. When they arranged a ball, romantic maidens yearned to be there. At most other people's balls, a fair sprinkling of the Blues had an automatic place on the guest lists as the most eligible young men in town.

The regiment had more than its share of rakehells, addicted to gaming tables and ladies' beds. In his younger, wilder days, Oliver had been one of those wicked boys, in Bertie's fond description, included among the reprobates whom the queen judged to be undesirable companions for her heir. But as a middle-aged bachelor, the colonel was an altogether different man, a Lancelot ready to lay down his life for his beloved princess in the unquestioned belief that the emotion and the act of love had nothing in common.

He thought she came as close to perfection as a woman could. When his prince was not there to escort her, Oliver was at her side. As a matter of habit, she invited him to partner her in the first waltz after supper, conscious of nobody else on the dance floor. The adder tongues of gossip could find nothing but platonic admiration on both sides. "The Princess," one seasoned observer concluded, "never gave any real occasion for scandal. I think it must have been due to Oliver Montagu's care for her. He shielded her in every way, not least from his own great love. . . . But she remained marvellously circumspect."

The security that Oliver's undemanding attention gave her made the advent of Lillie no more significant than the addition of another spadeful of sand to a child's seashore castle. She did not object when Bertie made his latest love a dinner guest at Marlborough House. Lillie played her part in the game without missing a cue. She found the princess "wonderfully lovely and faultlessly dressed. . . . Her grace and fascination were such that one could not take one's eyes from her."

In that same year, Bertie saw to it that Lillie was presented to the queen. Since neither he nor his mistress talked to others about such things, only they knew whether the presentation was prompted by her desire for her place in Society to be acknowledged with all formality or his wish to give her this credential.

Queen Victoria's "drawing rooms" were held at three in the afternoon in Buckingham Palace. An invitation there was more than a pleasant piece of flattery. It was essential as the ritual by which a girl, or a woman, became a fully fledged member of her class. Bertie sat through so many of the functions that they were one of the many institutions of his mother's that he abolished after her death.

They were designed primarily for eighteen-year-olds, to the milestone a girl passed when she left the schoolroom, put up her hair, and made her debut in the universe of the few hundred families in which her parents hoped she would find a husband. Shiny noses predominated over Paris gowns. Only professional beauties were expected to wear lipstick.

"We looked askance at privateering, piratical matrons, lovely as some of them were," one lady of the court recalled, and her reference fitted Lillie as snugly as a glove.

A row of royalties lined up beside the queen in descending order of rank while a string band explored its repertoire of sentimental music. The debutantes were required to attend in full evening dress and yards-long trains, with three feathers in their coiffures representing the *fleur de lys*. Each of them needed a "presenter," an older woman relative or friend who had undergone the same initiation in her day. A state coach, hauled out from the family stables or rented

202

for the day, was the only conceivable means of arriving for the pageantry. Lines of them filled the mall and wound along the roadways of St. James's Park, waiting their turn to unload their fluttering passengers under the stares of the crowd that looked forward to these afternoons as one of the prettiest free sights of London.

The idea that Lillie should come face to face with the queen, for whose health she had prayed on her knees every Sunday as part of the Church of England service, was born at a country-house party in Kent. She and the prince were guests of Lord and Lady Conyngham, whose daughter Jane would be one of the season's debutantes. Should not Mrs. Langtry be presented, too? The unspoken thought was that it would add to the illusion of discretion for the prince's mistress to be an accredited lady of Society.

Lillie was in two minds about the plan. It was unthinkable to be treated as little more than a younger Skittles, debarred from the presence of respectable women or kept out of sight like a demimondaine and served with champagne, which the prince rated as suitable for such companions. Ladies at night merited whisky-and-soda, in his opinion, though he would say, "There's not much difference nowadays." Yet gossip claimed that the queen would never consent to receive Lillie. The prospect of a royal rebuff in public frightened her, which was enough to convince her that the fear must be overcome. She must test her courage, as she had all her life.

The prince prepared the way with unfailing regard for detail. In March his mother made one of her rare excursions from Windsor to hold a Tuesday levee at the palace. In recognition of Edward's loyal forbearance, the prince personally presented him to her, with his nervousness fortified by the initialed gold cuff links he wore in his starched white shirt. They were a souvenir gift in advance from Bertie. Her Majesty was sufficiently intrigued with Mr. Langtry to spare him five minutes of her carefully regulated time.

On the May morning of her own presentation, the

prince bolstered Lillie's morale by sending her a bouquet of pale yellow Marechal Neil roses for her to carry when she met the queen. She had already planned defences of her own. She would appear at her best in ivory brocade garlanded with the same fresh-cut roses, including the nine-foot train, lined with matching yellow silk, that hung from her shoulders. She minimised to herself the importance of appearing at court anyway. She refused to be so overwhelmed as most other women.

Beyond that, she was counting on possibly not seeing the queen at all. Victoria usually made her departure from the throne room when she grew weary from standing towards the end of the afternoon, leaving Alexandra to receive the last in line. She knew she was on safe ground with the princess. Lillie would arrive as late as possible and hope to avoid a confrontation with Victoria.

She had her mother, who was staying with her, help fit her into her low-necked gown, a task no maid could be trusted with. Mrs. Le Breton was severing her ties with her lustful dean. The simmering scandal of his behaviour on Jersey continued to be kept from boiling over. That was vital if Lillie's precarious reputation was to escape further damage. She would have a house built for her mother's use next to hers in Bournemouth, where the two women could support each other in the appearance of provincial respectability.

As a finishing touch, there were three ostrich plumes, the longest Lillie could find, to be fixed with the white tulle veil in her hair. The word had been circulated by the court among the guests for this afternoon that the queen disapproved of the tiny feathers that had become the fashion. Her sight was beginning to fail, and she wanted to be able to *see* what the girls wore on their heads when they kissed her hand. But Lillie's choice was deliberately arrogant. The three swaying ostrich plumes brought instantly to mind the coat of arms of the Prince of Wales and the accompanying motto, *Ich dien*—"I serve." She intended to be recognised as the prince's woman. She would give the court something else to whisper about. Instead of piling up her hair in a pompadour, she wore it coiled low on the neck in a Jersey Lily knot.

She was too tense to eat anything before she set out with her cheerful sponsor, Lady Romney, in the coach she had provided. They were last but two in the queue entering the palace in the fading sunlight, and the surging crush of spectators irritated her. Her calculations had gone awry. Waiting to be called from the palace crush-room with the weight of her folded train dragging on her arm, she heard that the queen was still receiving.

Lillie fiddled with her veil and her pasteboard invitation card, mentally rehearsing how to handle the train when she handed it to the pages to spread behind her and, more demanding, how she could catch it up on her left arm, as the drill called for, after she had made her obeisance, to contrive a dignified backwards exit, keeping her eyes respectfully fixed on the royals. She felt confident about her curtsey; she had practised it until her knees ached. Yet she had often heard the stories of ladies who tripped as they bent their legs, or toppled over and had to be propped up by pages or even cling to the plump royal fingers for support.

The tiny, commanding widow of Windsor was waiting to inspect her. A rare fit of trembling seized Lillie at the sight of her, in a short-sleeved black gown with a velvet train. A diamond crown, veil, and black feathers made up her headdress. The Order of the Garter's blue ribbon traversed her bodice, diamonds and jewels studded her corsage, strands of pearls encircled her neck. She looked grave, tired, and shatteringly imperious. Next to her stood Bertie, with Alexandra beside him.

The precious invitation card was normally handed to the Earl of Mount Edgcombe, the newly appointed Lord Chamberlain, before he called the next name. He dispensed with that formality as Lillie approached. She managed her train superbly. All emotion was hidden in her tranquil face. "Mrs. Langtry comes next, Your Majesty," she heard Mount Edgcombe call.

A memory of her father flickered across her mind at that moment. As a child, sitting on his knee, she had heard him tell time and again of how the queen and the prince consort paid a call on Jersey when Lillie was five years old. They landed from *Victoria and Albert* at St. Helier and drove up the hill to inspect the only boys' private school on the island, Victoria College. The young dean was standing with a quill pen for her to sign the visitors' book. The pen failed to write, so she let it fall from her fingers while she waited for another. Lillie fancied that the look she saw now on the sagging cheeks was the same as her father spoke of.

It seemed to her that Her Majesty extended her hand reluctantly. Lillie executed a flawless curtsey and kissed the fingers that had discarded her father's pen so rudely twenty years ago. She received not a word or a trace of a smile from Victoria.

A curtsey to the prince brought a twinkle to his eyes. Another to Alexandra, and she smiled in recognition. Then on down the line until the train was deftly gathered up by a page and flung over her extended left arm for the final exit. Lillie was satisfied that she had carried the whole thing off with appropriate élan, but she doubted whether the effort was worth the trouble. "To be seen only for a moment as one was hurried in and out of the Presence made it seem a great deal of labour lost," she said afterwards. She wondered what the queen had thought about the ostrich plumes, but she was too independent to care.

She went that night to a ball in Marlborough House. In the middle of a royal quadrille, Bertie mentioned that his mother had stayed on only to satisfy herself as to the appearance of Mrs. Langtry, and she was annoyed with her for being so late.

"You rather overdid it with the ostrich feathers," he said.

"At all events, I *meant* well," Lillie answered.

Their affair continued with no pricking shame on

either side. The Court marvelled that the prince, in his fashion, remained faithful to her. He went to Sandringham as usual for Alexandra's birthday on December 1. The husband and wife spent a quiet, rare day together. Bertie, Alix told the queen, "quite overwhelmed me with lovely presents."

❧ VIII ❧

The New Year saw the queen and millions of her people in deep distress, Victoria tearful over the death of a daughter, her subjects because hunger haunted fields and factories. Everywhere in the land, trade and agriculture were close to collapse. In the industrial north, half the labouring classes were out of work and the rest on short time. Mills that spun cotton for the world to wear stood silent. Iron and steel furnaces on which British prosperity depended were blown out. Miners huddled in the cold outside locked pithead gates or burrowed in slag heaps for coal to warm their homes. A wave of bankruptcies erased some of the easy fortunes that the decade had produced. Only the banks and the great landowners who still composed the bulk of Society stayed secure, as they believed God had intended.

The prince showed stirrings of concern, if not of conscience. When Disraeli wanted him to help launch a national fund collection to relieve suffering, he leapt at the opportunity to make himself useful at last. "I am entirely at your disposal, and ready to do anything you think proper," he told the Prime Minister. The Liberals quashed the plan. They were convinced that it was nothing but a manoeuvre to shore up the faltering Tory government. Bertie had to content himself by attending an unprecedented total of nineteen debates in the House of Lords, while he lent his name to any worthy charity.

The queen added to the universal gloom by ordering the Court into deep mourning for her gentle-faced daughter Alice, Grand Duchess of Hesse. Diphtheria broke out that winter among Alice's family in the turreted, mediaeval castle at Darmstadt, the capital of her adopted country bordered by the Rhine. Her little daughter Mary was the first to die. Another daughter, fifteen-year-old Victoria, attempted to take over the reins of the household when Alice was infected.

Bertie had taken Alexandra to Windsor for the annual pilgrimage to Albert's mausoleum on the anniversary of his father's death when a telegram brought the news of his sister Alice's end. "I wish I had died instead of her," Alexandra said.

When Victoria mourned, the functions of the Court came to an abrupt halt. Formal dinners and receptions were cancelled. Anything that smacked of disrespect for the departed was forbidden. She personally went into seclusion and saw no reason why her family and household should not follow her example. The tone of the country was as black as the borders of the notepaper which she used exclusively throughout her forty years of widowhood.

Society life in London was scarcely affected, since none existed at this time of year. From October to February, the capital was deserted by anyone of consequence. Shutters sealed the windows of the mansions of the town. Lords, ladies, and the new rich who emulated them wintered in the country, where hounds and horses filled the courtyards by day and the windows blazed with light as dusk fell over hushed woods and fields, where farmboys worked for half a crown a week. Court mourning made little impact here.

The prince's life with Lillie at its centre was conducted on a circuit of such houses owned by his friends. They were given no alternative but to welcome her. He imposed his will by the implicit threat that unless she were a guest, he would no longer honour the place with his presence. Bedroom arrangements must be to his liking, too, with due regard for discretion, so that convenient accommodations were provided for Mrs. Langtry close to his own.

Competition ran high among the rich to be recognised as a host to the prince and Lillie. It was an expensive undertaking. It might entail reserving a permanent suite of rooms in the house for His Royal Highness and refurnishing them to impress or amuse him on every visit. To tempt his appetite at the table, a special chef would be brought in during his stay, though the length of corridors stretching between kitchens and dining room could make the serving of suitably hot dishes well-nigh impossible.

Entertaining the prince demanded weeks of preparation in advance. He wanted to know in good time who else would be there, and he had Lillie's name added if it was missing from a list. Once any other guest had accepted the host and hostess' invitation, only death or a contagious disease were sufficient excuse for not arriving.

The prince expected every meal to be served on the stroke of the hour and the rules governing what should appear on the table to be followed to the letter. Any cultivated person was aware that if more than a dozen sat down to dine, there must be two kinds of soup, two fish dishes, and a minimum of two entrées, one brown, one white. He drew the line at ever making himself one of thirteen. At one gathering, he allayed his superstitions by noting that one lady of the otherwise unlucky number was in an advanced stage of pregnancy.

He was equally punctilious in the matter of tipping. The head gamekeeper received a pound note. Ten pounds were left on the prince's departure to be divided among the servants of the house. If Bertie was compelled to leave ahead of Lillie, she was handed the money for the *pourboire*.

Making the rounds of country houses enchanted her, and her pleasure sharpened his. There were cynics who claimed that the larger the house and the more numerous the flunkeys, the worse would be the food, but she dismissed them to the same objectionable category as Disraeli, a man of Byzantine taste, who shunned rural living. It "involves a good deal too much both of eating and dressing," he complained.

The prince might descend for a weekend or longer with Lillie and perhaps a dozen of his companions like Suffield, Oliver Montagu, one or other of the Beresford brothers, and the permanent butt of his practical jokes, Christopher Sykes. Landowning dukes had no need to regret the expense. Other people drove themselves into debt for the privilege of having Bertie and his party under their roof. Lord Hardwicke was one, and another, Lord Dupplin, inventor of the tailless dinner jacket which Bertie took to with gusto. Charles Buller, with only a thousand pounds a year to live on, ran up such bills that he had to resign his commission in the Blues. The prince found a job for him as guardian of his Indian collection on display at the Paris Exhibition. Bertie had a way of trying to take care of his own. Even after Buller was imprisoned for writing a worthless check, Bertie continued to help him.

Christopher Sykes squandered a fortune on his master. Lillie, a target for many a man's attention, felt secure with the tall, solemn Yorkshire squire with the pale eyes and tawny beard who, at forty-eight, remained a bachelor. He treated her, she thought, almost too politely, but that was reassuring and his manner towards all women. On the circuit of country houses, including his own three-thousand-acre estate at Brantingthorpe, he was so unfailingly deferential to the prince that Bertie amused himself by pouring brandy over the Yorkshireman's head and teased him by pretending to stub out a cigar on the back of his hand to see whether smoke would emerge from his ears. That struck his cortège as almost as funny as the princely prank in pre-Lillie days of putting a dead seagull in bed with Christopher after he had retired from a royal ball, staggering drunk.

Sykes was on the road to beggaring himself when Lillie knew him as the prince's host at endless house parties. She had no idea of his problem in keeping up with men like another Rothschild, Alfred, who made her his guest of honour at an otherwise all-male "adoration dinner," climaxed with the gift of a handsome piece of jewellery, at his house on Seamore Place. The time came when Christopher faced bankruptcy. As soon as Bertie realized his loyal companions' predicament, he arranged for richer friends to put up enough money to keep Sykes out of court, but Lillie expressed no pity for him.

She was caught up herself in wild extravagance with never a thought of the cost. The Jersey woman who had made a plain black dress a symbol of her independence had to attire herself now as an equal, at least, of the fanciest fashion plates in the land. She had her negligees lined with ermine to delight her lover and her ball gowns trimmed with silver fox. She arrived at one Marlborough House ball in yellow tulle draped with gold fishnet on which captive, preserved butterflies were loosely pinned. Bertie, up early the next morning, went around the floor, retrieving them as souvenirs. While the queen mourned and England foundered into dark depression, the first obscure words of public criticism appeared in print. *Town Talk* was a mischievous weekly magazine, printed in an alley off Fleet Street, the heart of England's national newspaper industry. Its twenty-seven-year-old editor and proprietor, Adolphus Rosenberg, was a newcomer to a sturdy tradition of journalism that specialized in pillorying royalty and the rich. Similar publications had flourished in Victoria's younger days, but they had been suppressed for forty years. Only now were they reappearing with titles like *Paul Pry, Puck,* and *Tomahawk,* enraging the men who were their targets.

An editor who published such paragraphs ran the risk of physical attack as well as prison. When *The Queen's Messenger,* a competitor of *Town Talk,* printed a series of articles criticizing Carrington, who briefly inherited Nellie Clifden from the prince, he laid hold of photographs of the author, Grenville Murray, then waited for him at the exit of his club. "I am

Lord Carrington; you know where to find me," he said in the classical challenge to a duel. When Murray smiled, he earned himself a thrashing with a horsewhip. He was then put on trial and found guilty of libel.

Rosenberg, a married man with two children and his elderly Jewish parents in his care at his suburban home on Brixton Hill, trod carefully at first. In his January 11 issue, he wrote:

I wonder how the husbands of the "beauties of Society" like their wives to be shown about in a "visitors-are-requested-not-to-touch" sort of way. I don't believe they are husbands at all—only dummies. Some of the beauties, I'm afraid, have too many husbands.

He was less circumspect when he returned to the theme in the pages of *Town Talk* three months later. Broad hints of scandal at the apex of the pyramid were good for sales of his magazine. He wrote:

About the warmest divorce case which ever came before a judge may shortly be expected to come off. The respondent was a reigning beauty not many centuries ago, and the co-respondents —and they are numerous—are big "pots." The poor husband is almost frantic. "Darn this country," he says: "Nothing belongs to a fellow here. Even his wife is everybody's property." Oh, that woman! I myself loved her. I bought her portrait —oh, years and years ago—in thirty-five different positions, and wept over it in the silent hours of the night. And I am not even a co-respondent.

He followed up in his next two issues with stories of misunderstanding between the prince and Alexandra, speculating that she was on the point of returning permanently to Copenhagen.

In the London clubs Rosenberg was branded as a damned radical. That was the name the English applied to those Marxists and Socialists whose unprincipled appeals to the poor were causing alarm to the rulers of Germany, France, and Russia. In Paris one of Bertie's political acquaintances, Léon Gambetta, the Chamber of Deputies' one-eyed hero of the Franco-Prussian War, had seen his force of Democratic-Republican moderates split when Georges Clemenceau proclaimed himself an out-and-out radical.

The true radicals of England preferred to be called "advanced Liberals." They advocated much the same programs as their compatriots overseas. The oath of loyalty to the queen required of all Members of Parliament should be done away with, they said, and Members paid a living salary to end domination of law-making by the rich. The radicals sought to break the power of the House of Lords and to establish an effective income tax. They stood for free education for every child and a vote for every adult. The railways, they preached, should be nationalised like the post office.

What inflamed the ruling classes perhaps most of all was the radical belief that England must be involved in future wars only after a majority vote in Parliament. War itself, the radicals insisted, ought to be abolished and quarrels between nations resolved by arbitration. In the nightmares of the rulers, radicalism meant bloody revolution, with the churches burned and the queen massacred, along with the aristocrats and clergy.

At the end of May, Rosenberg was ready to name names. He muddled one fact at least in subscribing to the myth, prevalent even among people who claimed to know her, that Lillie had arrived from the United States:

I am informed that Mrs. Langtry, being tired of London life, is about to return to her American home, accompanied by her husband. She will probably remain here until the end of the season, so photographers ought to make hay while the sun shines.

Whether Mrs. Langtry is disappointed that her reign as a beauty of Society was short-lived, or whether the commission on the sale of her photos didn't come in quick enough, or in sufficiently large amounts, I have not been enabled to learn. My own opinion is that Mr. Langtry—how strange that name sounds!—has asserted his position and commanded my lady to pack up. But I can hardly believe that after all.

The following week, *Town Talk* contained only a single paragraph on the theme that increasingly obsessed its editor: "I am informed that Mr. Langtry has announced his intention of breaking my neck. Now, if the brave gentleman wants to go in for neck-breaking, surely he can find plenty of his friends (?) who have injured him more than I have."

By this time, another London season was in full swing. The queen had endeavoured to cheer herself with a month in Italy at the Villa Clara on the shore of Lake Maggiore and was back in Windsor Castle. On a timetable as precisely timetabled as a railway's, the prince had enjoyed a springtime holiday at Biarritz, evidently with Lillie at his side. The "Earl of Chester," as he wished to be known on this occasion, arrived behind four horses for breakfast at the Hotel de Londres in San Sebastián, "accompanied," as the official accounts carefully reported, "by Mrs. Bellairs, the British Counsul at Biarritz, by his secretary and one other person." The earl met with trouble after the meal, not from Nihilists or radicals but from the horses, a constant source of danger between the shafts of anyone's carriage.

Even the best-trained royal animals could be skittery when a crowd started to shout and wave Union Jacks. A stand-by carriage was an essential part of a public appearance. The skittery San Sebastián team took fright as the prince and Lillie turned out of the hotel into the Avenida la Liberdad. Kicking heels broke the front of his carriage and threatened to smash into Bertie. He remained a picture of calm. "It is nothing," he growled, helping Lillie down and setting off on foot with her to see the sights of the town.

He was back home in time to see his brother Arthur, Duke of Connaught and the queen's third son, married to Princess Louise of Prussia in Windsor Castle. Attendance was a duty; the two brothers had little in common. Their mother had perhaps hinted at her disapproval of Bertie's alliance with Lillie when she said at the time of the duke's engagement, "It will be *most essential* that Arthur does not *consult* the Prince of Wales as to his plans in any way, or take the House at Sandringham with its very irregular hours and way of living as an example."

Spring brought daffodils, crocuses, and sheep to the Park, and the inexorable calendar of Society festivals calling for the prince's attendance: drawing rooms at Buckingham Palace and levees at St. James's; trooping of the colours and the Derby in May; banquets, receptions, garden parties, and balls; the opera and the theatre; foundation stones to lay and hospitals to visit. In the background to relieve the tedium there was Lillie.

It was all "a dream, a delight, a wild excitement," she said. She intrigued him, her childish sense of fun, as simple as his, that had her sliding down the stairs of one august country house on a silver salver. She tried riding to hounds at Lord Manners' place, Quenby, in Leicestershire, but gave it up as hopeless and cheerfully accepted the ignominy of trotting along the lanes as a follower on a hack more docile than a hunter. She kept up the displays of herself in the Park. Her need for sleep matched Bertie's, so she could dance until daybreak, then be wide awake to take out Redskin for a misty, early morning canter with the prince, though she had acquired a brougham and a chestnut harness horse to pull it from the Norfolk Street stable.

The fun of Ascot races, which she saw as his guest, was spoiled for him this year. He had used his influence to have his protégé, Louis Napoleon, sent to the Transvaal in South Africa, where white imperialism, British and Boer, was running up against black resistance in the person of King Keshwayo and his army of forty thousand Zulu warriors. Louis Napoleon, a volunteer, was out on reconnaissance when he was ambushed and impaled by a Zulu assegai.

Another Prince Louis filled the gap left in Bertie's circle. Louis Battenberg took up Uncle Bertie's longstanding invitation to join him as a ship's officer under Charlie Beresford aboard *Osborne*. On the face of it, it was a surprising decision: He had recently been offered the opportunity to become the ruler of Bulgaria.

The throne of the little kingdom on the Danube had been vacant since its freeing from the Turks by the czar's armies a year ago. The Congress of Berlin, in setting the terms of peace, recognised the need to fill it. A delegation of Bulgars came from Sofia to approach Louis as their first choice.

He declined, primarily because he had dreams of advancement in the British navy, which he made his life's great love. Possibly, he sensed too, that "Prince Louis I of Bulgaria" could only be an empty title, rewarding in terms of gold from St. Petersburg, but dependent on the will of Russia. Bulgaria was a puppet principality of the czar's. The statesmen of Sofia were intent, however, on setting up one Battenberg or another as the Russians' nominee. After Louis, they chose his younger brother, twenty-two-year-old Sandro, as Prince Alexander I. He assumed the throne in April, the month when Louis took up his lighthearted duties aboard *Osborne*. In the same month, the czar escaped another Nihilist attack in St. Petersburg. A groom's son missed him with all four shots from a revolver.

Lieutenant Louis delighted men and women alike. In his middle twenties he possessed much of Uncle Bertie's charm and none of his evil temper. He could dance, swim, ride and even play the piano on command to accompany Affie's squeaking violin. Alexandra found him "noble." The queen enjoyed the tales he told so much that she would draw him to her side and laugh until her lace cap fell awry. To Bertie, he was a splendid fellow, a perfect playmate who must be enrolled in the Marlborough Club and taken along on every possible occasion. He was just the man to appreciate the charms of Mrs. Langtry. Bertie was delighted to introduce them to each other.

He was too worldly and too promiscuous in his own habits to be surprised at the result. It was more than likely that he had foreseen what was bound to happen when his handsome, gentle-mannered nephew encountered the most dazzling woman in England. Louis was enraptured with Lillie, and she encouraged him. He was in love with her, and she loved him well enough to share his bed whether in Marlborough House or in some country manor which they visited together as members of Bertie's entourage. Louis would marry her if she became available. Since marriage to Bertie could not even be dreamed of, the not quite impossible vision of becoming Louis' bride could find a place in her ambitions. Possibly that would have been a suitable reward for both his favourite princeling and his favourite mistress in Bertie's judgement.

Louis was a natural candidate for the strictly limited entertaining that Lillie carried on at 17 Norfolk Street. She practised only on intimate friends, who would not be condescending about the size of the house and her shortcomings as a hostess; *Mrs. Beeton's Household Management,* selling in the thousands, was not for her. She judged her efforts to be "distinctly defective," but Louis could be relied on not to deride one of her pet tries at decor. Floating a yellow water lily in a blue glass bowl was Jimmy Whistler's idea.

Lillie's reputation as the most fascinating woman in London was overshadowed that season by another newcomer. Oscar Wilde hurried away on a train to Folkestone to be among the first to welcome Sarah Bernhardt of the Comedie Française as she stepped ashore from the Channel steamer. He spread an armful of lilies at her feet lest he would otherwise pass unnoticed. Bertie was well acquainted with her as a result of his visits to Paris. The stir she created among the English immediately started to grow when he took a box for the run of the French company's stay at the Gaiety Theatre.

Lillie made a return call one morning to Eaton Place to be introduced to the wraithlike Frenchwoman with the frizz of auburn hair at a welcoming breakfast given by a former neighbour who had imported the company, Sir Algernon Borthwick, proprietor of *The Morning Post*. Sarah, who spoke no English, had her manager, snowy-haired William Jarrett, act as interpreter, but Lillie had kept up her French.

The tragedienne, daugher of an unmarried Jewish cocotte and a runaway father, had played the social role of the inscrutable vedette for years. She was dressed in a trailing white gown, beaded and embroidered, with her perennial bow of white tulle at her throat. Her enormous dark eyes burned as she concentrated to catch every word of conversation, then interrupt before the sentence was completed. For once, Lillie stood in awe of someone, and Sarah seemed to approve of her. "With that chin, she will go far," Bernhardt commented later.

Lillie dashed off her impressions of the woman she suddenly felt the urge to emulate. "This great and overwhelming artist was almost too individual, too exotic to be completely understood or properly estimated *all at once*." She listed for her own edification the qualities she saw in Sarah—"superb diction, lovely silken voice, natural acting, passionate temperament, fire." Only two words could do her justice; they were "transcendent genius."

Jealousy was rare in Lillie. She was too sure of herself and her status with the prince to be piqued when Sarah set about conquering the city and Bertie, too. Ostensibly, the Comedie Française had no stars. Its program consisted of two comedies by Moliere, *Le Misanthrope* and *Les Précieuses ridicules,* in which she did not appear at all, and one act from Racine's tragedy *Phèdre,* which she had made her personal triumph. She had an instinct for publicity that ranked her with Phineas T. Barnum, the circus king.

Bertie joined in the cheering when he saw her on

opening night from his box with Alexandra and his brother-in-law, Crown Prince Frederick. From the minute she made her entrance—it was after ten o'clock —Bernhardt was "the divine Sarah" to the critics. There had been no one like her, they raved, since the legendary Rachel, dead now for almost twenty years, who in her day had also had London at her feet.

Lord Dudley displayed Sarah in his carriage in the Park. The lord mayor gave a luncheon in her honour in the Long Parlour of the Mansion House and personally escorted her around the state apartments there. Squire Bancroft, another luncheon guest and the most celebrated actor-manager of the English stage after Irving, felt it polite to apologise for the marble busts of Lord Nelson and the Duke of Wellington. They had been less friendly to the French in the battles of Trafalgar and Waterloo.

Oscar was smitten with the fancy that Sarah's intense, narrow face in profile was the exact replica of a Roman goddess'. He was not satisfied until he took Lillie off for a day in the British Museum, prowling among the collections of vases, coins, and intaglios to find the original. Lillie bore up well under his infidelity to "the New Helen." She decided that Bernhardt "filled the imagination as a great poet might do."

At first she was equally calm about the prince's disaffection. She saw *Phèdre* when Bertie returned with her to the Gaiety. "I would give all my beauty to be just one part so great an actress as she," Lillie said afterwards. She went with the prince and Alexandra to the opening of an exhibition in a house on Piccadilly of ten paintings and eight pieces of sculpture which Sarah had included as part of her baggage. A hundred invitations were issued; twelve hundred people presented themselves at the doors. Sir Frederick Leighton, newly knighted, pressed his compliments on Sarah for these unsuspected skills of hers in other arts. Gladstone spent ten minutes talking with her. Bertie bought one picture and commissioned another.

The Barnum strain showed when Sarah spent the proceeds of her sales. From Mr. Cross' menagerie in

Liverpool, she bought a cheetah, a wolfhound, and seven chameleons, which she wore one at a time on her shoulder, held by a thin gold chain, to match any dress in her considerable wardrobe. She had the whole collection with her in a rented house at 77 Chester Square, together with four dogs, her parrot, Bizibouzou, and Darwin, a caged monkey.

Lillie had to conclude that the prince had eclectic tastes in women. In herself were exemplified the ideals of the age, which worshipped tiny waists, broad shoulders, and broader hips. Bernhardt, she told herself, could not be judged as beautiful by those standards. There was nothing sensual in Sarah's slim, supple body and white face; no roundness; no tempting flesh. "The masses," as Lillie was fond of calling the multitude of Englishmen, dismissed Sarah as a skeleton only because they did not appreciate her rare beauty as Lillie—and Bertie—did.

If the prince had been unremittingly faithful before, which seemed improbable, he was not now. Sarah began to receive calls to Marlborough House. After one of them, she scribbled a note of apology to the maestro of the French company, Edmond Got: "I've just come back from the P. of W. It is twenty past one. I can't rehearse any more at this hour. The P. has kept me since eleven . . . I'll make myself forgiven tomorrow by knowing my part."

A groundswell of sympathy for Lillie began to develop, with undertones of xenophobia. She could be regarded as almost an English *lady,* after all, and far more suitable for the prince therefore than a French *cocotte,* "a woman of notorious, shameless character," as one horrified matron confided to her diary. "London has gone mad . . . Not content with being run after on the stage, this woman is asked to respectable people's houses to act, and even to luncheon and dinner; and all the world goes. It is an outrageous scandal!"

But Sarah's hold on the prince's attention was secure. On a future evening in Paris, when she was playing in a drawing-room melodrama about Russian

Nihilists, entitled *Fédora,* he mentioned that he would like to have been an actor himself. She immediately dressed him for the role of Vladimir, Fédora's husband, whose corpse is brought home to her in an early scene. Bertie made his theatrical debut lying on a bier on the stage of the Vaudeville Theatre.

Alexandra learned to accept Sarah, too. When Bertie introduced her to his wife the following year, Alix took the gardenia she was wearing, pinned with a pearl brooch, and fastened them both on Bernhardt's shoulder. Eventually the queen, after a prolonged search of her conscience, received Sarah, too, and asked her to write a line or so in her ever-present birthday book. Sarah took book and pen to kneel on the floor before Her Majesty while she scrawled over one full page, *"Le plus beau jour de ma vie."*

Lillie's name appeared more diffidently in another volume of record-keeping. On an autumn visit that year to Cunliffe Brooks, a new-generation businessman, in Scotland, she drove to Balmoral Castle, a few miles away. She had reservations about inscribing "Mrs. Edward Langtry" in the visitors' book after her one previous encounter with the queen. The rest of the party persuaded her that she must, or risk offending Her Majesty. Victoria came in twenty minutes after they had left and glanced with customary curiosity at the page.

"I should like to have seen Mrs. Langtry," she said. A servant was sent on horseback to try to overtake the unseen guest, but he was too late. Balmoral did not strike Lillie as a place in which she would care to linger. "Bleak and uninteresting" was her delivered judgement.

The queen's desire to see more of Mrs. Langtry might have been stirred by a lawsuit into which Lillie was being dragged. Throughout the summer, Adolphus Rosenberg had been bandying her name in his columns. In June *Town Talk* reported: "There has been lately a rumour that Mrs. Langtry was about to appear in the divorce court, with more than one il-

221

lustrious co-respondent. This rumour is, like many others, without the least foundation."

He was evidently improving his sources of information about her. "Mrs. Langtry does not hail from America, as is popularly supposed," he explained two weeks later, "but was born on the island of Jersey, being the only daugher of the Reverend Dean of Jersey, Mr. Corbet Le Breton, M. A. Mrs. Le Breton, the mother, has recently abdicated her throne of quietude, the deanery, for more fashionable realms."

A few days before Sarah and the Comédie Française sailed home in July, Lillie was pointedly put in her place by the prince. People who saw the incident read it as a sign of resentment on her part of Bertie's preoccupation with the *piquante* Frenchwoman. They wondered what else could have prompted her into such an exhibition of lese majesty.

The Royal Albert Hall was taken over for a grand fete to raise money for endowing a bed in the French Hospital, Leicester Square, exclusively for the use of French actors and actresses falling ill in the British capital. Sarah was one of the leading lights of the Comédie Française who graced the twenty booths. Bertie brought Alexandra and their daughters, with Louis in tow.

Lillie, in a brocaded dress and yellow bonnet, adorned the refreshment stand of the Countess de Bülow, wife of a German diplomat, where a cup of tea cost five shillings with milk and sugar or one guinea if Lillie took the first sip. Two policemen had to part the crowd that gazed on her so that Bertie could buy a box of bonbons.

The royalties moved on to Sarah's stall. Alexandra paid ten pounds for a pair of blue-eyed white kittens, and the prince handed over a fistful of notes for an oil portrait which Sarah had painted and commissioned another from her. A sizable proportion of the five thousand patrons of the fete knew enough about the unspoken rivalry between Lillie and Bernhardt to watch every move made. Sarah's stall drew the most money, with 256 pounds taken in when the proceeds were counted. After leaving Bernhardt, Bertie strolled back to Lillie for a cup of tea.

Lillie poured it and, unasked, touched the rim to her lips before she gave him the cup and saucer. He set them down on the counter, saying firmly, "I should like a clean one, please." She served him another in silence. He put two gold sovereigns into her hand and walked away.

For a week or two *Town Talk* ignored her, while it pursued other royal tidbits. Alexandra, it said, was taking "too active an interest in the domestic arrangements at Marlborough House." Then Rosenberg rattled the skeleton of the morganatic marriage of the queen's first cousin, George, Duke of Cambridge, to the actress Louisa Fairbrother. George, commander in chief of the British Army, was sixty and Mrs. Fitz-George, as she was known, four years older. The law stipulated that George required the queen's permission to marry. He had neglected to ask for it, so for Victoria, Louisa did not exist and neither did the three sons she had borne the duke. Bertie, however, had a high regard for the old man.

On August 30 a new issue of the magazine went on sale. It caused a sensation among its readers and thousands of others who tried to lay hands on a copy. "A petition," it stated unequivocally, "has been filed in the Divorce Court by Mr. Langtry. H.R.H. The Prince of Wales, and two other gentlemen whose names up to the time of going to the press we have not been enabled to learn, are mentioned as co-respondents." An accompanying article headlined "Who Is Mrs. Langtry?" summarized the few known facts of her career. It "is not intended to bias the case," wrote Rosenberg, "and must be read as indicating the public and not the private life of the much-photographed lady. On the coming divorce case itself I would rather not at present comment."

If it was a trial balloon, nobody attempted to shoot it down. Encouraged by soaring sales and silence from the protagonists, Rosenberg put out a poster to promote his next week's issue: "The Langtry Divorce

Case: Further Particulars." There were not many, but they were persuasive that the story was not pure invention. "I now learn," he wrote, "that a few weeks ago an application was made that the case be tried *in camera,* and I believe the learned judge acceded to the request."

Another week passed, and Rosenberg supplied more details. "I am informed that the Langtry divorce case will be one of the first to be tried when the Court reopens in November. It has been finally decided to try the case *in camera,* and so scandalmongers will be deprived of a fine opportunity. Mrs. Langtry has, I understand, filed an answer, denying the adultery, and, as far as I can learn, the petitioner will find it exceedingly difficult to make good his case. . . . Of course, there will be a great outcry against the case being tried privately, but I don't see why anyone need be dissatisfied, especially as the details are not likely to be at all creditable to us as a nation. I don't care about being more explicit."

Still no response was made or denials issued. *Town Talk* ploughed ahead with a claim that the Home Secretary in Disraeli's Cabinet, R. A. Cross, had warned managers of the music halls to make sure that no stage comedians cracked jokes about the Langtry case. That was followed up by an invitation to Henry Labouchère, editor and founder of a rival publication, *Truth,* who had scoffed at the whole story. "Go to Somerset House . . . to see the petition," Rosenberg urged. "If he doesn't care to bother himself so much as that, let him ask their Lordships Londesborough and Lonsdale."

The prince's views on divorce were so rigid that it was unlikely that Lillie dare broach the topic at all unless he started the discussion. Divorce, Bertie considered, was a subject "which cannot be discussed openly and in all its aspects with any delicacy or even decency before ladies." But someone or something persuaded Rosenberg in the course of the next few days that royal bargaining was taking place behind the scenes.

"I am now informed on authority which I have no reason to doubt," he declared on October 4, "that Mr. Langtry has withdrawn the petition which he had filed in the Divorce Court. The case of Langtry v. Langtry and others is therefore finally disposed of, and we have probably heard the last of it. It is useless for the sixpenny twaddlers to deny that Mr. Langtry ever filed a petition. He did, and as I have said before, an application was made to Sir James Hannen to hear it privately, and he consented. I am told also that it is not unlikely that Mr. Langtry will shortly be appointed to some diplomatic post abroad. It is not stated whether his beautiful consort will accompany them."

Five weeks had gone by since *Town Talk's* original statement that Edward was bringing suit, and no word had been heard from him. Rosenberg's forecast that "we have probably heard the last of it" turned out to be disastrously wrong for him, but for reasons which at first seemed coincidental. In the same pages that week he ran an article mocking Mary Cornwallis-West. Each corner of the backyard of her house on Eaton Place contained a little photographic studio, he claimed. Mary hurried between them, changing costumes, to satisfy photographers' demands for more pictures of her. She charged commission for her services and personally drove around the shops collecting her fees.

Within a week, her husband, William, Lord Lieutenant of Denbighshire, sued Rosenberg for defamatory libel, "filthy and foul." Rosenberg was arrested. At his first hearing before the Guildhall magistrates on October 11, he was stunned to see another lawyer rise to present a further, unrelated charge against him: Six issues of *Town Talk* had libelled Mr. and Mrs. Langtry. To amazement in the courtroom, the magistrates agreed that Rosenberg should stand in double jeopardy. When he could not raise 2,000 pounds in bail money, he was locked in gaol.

His trial finally began in the Central Criminal Court on October 25 before Mr. Justice Hawkins, renowned as a vindictive judge. Additional indictments were levelled against the editor there for libelling Lord Londesborough, who was allowed to sit on the bench that day with the lord mayor, sheriffs, and aldermen of London. The case had escalated into a *cause célèbre*.

The Langtrys had a team of three high-priced counsel, led by the rotund Sergeant Parry. Parry had appeared for Whistler in his suit against Ruskin and had possibly been recommended to Lillie by him. Neither she nor Mary Cornwallis-West was in court, but their husbands were. To be there, Edward had interrupted what Lillie described to her friends as interminable fishing trips. The Cornwallis-West matter was put aside to give precedence to the Langtry business. Sergeant Parry opened:

"Mr. and Mrs. Langtry live in the best and highest society. They have for some time been honoured with the acquaintance and, I might say, the friendship of Their Royal Highnesses the Prince and Princess of Wales, who have frequently visited them at their residence. . . . The lady of whom this libel has been published is of great personal attractions and beauty. Hence it has been that the defendant and those who are associated with him have thought fit for the purpose of profit, and for the sale of their vile publication, to make her the subject of obloquy and defamation."

A junior counsel led Edward through his paces after the *Town Talk* articles had been read into the record. The regiment of newspaper reporters in the overflowing courtroom included them verbatim in the tens of thousands of words that appeared day by day. If Edward suffered one of his usual attacks of nervousness, he hid the symptoms well. Immaculately turned out, he made a sober, convincing witness, the model of a gentleman wronged.

"You have heard the libels that have been read," said his lawyer. "Is there a single word of truth in them?"

"Not one single word," answered Edward forth-rightly.

The judge made a learned interjection: "That is, so far as the matter is within his knowledge."

No, said Edward in response to further questions, he had never filed suit for divorce or even considered such a step. He had "always lived on terms of affection" with his wife and "am living with her still at Norfolk Street." When the trial was over, he went back to his routine of fishing trips.

Rosenberg's defense was pitifully frail. He had been misled, he swore, by an informant whom he volunteered to name but was not allowed to. His counsel was reduced to begging for mercy on the grounds that his client was a hard-worked family man of good character. It did him no good. His lawyer managed to introduce one ironic thought that was current among the spectators: "Far be it from me to suppose that the Prince of Wales could for a moment depart from that morality which it is his duty to exhibit. . . ."

Rosenberg was sentenced to eighteen months in prison. "I regret," said Mr. Justice Hawkins, "that I cannot add hard labour." A timely example had been set. Every newspaper and magazine in the country would be circumspect in future about mentioning Lillie. "Never in print" became something of a watchword of hers.

But Rosenberg could not stay entirely clear of the subject which had cost him his freedom. He had begun serving his sentence when *Town Talk* aimed one more dart: "Sergeant Parry did not long survive his exceptionally vindictive speech against Mr. Rosenberg in the Langtry libel case. The amount of forensic ammunition which this portly advocate wasted on that occasion was noticed even by persons unfriendly to Mr. Rosenberg. But I never forget the ancient aphorism, *De mortuis nil nisi bonum,* and instead of saying anything further of that *cause célèbre,* I simply inscribe on the late Sergeant's tomb R.I.P."

The matter was dropped there until Rosenberg

came out of prison. When he returned to worry the subject like a dog at a well-chewed bone, he ran on firmer ground.

The clash of wills between Lillie and the prince was soon forgotten. Neither of them could see any reason to interrupt their relationship while the libel case moved towards its climax. Cowes provided the setting again after Alix obligingly departed for Copenhagen for a month's stay with her family.

The English summer weather was disappointing, but the rain that fell most days could not douse the spirits of Bertie's entourage. Charlie Beresford's fondness for a joke brightened one afternoon. Commander the Right Honourable Lord Beresford was captain of *Osborne* at this time, but a previous command of his, the armour-plated warship *Thunderer,* lay within easy sailing distance. The ironclad's accommodations lay below the waterline with air supplied by the same hydraulic system that worked the loading gear for her heaviest guns.

Thunderer made a bizarre choice for a tête-à-tête with a "royalty," but Lillie went aboard. Four years earlier, as the ship underwent speed trials, one of her boilers had blown out and filled the stokehold and engine room with scalding steam for an hour. Crewmen raced over the decks, tearing their clothes from their seared bodies. Thirty-six of them died in the disaster.

On the afternoon that Lillie shared a cabin, Charlie turned off the air supply, turning two faces an increasingly deep shade of scarlet. She joked about the incident nearly half a century afterwards, without giving a clue to the identity of the "royalty" with whom she spent a passionate afternoon. That was the only incident of its kind that she touched on in her reminiscences. Almost certainly, her companion on that occasion was Louis. Perhaps she traced to that particular interlude *corps à corps* one of the epochal turns of her life.

The frivolous months afloat had worn thin for Louis Battenberg by the time autumn came. As a dedicated navy man, he wanted greater challenges. Once again he politely refused Uncle Bertie's appeals to him to stay on in *Osborne*. Instead, he elected to go back on the inactive list on half-pay until a more demanding seagoing appointment was open for him. Meantime, he kept the prince company on his excursions and occupied the room reserved for him at Marlborough House.

Alone or with the prince, Lillie was accepted in Society except in the upper reaches where Victoria's old-fashioned views predominated. Any rich banker or businessman with aspirations to be close to the prince welcomed Mrs. Langtry. She was shrewd, well-informed, and she had a gift for mental arithmetic which appealed to an entrepreneur. Without specific evidence, they reasoned that she must have influence with the prince, which they could turn to their own good use.

Old attitudes were melting fast in the heat of friction between the secure past, when farmlands represented the country's wealth, and the new era of coal and iron. As a free spirit who had achieved precarious respectability, she was as much a symbol of the times as the telephone and electric light, which was slowly replacing oil lamps and gas jets. Impervious to change, the queen believed that when she died, her kingdom would perish with her. Bertie's historic role, half-consciously performed, was to let in enough fresh air to prevent England becoming a national mausoleum. His delectable mistress was an accomplice in his task of securing the future.

Rothschilds and Sassoons opened their doors to her. Staying with the Reuben Sassoons at their Georgian house in Brunswick Gardens, Brighton, she was one of the sights of the seafront promenade, riding in his victoria with her host, who had inherited the dark complexion of his ancestor, Sheikh Sassoon Ben Salah of Baghdad. "Here's Desdemona with Othello," the inhabitants used to say. Politicians paid their respects to her, especially members of the Opposition, who could smell that their day was coming after six years of Disraeli's government. Gladstone made a personal point of not forgetting Lillie.

Songs continued to be written about her and the sheet music sold in tens of thousands of copies. Now an opera was in production that owed its title to the tide of her popularity. The prince took Alexandra to the first performance of *The Lily of Killarney* by the Carl Rose Comany at Her Majesty's Theatre. He escorted Alix, too, when the Haymarket Theatre reopened soon after Christmas, under the new management of Squire Bancroft, who had torn out the old "pit" behind the stalls and built a second gallery, aiming to make this a showpiece of London. The idea of becoming an actress had tantalised Lillie since she saw Bernhardt's triumphs with Londoners and with Bertie. Bancroft would be a useful man to cultivate, since Sarah was due back for another series of performances at the Gaiety, this time with her own company, before she set off to New York.

The paths Lillie trod crossed Alexandra's with increasing frequency, with no evidence of hostility ever shown by the princess. An unwritten law said that no gossip of any kind was to be repeated to her. When wife and mistress met, they spoke of trivialities, not people, never about Bertie. In private, Alexandra took refuge in a thought which the endless, expensive presents that her husband plied her with made it easy to believe: "After all, he always loved me the best."

Far more than Lillie had need to, the princess lived on the adoration of crowds. She made sure that she would be the best-dressed woman at any ball, with her girl's figure revealing no trace of age, gliding across the floor on Oliver Montagu's arm in an aura of her unique violet perfume. Lillie was hard pressed not to be overshadowed. "I spent every possible moment planning bizarre hats," she remembered, "and ordering and trying on elaborate frocks." Dressmakers could not do too much to claim her as a patron, but the bills mounted higher and higher.

A ball began after the theatre ended and lasted until the night sky began to lighten. A town house of consequence had its own ballroom, bright with banks of flowers and garlands draping the walls, the sparkling gas chandeliers and sconces. That season, the fad persisted for Hungarian string orchestras, the musicians decked out like Hussars in short, heavily braided red and blue jackets. State balls at Buckingham Palace struck Lillie as rather too staid. Ladies glistened in their family jewels, the men looked imposing in court dress and decorations. Scarlet-coated footmen served supper on the gold service, the gold tazzas on the tables were filled with fruit and flowers from the gardens at Frogmore. It was a joy to behold, but only limited fun. Formal square dances made up too much of the program to suit her. The crowd on the whole was slightly antique in spite of the inevitable leavening of ramrod-straight officers of the Life Guards and the Blues.

She much preferred to dance at Marlborough House, where there was room for five hundred guests at a time and the prince and princess mingled with all of them. Usually two orchestras played simultaneously there, one in the ballroom, where stately quadrilles had pride of place, and Hungarians in the conservatory for livelier waltzes, gallops, and old-fashioned polkas, danced in two enormous rooms on the garden front. The most fun of all, she thought, were the fancy-dress affairs which the prince sometimes held. She was disappointed that she had not made her mark in time to enjoy the most spectacular evening of all five years ago, when he wore a wig of fair cavalier curls to his shoulders to impersonate Vandyke and led a Vandyke quadrille with the wicked Duchess of Sutherland. A winter ball at Sandringham brought an invitation for Lillie. The code of discretion made it inadvisable for her to stay under the prince's roof while Alix was there. Some Norfolk neighbours, the accommodating Lady Romney and her husband, made room for her. Louis, one of her favourite partners on the dance floor, was at Sandringham, but the whole arrangement was somehow irritating. "While a very spacious house, Sandringham is not palatial," she said, though it seemed comfortable and livable. The big central hall had to be put to use as a ballroom.

In February, Louis was briefly missing from the circle. Trouble had already developed with Bulgaria's overlord, the czar, over Sandro's high-handed methods on the puppet throne. The young prince had been summoned to St. Petersburg, where Louis and their father went to confer with him as guests in the Winter Palace. A visit to Russia was a hazardous undertaking. Two months earlier, another attempt had been made on the life of Alexander II. This time two innovations of the age, electricity and dynamite, invented by Alfred Nobel, were put to work. On the railway tracks outside Moscow, an electrically fired land mine was exploded to destroy a royal train. By a fluke the czar was following in another.

The train carrying Louis ran late into St. Petersburg. The Czar ordered dinner to be delayed while Sandro went to the station to meet his brother and father. The dining room of the Winter Palace stood empty of guests when it rocked under the blast of one hundred and fifty pounds of dynamite hidden in the cellar two floors down beneath the guardroom floor. Ten Finnish Guards died; fifty-three others were wounded. That was the fifth bid to annihilate Alexander II. The sixth waited thirteen months away.

The omens Lillie saw in the spring promised to make 1880 a good year for her, possibly the best she had known to date. A general election in March wafted the Tories out and the Liberals back into power. The queen was so distraught at Disraeli's overthrow that she vowed she would rather abdicate than see Gladstone, *"that half-mad firebrand* who would soon ruin everything and be a Dictator," succeed her beloved Prime Minister. Along with the majority who had voted for Gladstone's party, Lillie expected her old mentor to be sent for by Victoria to form a new government. For weeks on end, the queen tried to stave off that evil day, and the country grew restless with the delay. The Lords Hartington and Granville, official leaders of the Liberals, since Gladstone was nominally in retirement, or anybody else would be preferable to the white-locked moralist who denounced imperialism.

With his mistress' total approval if he had discussed the business with her, Bertie felt compelled to intervene. The letter he wrote to Ponsonby, Her Majesty's private secretary, was intended for his mother: ". . . Mr. G. will, I am sure, do all he can to meet the Queen's wishes and be conciliatory in every possible way. . . . Far better that she should take the initiative than that it should be forced on her."

Victoria snapped that her heir "has *no* right to meddle and *never* has done so *before*," but at last, on April 23, she sent for Gladstone to appoint him her new Prime Minister. The strange, imprudent old man repaid what he could only have fancied was his indebtness to the prince's paramour. He wanted to help the prince in seeing that nobody in Society coldshouldered Lillie. He was eager to have her use his name as a social credential. He trusted her implicitly, so he confided to her the code known at only the top levels of government which enabled a few special people to send him letters enclosed in double envelopes. Gladstone's private secretaries gave him these unopened. The queen, meanwhile, continued to refuse Bertie any sight of her own secret documents.

Lillie's political coup was followed by a dazzling celebration. T. G. Freake was one of the new rich, a factory-owner who had made himself a millionaire. He and his wife decided to make a social splash at their house on Cromwell Road, South Kensington, by staging a party with *tableaux vivants* as the main attraction. They enlisted the help of the Royal Academy in preparing the settings and enrolled their neighbour John Millais, too. Lillie was essential to their plan; they wanted to be certain of the prince's attendance. She and Millais worked together in the magnificent new house he had moved into at Palace Gate, with its Italian marble staircase, a marble fountain playing on the first landing outside his studio, and views from its windows of the arching trees over

233

the avenues of the park. Lillie was a constant visitor there, greatly taken with the self-proclaimed Jerseyman who had earned himself a fortune.

The two of them decided that Lillie should be "Effie Dean" again. The scene as Millais had painted it was duplicated exactly at the Freakes'. The male model who had posed as the outlaw Geordie Robertson was conscripted to appear with her. She had only to pose, not to act, but the prince and the rest of the fashionables who flocked to the Freakes' agreed that the effect was, in the latest catch word, electrifying. Lillie's tranquil beauty had never been seen to better effect. Once again, the thought of the theatre crossed the mind of the undisputable supreme attraction of the *tableaux vivants*.

She had come perilously close to being a pauper. Apart from the inconsequential investments Edward had made, the sole source of income for the Langtrys was property owned in Ireland. That green, overcrowded island was in turmoil. The appalling weather of the previous summer had ruined the potato crop there, as it had blighted agriculture in England, where farmers' losses had to be counted by the millions of pounds. Famine had returned among the Irish on a scale approaching that of thirty-odd years ago, when thousands died and hundreds of thousands emigrated to the United States.

In the new world, the most embittered of them had started the secret society that the British called the Fenians. It was devoted to throwing off English rule and making their homeland an independent republic. Terror was the weapon. Two years ago the Earl of Leitrim, with his clerk and driver, had been shot dead without a chance to open fire with their own revolvers on the way home to Milford, County Donegal. The self-styled "Captain Moonlight" and his gang were setting fire to the houses and hayricks of the detested English landlords and maiming their cattle. The Langtrys' rents were a casualty of undeclared war.

Edward crossed the Irish Sea from Liverpool to investigate. It was easier to draw milk from stones than collect arrears from his desperate tenants. He came back empty-handed, but Lillie's debts still soared. She had no more sympathy for the Irish than for him. Her comments on the famine were as self-centred and callous as anything she ever said: "I suspected the good-natured, happy-go-lucky Irishman of refilling the pigsties and rebuilding the entire village. . . ."

That was one subject, at least, which could not be discussed with Gladstone. The last time he had been in power, his Land Act provided for loans of public money to Irish tenants to buy out their holdings and curbed a landlord's power to evict them at a moment's notice. He wanted Bertie to spend his winters in Dublin as deputy for the queen, to draw Ireland closer in sympathy to England and make a suitable job to end the prince's idleness. Neither the queen nor her son had warmed to the idea. Now the problem of Ireland rested squarely on Gladstone's shoulders again. It would take five more years and three more political murders to convert him to home rule.

The surface of the summer was as tranquil as a trout stream. The queen continued to snub Bertie by refusing to share any kind of official document with him. She harassed him over the upbringing of Eddy and Georgie, who, she insisted, must not be contaminated by the people with whom her son kept company. There was a veiled reference to his mistress in one of Bertie's replies: "We both hope and think that they are so simple and innocent, and that those they have come in contact with have such tact with them, that they are not likely to do them any harm."

Lillie made a particular point of being friendly to Eddy after his father received a depressing report from the tutor, the Reverend Mr. Dalton, enumerating the boy's weaknesses: "Listless and vacant . . . this weakness of brain, this feebleness and lack of power to grasp almost anything put before him . . . a fault of nature."

Bertie may have listened to her cool assessment of the accomodations at Sandringham; he was finally having a ballroom built there. She went to Cowes again, but without Edward this year. Her standard explanation was that he had gone fishing or hunting, and she hinted at his extravagances. Some people believed that he had abandoned her and gone to America. She inspected the new racing yacht, *Aline,* that the prince bought, a sign of his readiness to take serious interest in another sport. With the Cornwallis-Wests, who had rented a house for the season, she watched Eddy and Georgie pay a ceremonial visit to the troopship *Jumna,* bound from Portsmouth for South Africa to fight the Boers, who were again making trouble for English immigrants lured to the new republic of the Transvaal in search of diamonds. One old soldier sat on deck with tears on his cheeks.

Her creditors grew uglier as the season drew to its end. Dominique had to stave off the tradesmen who came to dun Lillie, alone on Norfolk Street. Lillie could not expect to live indefinitely off the prince's erratic favour. She was too keenly aware of his nature to delude herself that she would escape the fate of all the other women he had courted, then put aside, yet never entirely deserted. Nothing could be easier than to take on another lover, perhaps a richer man, who would keep her, like Skittles, in luxury and glow with pride that he had inherited her from the Prince of Wales. But that recourse held no appeal for her.

She could console herself over some circumstances. There was still the house in Bournemouth, with her mother close by. And she had not yet had to call on Samuel Lewis, Society's renowned moneylender, at his offices on Cork Street off Grosvenor Square, though some of her friends recommended him as an honourable shark, for all his staggering interests rates, who squeezed the poor but never pressed an upper-class borrower for money.

A bigger problem was added to her load of them before winter came. She was at the Sunday dinner table in Marlborough House with the prince and princess when sudden pain turned her pale. It frightened her because for years she had not suffered as much as a touch of indigestion, but she refused to make a nuisance of herself. The inevitable Charlotte whispered to Alexandra, "May Mrs. Langtry be excused?" The princess showed immediate concern. Lillie must hurry home to bed, she said.

Half an hour later, she sent the prince's physician, Dr. Francis Laking, a newcomer to the household staff, to examine her and report back on her condition. Towards the end of the next afternoon, Lillie felt well enough to lie on a sofa. When the doorbell rang and the butler announced, "Her Royal Highness the Princess Alexandra," Lillie rose to her feet to curtsey, but Alix would not allow that. While the woman with whom Bertie had consorted for the past three years lay comfortably under a shawl, Alexandra made tea for them both. Their conversation centred on her perfume. How she admired the beautiful fragrance of violets the princess wore, said Lillie. The princess trusted it was not too strong a scent in view of Mrs. Langtry's condition.

Compassionate as always, Alexandra knew from Laking by this time that Lillie was in the early months of pregnancy.

IV
Rewards of Virtue

❧ IX ❧

The secret was so closely held that Edward knew nothing of it. Somehow she cajoled him into travelling across the Atlantic on a will-o'-the-wisp venture so that there was no danger of his catching sight of his wife. "I was packed off to America on some business which kept me dodging about Chicago and New York," Edward recalled bitterly years afterwards when he learned at last of Lillie's child.

She saw no occasion to write to him, except for a few lines telling him that their marriage must be considered over. She was to see nothing of him until more than a year had gone by. The prince allowed a few days to pass before he called at the house on Norfolk Street. She found no reason to start complaining to Bertie now. There could be no talk of an abortion though the operation was commonplace, whether performed by a discreet *accoucheur* in Mayfair or by a midwife with a bottle of gin and a knitting needle in an East End hovel. Lillie would bear her child and take the consequences, even if she had not wanted to conceive.

It was unthinkable for a woman in her circumstances to be ignorant of the methods of minimising the risk. Birth control made an intriguing topic in enlightened company so long as it was referred to as "neo-Malthusianism." The name commemorated the English clergyman, Thomas Robert Malthus, who preached that war and poverty were inevitable unless the world's population was held down to a level where there was food enough for all. Malthus had been dead for close to half a century, but means were available now, on a strictly limited basis, for giving practical effect to his warnings not among the poor, where the need was greatest, but among the more prosperous with access to an obliging chemist's shop.

Sheaths, originally sewn from animal gut, had been on sale in London for a hundred years and more, though pleasure-seeking males accepted current medical opinion that recourse to them often made a man impotent and was sure to disgust a woman. Such devices were spurned at the apex of the social pyramid. In Paris and Berlin, where more open discussion of the subject was possible, physiologists had concluded that "it is only necessary for women to abstain from sexual intercourse during a certain part of the month . . . this would leave them about the half of each month for the free indulgence of their sexual appetites, without the danger of adding to an overcrowded population."

English medical men were more inclined to advocate douching immediately after coition or, better yet, the use of a vaginal sponge. Lillie's unending search for knowledge under any heading may have made her one of the eighty thousand who bought a copy of a little book by a Scots doctor, George Drysdale, with a title that would not bear repeating only because of its length: *The Elements of Social Science; or Physical, Sexual and Natural Religion. An Exposition of the True Cause and Only Cure of the Three Primary Evils: Poverty, Prostitution and Celibacy*. Buried in its tightly packed pages was an effective manual for contraception.

"By far the best of these mechanical means," wrote Dr. Drysdale, "I should take to be the sponge, and it might be used during that part of the month in which fecundation can take place."

Bertie was too self-centred for his responses to anyone else's problems to be anything but slow. Once he realized they existed, he could be moved to sympathetic action, as when bankruptcy threatened Christopher Sykes or Charlie Buller's check was returned. Lillie would not compromise her dignity by pouring out a sad tale about her financial crisis. Whatever might be said, physical relations with the prince were over for the present, but they parted good friends. He would keep in touch with her and help if he was asked to.

In her fifth month of pregnancy, the sheriff closed in on Number 17 Norfolk Street. The contents of the house were to be auctioned off to pay her bills. Dominique contrived to save a few trinkets and pieces of jewellery from under the eyes of the bailiff's men by slipping them unnoticed into the pockets and handbags of friends who came hurrying with condolences. Laced in an unaccustomed corset, Lillie guarded herself from unwanted questions.

On one of her last nights in the house, she had gone to one more ball, this in Grosvenor House, where the aging Duchess of Westminster held court. In the middle of the hilarity, Lillie experienced a moment of realization as bitter as on the day she heard that her first love was her half-brother. By sheer effort of will, she had achieved every goal she had set for herself so far. She had taken her looks to market and sold them at an unheard-of price. She had a place in Society unmatched by anyone before her. She was a national celebrity, envied by half the women of England and admired at a distance by more than that proportion of men.

In the process she had lost her husband and any future hope of being considered "respectable." She had debts without hope of paying them. Her child could never in all probability know the presence of its father. If this was success, she had enjoyed all she could take of it. She excused herself from the crowd and wandered alone through the echoing, empty halls, the music of the orchestra growing fainter as she peered into the portrait faces in massive frames that hung on the walls. These were the ancestors of the richest man in England. She found them and everything they represented remote from her life. She would have to remodel herself. "But it is not an easy matter," she thought, "to change suddenly from the butterfly to the busy bee."

She pushed her way past the footmen at the entrance

doors. Park Lane was dark in the rain, and the pavement splashed with mud. She lifted the skirt of her white satin dress and ignored the grime that spattered her white satin slippers as she walked home around the corner alone.

As she left her house for the last time, a carpet flapped from an upstairs window, the sheriff's notice that an auction was about to begin. The stuffed black bear had already been sold to a friend but the imitation antiques, the Oriental rugs, the greenery-yallery bric-a-brac—everything that remained was going under the hammer. She felt an odd lack of regret. There was no cause to steel herself against tears. Self-pity was foreign to her.

The stuffed peacock with outspread tail feathers, shot and presented to her by dapper, little Lord Brook, had been saved from the auctioneer by young Lady Lonsdale, who bought it in advance to save for Lillie as soon as she could set up another home. Lillie wondered whether she ought to use it again as a fireplace fan. She was as superstitious as a Jersey *décompteuse* dabbling in witchcraft. A dead peacock supposedly brought bad luck. Possibly some of her present problems could be blamed on Brookie's present.

Mary Cornwallis-West saw her off at Waterloo Station. Dominique and perhaps Mrs. Le Breton travelled with her to Southampton. Nobody unaware of the truth would notice any perceptible thickening of her figure. She left London as imperiously as Cleopatra on her way to greet Mark Antony. She was already turning over in her mind what future means might be found for supporting herself and her baby.

A cottage was rented for her somewhere outside St. Helier. No matter how hard she tried, it was impossible to hide herself on the island. Before long, well brought-up young ladies were told to turn their eyes away if they happened to pass by the little house, just as they were never to look at a kept woman on the street. The island seethed with rumours, endlessly embroidering the facts known only by Lillie and those few in whom she confided.

Her fame as a rare social phenomenon had spread across the Atlantic, but American newspapers were as ignorant of developments as their London counterparts. On November 6 *The New York Times* knew only that:

> Mr. and Mrs. Langtry have given up their London residence, and for the present Mrs. Langtry remains in Jersey. Is beauty deposed, or has beauty abdicated? The result on London society will be the same. Public pets may be objectionable, but few could so well have survived the ordeal of public admiration and reserved so much of the natural good-hearted woman as Mrs. Langtry.

Another Le Breton was stirring up mud on the island, and *pus nou-s'etiboque la saltai, pus ou pu.* If the dean's parishioners needed anything more to prod them into action, this was it. With no public fuss, he was dismissed, and any churchwarden who tried to defend him replaced. He would still be listed in *Crockford's* as Dean of Jersey until he died. But the parish was put in charge of another man, the vice-dean, Philip le Feuvre, of a more dependable island family. William Le Breton was forced to leave and resume at sixty-five a life that he had given up thirty years earlier, serving obscurely in a London church in the slums of Marylebone.

Lillie's child could not safely be born on Jersey. England was out of the question. Concealment of a birth there, no matter who the parents, was an offence against the law. When the time of confinement drew nearer, she crossed to France and on to a house in Paris. The French were more lax about the question of birth certificates. Arrangements had been made to receive her there, which Bertie could easily have set in motion. All his friends had houses available. Some of the closest had three or four, like Jeanne, Princesse de Sagan, with a mansion on the Rue St.

Dominique, estates at Cannes and Deauville, and the Château de Mello south of Paris.

Lillie sailed from Jersey in winter weather more bitter than in the year in which she was born. In London the temperature fell to a record-breaking ten degrees; it reached two below zero elsewhere on the mainland. Snow halted all traffic in the streets and blockaded the theatres. In the estuary of the Thames, the blizzard sank a hundred barges. Coming home from dinner with the prince, Gladstone slipped on the ice of Downing Street and cut his head to the bone as he fell back against the curb.

Soon after she reached France, Bertie also made his way to the continent. Marlborough House glowed again with a thousand lights as the carriages rolled up under the porte-cochere, bringing the regulars to dine and dance to the music of two orchestras. The aristocrats, the millionaires, the equerries, the officers —the familiar faces were there to bid him *au revoir*. He was off to Berlin, without Alexandra, for the marriage of his nephew, arrogant Crown Prince William, to Princess Augusta Victoria, a daughter of Duke Frederick of Schleswig-Holstein-Sonderborg-Augustenborg.

The queen was delighted with the match. She had given the hand of her own daughter Helena to Duke Frederick's younger brother, Christian. It grieved her that ties were not warmer between England and Germany. She could not understand the hostility of Alexandra, who refused to forget what the Germans had done to Denmark in their invasion of 1863. This wedding was precisely what was needed in the queen's judgement to bring the two countries, and the families that ruled them, into closer harmony.

Berliners turned out in the tens of thousands to welcome Bertie. At a family dinner given by his sister Helena, he counted no fewer than fifty-four blood relatives among the wedding guests. After seeing his Willie married, the prince left for Darmstadt, which Louis Battenberg still regarded as his family home. What Bertie said or did there only he and his immediate party knew, but he made a detour to Paris on his journey back to London.

In Paris, by prearrangement, Bertie met Affie, Louis' former commander in his spell aboard *Agincourt*. Bertie's program made it feasible for him to be within reach of that city on March 8, 1881, when Lillie gave birth to a daughter. She named her baby Jeanne-Marie, possibly for Jeanne de Sagan. The prince delighted in rewarding faithful subjects. Nothing gave him more innocent pleasure than handing out a medal or recommending an honour; and his presence itself came into that category. But no one in a position to know left any record of his seeing Lillie and her baby, who was sired by another man.

Jeanne-Marie's father was off at sea again. Before she suspected that she was pregnant, Louis Battenberg was posted to HMS *Inconstant*, an iron frigate under the command of Rear-Admiral the Earl of Clanwilliam. The date was August 24, 1880. Louis remained passionately in love with Lillie. They had been admirably discreet in their lovemaking. Louis' thoughts were still of marriage, but Edward refused to be disposed of, and Louis' parents, Prince Alexander and Julie, were appalled at the idea of another morganatic blight on the Battenbergs. Their financial resources were skimpy, but a courtier was sent to London to discuss the matter of providing for Louis' illegitimate daughter.

Any protests he made were ignored. As a navy officer, he must do as he was ordered. His romance with Lillie was unknown to the queen, but she wanted him out of the country anyway. She was gravely concerned about the calf eyes which she had noted her youngest daughter, Beatrice, casting in Louis' direction. *Inconstant*—did Lillie find the name ironic? The frigate formed part of the so-called Flying Squadron with four other ships. One of those was *Bacchante*, in which two young midshipmen served, one relishing the life, the other uneasy in it—Prince George and Prince Eddy. The Flying Squadron would be gone for a year and would circle the globe before *Inconstant* returned to Spithead, off the Isle of Wight. Bertie heard from Affie the news that shook the civilized world. The sixth attempt to assassinate the czar had succeeded. He set off in a closed carriage, from the Winter Palace, which had been turned into a fortress rather than a home in the effort to preserve his life. The first bomb thrown halted the carriage on a St. Petersburg street. When the czar alighted, a young member of a group calling itself "The People's Will" lunged at him, a revolver in one hand, a dagger in the other. The assailant was grabbed by the Preobrazhensky Guard. At that moment, another bomb hurtled out of the crowd. The mangled, still breathing Alexander II was carried back into the palace, though his doctors held no hope for him.

Bertie had only a few days to spend in London before he left for the funeral in St. Petersburg. For once, he showed signs of being worn out by the emotional pressures of the past few days. At a requiem mass for Alexander held in the Russian Chapel on Welbeck Street, he stood with a burning candle in his hand and fell asleep on his feet, wax dripping onto the stone floor. He showed striking evidence, too, of his compassion for old friends in trouble. Among these, he counted the handsome young nobleman of mysterious origins. Count Mieclslas Jaraczewski, whom the prince met on the Riviera and brought to London. "Sherry and Whiskers," as Jaraczewski was nicknamed, had joined the magic circle of Sandringham and the Marlborough Club. When the charming scoundrel's luck ran out and he faced arrest as a confidence trickster, he paid a last call on Bertie, held a supper party at the Turf Club, and then, in his apartments on Bennett Street, dosed himself with prussic acid.

Before Bertie left for Russia, he went to Jaraczewski's funeral in Kensal Green cemetery. He laid two wreaths on the grave, one in his own name and one in Alexandra's.

The minute she heard of the assassination of Alexander II, Alix feared for the life of her sister Dagmar, "darling little Minnie," who was now the

Empress of Russia and an obvious next target for terror like her husband, who now ruled in his dead father's place as Alexander III. In spite of her fears, Alix left with the prince for the funeral. She must be at Minnie's side. Their journey began at Victoria Station. Two upsets disturbed her when their travels had scarcely started. A landslide on the tracks forced a change of route. And she was so reluctant to part with her pet dog Joss that she took him with her to the station. As she waved good-bye from her compartment windows, he slipped his leash and set off in pursuit of the rain as it gathered speed in the darkness. Suites in the Winter Palace waited for Bertie and Alix, though their host and hostess steered clear of the place for security's sake. The new czar and his empress stayed on in their old home, the Anitchoff Palace, encircled by a hastily dug ditch as a defence against the planting of mines. Alexander III was walled off from his subjects; Russia seethed. The only exercise he could take was to trudge around in the snow of a backyard garden. Shrouded in mourning, St. Petersburg was alive with tales of torpedoes hidden in the ice of the frozen River Neva and landmines buried under the Church of St. Peter and St. Paul. There, the decaying corpse of Alexander lay in an open coffin. Funeral custom must be observed and every relative was expected to place a final kiss on the shattered cheeks.

Bertie left for home as soon as he decently could, four days after the ceremony. Alix was determined to spend more precious time with Minnie in spite of Victoria's objections that that could conceivably cost the princess her life. The queen was concerned for her own safety. New precautions must be taken for her travels. Railway workers stood guard at half-mile intervals along the entire track when she travelled from Windsor to Osborne. A pilot engine ran ahead of the royal train as a defence against hidden dynamite.

The prince resumed the unperturbed rounds of his pleasure, a day's hunting with Carrington's bloodhounds, a box at the theatre, calling at Curzon Street to ask after the health of Disraeli, who lay on his death-bed. In France, Lillie had little time for doting on her daughter. The task of making money for herself must take precedence over that. She had to go back to the city where people of influence might help her as soon as she possibly could.

A whisper of what had happened to her reached Adolphus Rosenberg. She had only just moved into modest, rented apartments on Ely Place when, in the May 14 issue of *Town Talk,* he rehashed the Langtry libel suit and printed, apparently coincidentally, an article entitled "The Queen's Old Stocking," concerning the drain on public funds caused by government support of the royal family in all its ramifications. Else-where, in a column of Society gossip, he wrote: "I am exceedingly gratified to hear that the Hon. Miss Tabitha Grimalkin (real name suppressed for obvious reasons) has returned to town quite restored to health. The darling baby girl is also well." "Grimalkin" was a pet name for a cat or for a malicious old woman. Rosenberg liked to play with words. He was some-thing of a scholar, too, who hoped, perhaps, that Lil-lie's curiosity would drive her to a dictionary, find that "Grimalkin" derived from the French *grimaud:* "dunce."

She still had the Red House, as it was known to the townspeople of Bournemouth. The property records registered a minor change in the list of leaseholders. Now "Mrs. Langton and family" were the occupants. The urge to leave a benchmark on the places she lived in asserted itself again when Jeanne-Marie was taken into her grandmother's care in the house which the prince had provided for a different purpose less than four years previously. In the masonry above a window of the south wall facing the sea there soon appeared the birth date, 1881.

Rosenberg tantalised his readers the following week with one more veiled reference to what he believed to be the truth about Lillie: "I really don't know why we should blackguard the memory of Harry the Eighth. True, he had a great weakness for the fair sex, but, unless history lies, he *married* all the women he fancied, which is not a bad trait in a prince."

A piece of routine advice given to a newcomer to Society was "Never comment on children looking like their parents." Embarrassment was thus avoided in cases where the husband happened not to be the father. Bertie's reputation included the existence of bastard sons in France and England at most levels of Society. Jeanne de Sagan was one who had borne him a child, according to French belief. Her eldest son was so outraged by his mother's continuing affair with the prince that he once tossed all Bertie's clothes through a window of the Château de Mello into an outside fountain when he found them on a chair in the boudoir. Among the English in general, only the middle classes refused to countenance bastardy. Some social reformers, whose numbers multiplied, interpreted that as no more than a question of property rights. If a devoted employee or the struggling owner of a small business managed to put a few hundred pounds together, he wanted to be certain that his heirs, delivered of a wife whom he also legally owned, were his own beyond all doubt. The rich maintained a tradition for taking care of their bastards that dated back at least to the days of William the Conqueror, born out of wedlock himself. To the poor, illegitimate children were a phenomenon as tolerable and natural as a rainy day. Where poverty compelled a man and woman to share one cottage bedroom with their sons and daughters, incest often became inevitable, too.

Half the counties of England included among their population a youth whose prominent blue eyes and Hanoverian chin singled him out in the common fancy as one of the prince's offspring. Bertie's side of the family showed clearly in the faces of the children that Alexandra bore him. The legends credited him with illegitimate sons, but never with a daughter until now. Yet the few who knew about the baby felt sure that he was her father. In no surviving letter or recorded conversation did he bother to deny that Jeanne-Marie was his.

251

Subterranean belief in his virility flattered him, especially at a time when the queen was picking away at his pride by increasingly favouring his brother Leopold. Bertie blamed Leopold's influence for the near-crisis caused in the spring by their mother's unwillingness to ask Gladstone to form a government. Leopold was carrying out more and more public duties of the cornerstone-laying variety. Leopold was making public speeches. Early in the summer, Victoria rewarded her youngest son for his fidelity by naming him Duke of Albany.

The overriding reason for the prince's silence on the subject of Jeanne-Marie was his affection for her father. Scandal could blight the long-term career Louis wanted so passionately in the Royal Navy. He could not marry Lillie because Edward would not divorce her, for whatever reason—pride, principle, or the desire to punish her. In any event, it could not be taken for granted that either Lillie or Louis would choose to be man and wife even assuming that became possible. Louis had seen at close hand the consequences of his father's morganatic marriage to Julie, Countess of Hauke, and he may have set his sights higher than that, uneager to repeat a mistake. Lillie's scale of living could not be supported on a lieutenant's pay, which was Louis' principal source of income. As she grew older, she liked to pretend that money mattered little to her, but at this moment nothing was more important.

Louis continued to sail the seas. Its initial course took the Flying Squadron southward across the Atlantic. Uncle Bertie chuckled over the letters he was sent, telling how Louis had been ignobly lathered and ducked in obeisance to King Neptune when the ships crossed the line. Eddy, Georgie, and every man or boy aboard who was new to equatorial waters suffered the same rollicking fate.

Three days before Christmas, they anchored in the Plata River to spend the holiday at Montevideo. Then urgent orders from the Admiralty demanded a backtracking to Cape Town, to help put down the few hundred Boer farmers who were making trouble for British settlers in the area. By the time the squadron docked British troops had done the job for the time being.

Louis savoured every minute of his stay in a free-and-easy city whose streets blazed with winter sunlight and colour, from the costumes of the blacks to the hues of the inhabitants' skins—Zulus, Kaffirs, Malays, Hindus, bronzed Boers, and British. England and his days as the princely gadabout of Marlborough House belonged in a different universe.

The next set of orders to Rear Admiral Lord Clanwilliam, who was beset with heart trouble that confined him increasingly to his quarters, had the squadron set sail for Australia. The ships were soon pounding eastward along the fortieth parallel in the teeth of wild gales. *Inconstant* could easily outrun her companion vessels. She saw them fall out of sight over the horizon at her stern. Sails were shortened until three sets of masts appeared again—all but *Bacchante*'s, with Eddy and Georgie aboard.

A full day passed without sight of the missing ship. Forty-foot waves churned the ocean surface. Fear spread through the rest of the squadron that *Bacchante* had foundered, with the loss of all hands and the succession to the throne of England destroyed.

Telescopes failed to spot her making slow headway, her rudderpost broken by the mountainous seas. With her rudder disabled, she had veered uncontrollably, in imminent danger of swamping if she veered broadside on. Her captain, Lord Charles Scott, had saved her only by ordering his crew of two hundred men up into the forward rigging, to cling there and serve as a human headsail, holding her into the gale.

Her companion vessels could do no more than continue for Australia. Electric telegraphy depended on cables. Messages to and between ships at sea were impossible until Marconi's day, two decades later. Not until a blinker signal was received from a lighthouse did they learn that *Bacchante* had made port in Albany for repairs. Eddy and Georgie were taken off and transferred aboard *Inconstant,* under Louis' wing.

The death of another brother reinforced Lillie's superstitions about the malevolence of a dead peacock. Maurice Le Breton, working his way up in the Indian Civil Service, made the mistake of shooting one accidentally. Shortly afterwards, the men of a local village asked his marksmanship to be put to further use. Would he oblige them by killing a man-eating tiger that haunted the jungle outside their fence? Maurice was pleased to help. His first shot only wounded the animal. It sprang at him before he could fire another. He scrambled up the nearest tree but not in time to escape the tiger's claws raking his legs. He survived the attack, only to succumb to blood poisoning on June 2. That left two of her six brothers living. Lillie's own stuffed peacock had been given back to her by Lady Lonsdale to help furnish the Ely Place apartments. Sorrow over Maurice was matched by the thought that she must rid herself of her fireplace screen before it caused her any more harm. There was no time to mourn for him as she had for Reggie.

Her friends pressed on her a dozen different ideas for launching a career. Whistler thought enough of some caricatures she had drawn of him to urge her to study painting as a profession. She knew she lacked real talent. Frank Miles' recommendation was for her to capitalize on her sobriquet and take up market gardening. Oscar was against that. "It would compel the Lily to tramp the fields in muddy boots," he jeered.

The avenues open to a woman of business ambition were severely limited. A working-class girl could be a servant or a factory-hand. A middle-class girl was expected to stay at home until she married, unless harsh need compelled her to become a governess, give music lessons or perhaps take in embroidery. Higher than that on the pyramid, there was little a woman could turn to without loss of status. Run a dressmaking salon or a millinery shop? Lillie could raise no enthusiasm for either.

She was tempted to try selling her name for an advertisement and disregard the shock that would cause fair-weather friends. A lady did not lower herself to endorse a bar of soap or a bottle of patent medicine for a fee. Yet money was to be picked up for the asking, as Lillie's enquiries showed. The new era of publicity had begotten fresh tricks in the trade of advertising. Madame Tussaud was reputed to pay one hundred pounds a month to advertise her waxworks museum on the knifeboards dividing the upper-deck seats of the Atlas Company's London omnibuses. Messrs. Rowland & Son spent ten thousand a year extrolling the virtues of their Macassar oil in newspapers and on hoardings. A similar sum was budgeted for Dr. De Jongh's miracle-working cod-liver oil.

The pill-makers ranked as the biggest spenders of all. Mr. Holloway, who had made himself two million pounds in the business, paid out thirty thousand a year to promote his products. He was put in the shade by Mr. Humbold of New York City, "the largest advertiser in the world," according to reports she read, whose exhortations to try his line of pills and potions cost him two thousand pounds a week.

But she was not ready yet to move in that direction. The dream of following Bernhardt, however far ahead she would always be, preoccupied Lillie at Ely Place. She spoke about it often enough for the rumour to start up that she was taking lessons in acting. There was not truth to that. When she mentioned the subject to Ellen Terry, all she received was discouragement: Acting would be too rough a life for a woman as spoiled as Mrs. Langtry. But the rumour was enough to bring a caller to her door one early summer afternoon.

Henrietta Hodson was a dominating personality with cropped grey curls, a pugnacious jaw, and a no-nonsense look in her commanding brown eyes. She had been an actress of sorts until she had an affair with Henry Labouchère, who was persuaded to marry her. "Labby" made a good match. The year after their wedding, he inherited 250,000 pounds from his grandfather. He proceeded to become part proprietor of *The Daily News,* then founded an opinionated weekly magazine which he called *Truth.*

Labby had been caught in Paris when the Germans besieged the city. His despatches from there made his reputation as a journalist, but Liberal Party politics, verging ever closer to Radicalism, were his principal occupation now. The paragraphs he wrote for his magazine were as pointed as his speeches advocating, among other things, the abolishment of the House of Lords. He was witty, indolent, and Lillie found him to be almost as formidable a figure as Henrietta when she met him two days later.

Henrietta took charge of the situation from the minute she strode into Lillie's tiny drawing room. She had heard, she said, of Lillie's interest in the theatre. She had come to enroll her in some amateur theatricals which Henrietta was organising in the cause of a local charity at Twickenham, a green suburb of London where Henry had bought a house.

Lillie believed what she heard with no suspicion that dumply little Mrs. Labouchère had any other motive but helping her. That was ingenuous. Henrietta's heart was set on having Labby appointed Her Majesty's Minister to the United States in Washington, D.C. She intended to hound Gladstone about it, and, with the rest of London, she knew of his friendship for Lillie, irrespective of her relationship with the prince. Any influence Lillie might bring to bear could be useful. She was exactly the right sprat to catch a mackerel for the Labouchères.

A curious lack of will showed in Lillie from the beginning of knowing Henrietta. It seemed as though the struggle of remodelling her mode of living, with Jeanne-Marie hidden in the background, momentarily weakened her steely resolution. Possibly Henrietta, childless and in her forties, represented a parent— mother or father. The scandal-mongers, who let nothing Lillie did escape them, murmured about lesbianism, but that was the wildest kind of conjecture.

She paid her first visit to Twickenham as a guest

of the Labouchères in the grotesquely turreted villa on a bank of the Thames that Alexander Pope had once owned. She stayed there for some days while Henrietta walked her to and fro across the lawn, rehearsing her lines as Lady Clara, the part she was to play in *A Fair Encounter,* a twenty-minute sketch in which her instructress would be the only other performer. Labby grumbled that a flock of sheep would do less damage to his dried-up grass that sweltering July, when the temperature reached an unprecedented 98 degrees in the shade.

He was a baffling paradox, who went out of his way, as Lillie thought, to belittle her efforts. "Why did you do that?" he would growl as she tried out some new inflexion or a different gesture. She had no ready answers. He was equally disparaging when Henrietta brought up Lillie's financial problems.

"She can't act," he said flatly as though she were miles away. "She can't write, she can't do housework, she can't even cook. What can she do?" Lillie did not take kindly to Mr. Labouchère. She disapproved of his habit of sending out the footman to the nearest ham-and-beef shop for sandwiches for luncheon. She found his political opinions "preposterous." It was hard to believe that she would put in a kind word for Labby with anyone.

She was trembling uncontrollably as the curtain went up in Twickenham Town Hall for the Saturday evening performance, to reveal Lady Clara smiling fixedly at a bouquet of roses, her mind a blank. Henrietta waited behind a closed door for her entrance cue. Seconds passed in silence, and Lillie's smile began to tire. Over the improvised gas footlights, Henrietta's fierce whispers could be heard, prompting her protégée. Gradually, Lillie took hold of herself, and her debut was over before she felt panic again. Tempting fate once was enough. "I swear that I shall never do it again," she said, but Henrietta was not prepared to indulge such whims. Lillie, she vowed, was destined to be an actress. She set about finding something more ambitious for her next appearance.

Bertie intervened to help as soon as he appreciated the merits of the idea. The theatre and all it entailed increased its fascination for him that season. He tried to see a play or an opera on an average of at least once a week.

Bernhardt was back in London to star in *La Dame aux Camélias,* and he asked Ferdie de Rothschild to give a supper party for her, which turned into a dismal disaster. None of the ladies could bring themselves to speak a word to Sarah, but she cared nothing about their snubs. She was bursting to talk about her victories in New York—the street outside Booth's Theatre aglow with electric light for her opening, the ecstatic crowd that serenaded her at midnight in the Albemarle Hotel on Madison Square.

When the season ended, Bertie even succeeded in breaking down his mother's resistance to seeing actors and actresses indulge themselves in frivolity. The queen saw a play for the first time in twenty years when he imported a touring company to Abergeldie Castle to perform "The Colonel," a comedy, loosely based on George du Maurier's blistering skits and sketches in *Punch,* which made greenery-yallery aesthetes the butt of its jokes. Victoria responded in kind by holding a birthday ball for Bertie at Balmoral.

Lillie stayed with the Labouchères when rehearsals for her next appearance began during the St. Martin's summer that warmed southern England, bringing a second crop of strawberries to the fields in the middle of November. She was being coached for the part of flighty Kate Hardcastle in Oliver Goldsmith's *She Stoops to Conquer* in a charity matinee to raise money for the Royal General Theatrical Fund. She would be the only unpaid amateur in the cast, supported by some of the most illustrious actors of the day—Arthur Pinero, Kyrle Bellew, Lionel Brough, and others—who volunteered their aid. Provided that she could only stand on her feet and speak her lines, she would outshine everyone else as the attraction that guaranteed the crowds. Curiosity-seekers, distant admirers, friends and denigrators, would all be sure to attend to see her succeed—or falter. Squire Bancroft was happy to lend his Haymarket Theatre for the purpose.

She was perfectly willing to be used for the publicity which was inevitable. She was inured to public hunger for a glimpse of her or for news about her, fabricated or not. Only the reality of the work involved depressed her. Bernhardt made it appear so easy, but Ellen Terry had been right: It was a rough life. Endless rehearsals for ten hours a day on a darkened stage made for a dull, monotonous existence. They were the hardest days of labour Lillie had ever spent. Henrietta grew hypercritical. There was no pleasing her.

Lillie was obsessed by the realization that being an actress was déclassé. Actors stood in the same pariah category as tradesmen. They could never be admitted to court. The preposterous men and promiscuous women, their faces pitted from painting them for a living, were regarded by Society as clowns and maskers, no more important than jesters had been to earlier kings and queens. They could strut and weep behind the footlights, but they were outcasts from the drawing rooms that Lillie had made her own stage. Whoever had heard of the queen bestowing a knighthood on an *actor?*

The man Brodribb, who called himself Henry Irving, was bringing a touch of unknown respectability, however, to what the mountebanks who worked in it called "the profession," as though it compared with the church, medicine, or the law. His production of Tennyson's *The Cup* at the Lyceum that year was a distinct step forward towards scholarly respectability. The reviewers applauded its "poetic achievement" and "scenic splendour." They were not sure whether he had been wise afterwards to alternate with the American visitor, Edwin Booth, in playing Iago in *Othello,* with Ellen Terry their irresistible Desdemona.

Working on the stage incurred a graver hazard than loss of social rank. Fire destroyed any number of theatres every year when gas was the sole means of lighting them. A stagehand touching a taper to the footlights signalled the start of a performance. Backstage, open jets flamed dangerously close to painted canvas scenery and transparent cotton scrims. Yet actors resented the introduction of electricity. The golden glow of gaslight, finely adjustable for sunsets or the glare of high noon, was much more flattering. But in the past few months, the Duke's Theatre in Holborn, the Park in Camden Town, and others in Manchester and Dublin had gone up in flames. A similar disaster in Vienna saw five hundred of the audience killed in a panic to reach the unlighted exits.

Perhaps the greatest cause of Lillie's present misery was the continual absence of Louis. The cruise of the Flying Squadron should have been over by now. He and his two young relatives had been royally entertained in Australia, with an outing with staghounds for Louis. He had seen the Fiji Islands, mountain streams, coconut palms and cannibals, still in process of being converted by missionaries from sacrificing parents and children to provide a feast of "long pig." From Yokohama, he had taken the train with Eddy and Georgie to Tokyo, where the mikado received them in a gold-embroidered tent and dined them in one of his palaces. Louis rode in the Imperial Gardens, where foreigners were seldom allowed to tread. But the cruise was far from over. Ahead lay Kobe on the coast of Honshu; St. Helena, where Napoleon had been exiled; and the Cape Verde Islands. On his left arm, Louis carried a tattooed dragon as a souvenir of Japan. He would not be home for another year.

Henrietta's possessiveness of Lillie sat poorly with one of her most persistent public admirers, Oscar Wilde. Oscar was pilloried every night in Gilbert and Sullivan's comic opera *Patience,* as popular as ever in spite of its move to a new home in D'Oyly Carte's imposing Savoy Theatre. "Art for art's sake" was derided now as a creed, and talk was increasing about Wilde's unconcealed fondness for young men. He resented Henrietta's influences with Lillie, which challenged his own. After one quarrel with him, Lillie found means for revenge. In a hired four-wheeler, she carried her stuffed peacock to his house on Tite Street and left it there in his temporary absence as a gift, and a curse. She was appalled to learn that Frank Miles had carried it off to decorate his own rooms before Oscar returned. The corpse of a peacock spelled evil. She was not in the least surprised when Miles finally lost his mind and died in an asylum for the insane.

Rehearsing was a torment. Occasionally, she would be pulled up short by the thought of her sheer audacity and wonder just what opinion her fellow-actors, who suffered her mistakes so politely, had of her. The test she was facing was more important than almost anyone else realized. The prince, who relished the company of actors in general, turned his persuasions on Bancroft over the supper-table. The actor-manager was willing to take her on under contract as a member of his regular Haymarket Company, of which Mrs. Bancroft was the leading lady, provided Lillie acquitted herself satisfactorily as Kate Hardcastle.

The promised salary was high enough to overcome her protests that she had never really wanted to go on the stage. She was no vain extrovert, dependent on a crowd's applause. Rather, as Suffield had detected, she was a Madame Récamier, at her best when she could impress an intimate group or a solitary man with her charm and her courage. But money was the prime necessity for survival and self-respect. It would end the embarrassment of accepting the "loans" which came to her by way of Alleno. The prospect of a contract with Bancroft was interpreted as a personal compliment by Henrietta, who promptly took on the added task of taking over as Lillie's business manager.

Crowds waited outside the gallery doors on campstools, munching sandwiches, through the chilly night before the performance on a mid-December afternoon. Everyone in England who read a newspaper or heard his neighbours gossip knew that the prince would be there with Alexandra and other royalties. Every seat in the house had been sold days before, and speculators were busy offering tickets at inflated prices. One of these entrepreneurs, according to *Town Talk,* was Henry Labouchère.

Reporters agreed that the London theatre had never before seen such an illustrious audience at a single performance. Society turned out in force to see the celebrated Mrs. Langtry's brief career take a new turn or, as some of them hoped, collapse in ignominy. Edward was back in London, but he did not attend. He had been in touch with Lillie through her solicitor, George Lewis, who made his house, a few steps from her apartments on Ely Place, his office and served his clients tea and advice simultaneously in the parlour.

Lewis had a reputation for knowing so many of Society's secrets that he dared not keep a diary. His talent for smoothing down scandal by settling out of court had made him a fortune; it earned him a baronetcy from Bertie the year after he became King Edward VII. Lewis made a popular dinner-guest with his fund of legal stories, few of them flattering to his unnamed clients. None of them, he would say with a smile, had ever in the long run kept a penny from investments they made on the Stock Exchange. "The trouble with you people at the top of the tree," he would tell his hosts, "is that there is nothing left for you to climb. Worse still, you have nothing to do."

Since that was not remotely true of Lillie, Lewis sympathised with her problems. It was he who had been instrumental in keeping Edward out of the country with a series of letters and cablegrams concerning illusory business in the United States, calling for Edward's presence there for months on end. Now Lewis agreed over a cup of tea that Edward might see his wife, to hear her arguments in favour of divorce, but no word about Jeanne-Marie.

Possibly Louis still loved her and would marry her if she were free. There was no way of knowing, except for her to take the first step. In the course of an hour's meeting with Edward, he refused to talk about divorce. He was too outraged, too stubborn, to intent on returning the slights he had suffered. He would not bring suit against her. She had no grounds for suing him when she would have to prove adultery on his part to satisfy a judge. He tried for a conciliation between them, but she would not think of that. When the footlights were lit for *She Stoops to Conquer,* she could look forward only to being Mrs. Edward Langtry, mother of a concealed child whose father could not be identified, for the rest of her days.

With a cigar between his fingers, the prince helped the princess down from their carriage, then left it to her to smile and bow her head to acknowledge the cheering as they made their way between the massive columns of the portico that framed the entrance to the theatre. As they took their places in the royal box, he looked plump, in good health and high spirit. Alexandra appeared thoughtful to the point of sadness. The audience resumed its seats, and the curtain rose.

The lords and ladies in the stalls fidgeted and whispered to each other, turning their heads to watch the prince and princess until Lillie responded to her entrance cue. She was statuesquely calm, as though she had walked the stage a hundred times before, and taller than people seeing her for the first time had imagined. For public inspection at close hand, she had chosen yellow satin chintz trimmed with golden fringe. An emerald-and-diamond brooch held the ends of the fichu around her shoulders. Her shining hair was knotted loosely in the style all England knew from picture postcards.

Applause stopped the play. The unmistakable sound of hisses came from some of the better seats. She gave a low, practised bow and a tilt of her head toward the royal box. Her expression was close to melancholy. Lionel Brough, as Tony Lumpkin, spoke his next line and eased her on to the end of the scene. The audience cheered again at that until she took a curtain call. She received an ovation when the performance ended. The crowd in her dressing room parted to make room for the prince and princess. Bertie clasped her hands to congratulate her. She had not felt at all nervous, she said, because she had been too intent on pleasing Henrietta, standing in the wings.

Alexandra gave Lillie a delicate kiss on the cheek. More than six hundred pounds was counted in the box-office till as the audience filtered out into the late afternoon dusk.

The next morning's *Times* confessed surprise to her "potential as an actress." The *Daily Telegraph* forecast stardom for her. The *Illustrated London News* that week acknowledged that "she is a gentlewoman and brings to the stage the stately grace and dignity of the best Society," but witheld final judgement. She "will have to work very hard and make repeated trials of her gifts and capactiy before it can be definitely ascertained whether she has any of the making of a real actress in her." She agreed with every word of that, as she signed the contract with Bancroft.

Only Rosenberg feigned surprise at all the fuss. "I don't like to say nasty things of this lady," he wrote in *Town Talk,* "but I don't think that she is quite as good looking as she is represented to be. Unless your attention were specially directed to her, she would, popularly speaking, 'pass in a crowd.' As a matter of fact, Mrs. Langtry's beauty has been much exaggerated." He could not resist an extra dig. " 'The life of an actress, by her husband,' is the title of a forthcoming book. I think the work will be written in a very acrimonious and pungent style." Edward stayed on in the city, but there was no further word from him.

The prince sent a note to Georgie, back again aboard *Bacchante.* "Yesterday we went to a morning performance at Haymarket Theatre and saw Goldsmith's comedy, *She Stoops to Conquer,* in which Mrs. Langtry acted with a professional comedy. It was her debut, and a great success. As she is so very fond of acting, she has decided to go on the stage and will, after Christmas, join Mr. and Mrs. Bancroft's company at the Haymarket."

At twenty-eight Lillie could begin to appreciate the significance of the hateful wheel of fate as Burne-Jones had imagined it in painting her as Mistress Fortune. Its sudden turn had taken her from the top to a different point on the perimeter, less exalted but more secure if she could hold to this new position. Another candidate had replaced her as probably the most beautiful woman in London, with an undisguised taste for pairing off with other women's husbands.

Lillie had seen Frances Maynard grow into an auburn-haired nineteen-year-old with passion explicit in her eyes and promised in her body. The set of her jaw was as firm as Lillie's. At her stepfather's house on Grafton Street and at her Essex estate of Easton Lodge, Frances idolized Lillie whenever she came to visit. Disraeli in his day had dabbled in matchmaking and suggested to the queen that Frances, with her thirty thousand pounds a year, would make a suitable wife for Leopold. On both sides of her family, Frances was vintage aristocracy: her mother, Blanche, a descendant of Charles II and his mistress, Nell Gwynne; her dead father Charles, a drunken colonel of the Blues, Lord Maynard's eldest son. Some of the family threw pats of butter at her grandfather's portrait above the mantelpiece in the library at Easton Lodge after his thirty-one-page will was read, naming five-year-old Frances his heiress.

Victoria approved of Disraeli's matrimonial plan. Frances, at seventeen, was summoned with her parents to Windsor, Castle. Leopold, however, was reluctant to be drawn into marriage. Her call on the queen was wasted, and Leopold lost his chance the next day when Lord Brooke, the donor of Lillie's stuffed peacock and an equerry of Leopold, took Frances for a walk in the rain and proposed under an umbrella. To the outrage of Victoria, Frances accepted him immediately.

For the past eight months, she had been Lady Brooke. The prince and princess headed the guest list at the wedding in the Henry VII chapel of Westminster Abbey, and Bertie signed the register. Brookie's best man was Leopold. Twenty-four hours later the bride and groom were required to dine with the queen at Windsor so that she might see for herself the man who had usurped Leopold. Frances wore her wedding dress.

Brookie had two qualifications on which to pride himself. Besides being one of the best shots in England, which brought him invitations to all the great country houses, he could see without fail both sides of any question. Frances relied on his tolerance. "From the beginning of our life together," she admitted later, "my husband seemed to accept the inevitability of my having a train of admirers. I could not help it. There they were. It was all a great game."

In the first year of her marriage, Lonsdale—called only Lord X in her memoirs—professed that he adored her. Frances was willing to be won until she overheard him whisper to Lillie, no longer the prince's preserve, as he helped her into her cloak at a party's end. "My darling," murmured Lonsdale, urging her to a later meeting alone. "Naturally, I was furious," Frances acknowledged, instantly jealous of the older woman, "and never again looked at him."

With his first volume of poems published at last, Wilde set off from Liverpool on Christmas Eve, wearing a bottle-green overcoat and a sealskin cap, to make a round of platform appearances in the United States. Henrietta was relieved to see him go. Now she could have her pupil's undistracted attention for more hard work. The queen passed Christmas at Osborne, the prince and princess at Sandringham, where labourers on the estate were presented with joints of beef to make sure their family enjoyed a good dinner in the season of good will to men.

Thirty-six hours after her appearance in *She Stoops to Conquer,* Lillie started rehearsing as a paid professional for Squire Bancroft. His forthcoming production was a new comedy on the improbable theme of the Crimean War. In *Ours,* as it was titled, Mrs. Bancroft was to be the leading lady and Lillie "Blanche Haye," a barmaid. She kept to herself her opinion that the whole piece was "silly and old-fashioned." If this was what earning a living entailed, she would not complain.

Christmas Day was spent in Marylebone with her father—"the dirty Dean," as Jersey called him now. Her mother and possibly nine-months-old Jeanne-Marie were there, too. That was the only break in rehearsals. The prince made an inevitable topic of conversation among the Le Bretons. He and Alexandra had opened a new infirmary for the Marylebone poor, built from parish funds.

Edward began calling at Ely Place and backstage at the Haymarket. His money had run out, and his family was unwilling to help him any longer. In times like these, with business slack everywhere, it was impossible for an untrained wastrel to find any remotely respectable work to do at the age of thirty-four.

He hinted that he would create a scandal with his knowledge of how she had existed for the past four years and how he had perjured himself on the witness stand for her if she turned him away. She could see no choice but to give in. She had George Lewis attend to the details. Edward was to be paid a monthly allowance from her salary. In return, she must see no more of him. If he pestered her again, she would cut off his only source of income.

The prince was away on a shooting party at the Earl of Stamford's place in Leicester, Bradgate Park, when *Ours* opened on January 19. Bertie arrived at the theatre from Sandringham nine days later to bestow his approval on Lillie's latest efforts and returned twice after that with groups of his friends, doing all he could to encourage her and drum up a public following for the play.

She had never been in greater need of whatever kindness this complicated, contradictory man could extend to her. The press notices had been heartening: "A most charming performance. . . . She will ascend to the highest roles of the romantic drama. . . . In her every word, gesture and movement, I see intelligence, perseverance, and volition."

But she missed him and everything he represented in her butterfly days. She found nothing attractive in this remodelled life as a busy bee. She yearned for the excitement of salons and ballrooms, country-house parties and delightfully idle carriage rides. Having to dine alone at five o'clock in time for another performance was an awful comedown.

His concern for Lillie set a chill wind blowing around the head of another of her stalwart followers. Gladstone, a model of moral rectitude, interrupted her at dinner one evening when he arrived with an armful of books, intent on rescuing her from her loneliness. "I heard of your venture," he told her. "It may help if I should sometimes read you passages from the greatest of all playwrights." Under his arm, he carried the plays of Shakespeare. In a series of calls, he proceeded to read entire scenes aloud to her, explaining their significance as he went along.

With equal carelessness about his public and private reputation, the Prime Minister had resumed his hobby of taking night walks in London streets in the hope of salvaging prostitutes. Lillie had made use of the two-envelope arrangement to confide some of her problems to him, but her distinctive, swirling handwriting was too familiar to pass unnoticed by his secretaries.

Liberal Party leaders secretly agreed in February that Gladstone must be warned of the risk he was running. Rosebery, on his way to becoming Lord Privy Seal in the Cabinet four years later, lost the toss of a coin and was delegated to approach the Prime Minister. Rosebery was no admirer of Mrs. Langtry, though the prince thought well enough of him to serve as godfather to his new-born son.

Bertie turned his mind to finding some appropriate means of showing his support for her and the profession that had made room without jealousy for the apprentice who won most of an audience's applause. Towards the end of the month, he let it be known that he was opening the doors of the Marlborough House to actors for the first time in history. To Sunday dinner, he invited an all-male cast, including Bancroft and Irving, Charles Wyndham and William Kendal, with a leavening of his personal friends— Sporting Joe Aylesford, Londesborough, and Carrington among them—for a total of thirty-seven. One of the men at table was saturnine George Lewis.

The players were "sandwiched in between ordinary mortals with more or less success," Carrington reported, acidly afterwards. "I sat next to Kendal, a good-looking bounder, who distinguished himself later in the evening by singing a very vulgar song which was not favourably received in high quarters . . . it was a dullish evening."

Lillie took it on herself to repay the prince's gesture. A week later she gave a midnight supper-party for him and the Bancrofts, which set London wondering whether she had lost her hold on him after all. Bertie did not arrive alone, but brought his younger brother Arthur, the Duke of Connaught, colonel-in-chief of the Rifle Brigade.

When *Ours* faltered, Bancroft reverted to a revival of *She Stoops to Conquer,* Rosebery went to see for himself the woman about whom he had warned Gladstone. The Prime Minister had taken it with good grace. The secret letters would be sent no more. Rosebery found her "passable" as an actress in what he called an appropriately titled play.

There was no way of persuading Gladstone to cease seeing Lillie. He used an early occasion to offer her some advice arising from the incident: "In your professional career, you will receive attacks, personal and critical, just and unjust. Bear them, never reply and, above all, never rush into print to explain or defend yourself."

Londoners were eager to believe anything about her. They speculated that Gladstone became her lover at the unlikely age of seventy-three. When the canard was repeated in a book published a generation later, she ignored for once the old man's counsel, which she had used to govern her behaviour for nearly half a century. His son brought, and won, an action for libel, and Lillie supported him. "It is hard, now," she said, "to have the blame fastened on me for things I never did and to be the weapon of attack upon the memory of a man for whom I have always had the greatest respect." In earlier times, she reflected, the author would have been horsewhipped.

If she counted on seeing Louis again, she had little cause to be grateful to Gladstone that summer. The rising tide of trouble in Egypt drove him to act as chauvinistically as Disraeli had ever done and order British warships, including *Inconstant,* to Alexandria. The Radicals denounced him as a jingo, quoting a flag-waving ballad of the music halls that swept the country, "We don't want to fight, but by jingo, if we do. . . ."

Native army officers were in revolt against the corrupt rule of Khedive Ismail Pasha, whom the British and French governments held in their pockets. England and France had taken over control of his bankrupt treasury to protect the investment of those countries' bondholders in the twelve-year-old Suez Canal, built at a cost of some 40,000,000 pounds to give passage of their warships and merchantmen between the Mediterranean and the Red Sea. Paying interest to them was given precedence over providing salaries for Egyptian officers, who often went empty-handed. The rebels' solution was a military dictatorship that repudiated the canal loans.

The situation took on the colouration of a holy war when Muslim Arabs rioted in Alexandria and murdered fifty European Christians in the dusty streets under the guns of the combined British and French fleets anchored in the sweltering harbour. *Inconstant* was still on her way, but Charlie Beresford was already at the scene, in command of a gunboat, HMB *Condor.* He dashed off letters to Bertie, seeking his intervention to persuade the British government to strike back. The prince was all too happy to oblige. A military expedition into Egypt might provide the long-awaited chance for him to see active service as a soldier. The rebel leader, Colonel Arabi, ordered heavy guns mounted at the harbour to menace the anchored fleet, exclusively British now that the French had withdrawn from a direct confrontation out of fear of becoming involved in all-out war. On July 11 the naval guns opened fire. By nightfall Alexandria lay in ruins from nonstop bombardment. Charlie Beresford was an instantaneous British hero. *Inconstant* was still at sea.

Lillie had by now suffered enough of the Haymarket Company for all the courtesies shown to her. She felt confident that she had picked up experience to earn more money than by playing second fiddle to Mrs. Bancroft any longer. The Bancrofts released her from her contract. She was ready to assemble her own touring troupe of players as the star and ostensible producer, though Henrietta would, in fact, be the real power.

They would exploit Lillie's reputation by displaying her in the ten major provincial cities of the British Isles with a repertoire of four plays. *Ours* and *She Stoops to Conquer* were obvious choices; she knew the lines. One of the two additions showed Gladstone's influence. Shakespeare's *As You Like It* would give her the opportunity to play Rosalind in buskin tights to flatter her marvellous legs. The fourth play was evidence that she took her critics seriously. One of them had written: "She will discover ere long that her real *forte* is in the character of heroines of genteel comedy." Tom Taylor's *An Unequal Match* was precisely that.

They opened in Manchester, the hub of the most extensive district of mills and factories in the world. There were flowers in her dressing room from Bertie. She took twenty-three curtain calls, and the stage-door mob unhitched the horses from the waiting carriages to haul her back to her hotel. In Bradford her path crossed that of the prince, who had come up to open a new technical school. He stopped to congratulate her at the Victoria Hotel.

In Edinburgh she received a Saturday-night telegram from him, asking her to make an overnight dash to London to be present, as a minor English institution in her own right, at a dinner for Keshwayo, former King of Zululand; the British obstinately spelled his name "Cetewayo." His power and his army of forty

271

thousand celibate black warriors, carrying assegais and shields of animal hide, had been annihilated by British rifles and field artillery in the Battle of Ulundi two years ago. Zululand was dismembered and thrown into anarchy and Keshwayo taken captive. Yet the sheer fortitude and mystique of the exotic warrior-king fascinated Bertie when Keshwayo was brought to England to be presented to the queen in the style of a Roman triumph.

Lillie gave no thought to any alternative but to arrive in London in time. There was no Sunday-morning train from Edinburgh, so she engaged one especially for the purpose. The hundred pounds it cost was more than likely to be recouped by the furore it would create when the story appeared in the newspapers. Calculated publicity was a subject in which she was starting to excel now that she had taken her talents to market.

With no effort on his part, Keshwayo challenged her eminence as an idol of the fickle London public. She noticed that in shop windows his picture postcard portrait had replaced hers. She attended the dinner in his honour and missed only her Monday performance in Edinburgh. Full houses for the rest of the run and the torchlight procession that university students put on to see her off on the train to Glasgow more than made up for the loss in ticket sales.

Adolphus Rosenberg scribbled a paragraph for *Town Talk:* "How can Cetewayo be said to have seen all the phases of our beautiful civilization? . . . He was not allowed to see Mrs. Langtry act, he never ever saw *Mr.* Langtry—but then he saw the Queen, and that is more than has been vouchsafed to millions of Her Majesty's most loyal subjects."

That summer a British expeditionary force landed at Port Said under orders to seize Cairo and destroy Arabi's army. When *Inconstant* finally reached Alexandria, Louis went ashore with a company of blue-jackets. They were armed with six Gatling guns, named for their American inventor, which spat out bullets at the turn of a crank. Their mission was to guard the khedive before he was restored to nominal power, backed by a remade native army under British officers. Louis led the march over the rubble of the city. He bedded his men down that night in the khedive's harem, which, he wryly noted, was as deserted as the streets.

In August and into September Bertie made his usual hegira to take the cure; shed some of the weight that a season's banquets added to his frame; and improve his digestion, which suffered from his incurable habit of bolting his food. He would also try to cut down his smoking, which otherwise began with a slim cigar and a couple of cigarettes before breakfast, followed by a dozen full coronas and a package of cigarettes before the day was over.

The spa he chose this year was Homburg, whose fragrant pine baths he found invigorating, and Ritters Park Hotel. Tennis had just been added to baccarat as another diversion of the town. Besides taking to the courts, specially installed for him, to supplement fencing as a weight-reducer, the prince took to a young American debutante. Miss Chamberlain, described as "a beautiful, accomplished and high-minded lady, as good and chaste as she is beautiful," won a place with the duchesses, demimondaines, and shop assistant who captivated Bertie. Scorning her where he had always welcomed Lillie, Alexandra labelled her "Miss Chamberpots."

Suddenly it seemed that America and Americans were leaving their imprint all over Europe with their money and their daughters. The idea of exploring what the United States had to offer her took root in Lillie's brain. Henrietta undertook to explore the possibilities. A cablegram to a New York theatre owner and producer brought him hurrying over to judge the prospect for himself.

Lillie found Henry Abbey an unprepossessing, flabby impresario, not at all the manner of man to attract her. He discovered that as a businesswoman, at least, she was irresistible. He offered her what was a standard contract: half the price of every ticket sold in return for her own services and her company's.

That was not good enough. She had Henrietta return to the haggling for the terms that Lillie knew Bernhardt had been given in New York. They included all travel expenses across the Atlantic and back. Abbey was too flaccid to hold out for more than a day or two. "Mrs. Langtry," he observed, "is as tough a businesswoman as she is a lovely lady. She may smell of delicious perfume, but nothing creases her hide except dollar bills."

Rosenberg caught wind of the negotiations. "Mrs. Langtry's terms are identical with those of the harpies," he wrote, "sixty percent." He underestimated her abilities by five percent.

She let the house in Bournemouth to a Mr. and Mrs. Holdsworth. She took a cottage on Jersey, where her mother and Dominique could take care of the little, brown-haired girl who was being taught to call her "ma tante." Over Labby's objections, Henrietta dismissed the cook and most of the servants from the house in Twickenham and muffled the furniture in brown holland covers. When he continued to object, she cut the buttons off his shirts as a parting gesture.

The company tried out its repertoire for two weeks at the Imperial Theatre. Bertie gave a farewell supper for Lillie. But it was Labby who provided the most sentimental send-off with a verse in *Truth* to mark her leaving:

Sing of Mrs. Langtry, a lady full of grace,
Four-and-twenty sonnets written to her face;
Now that face is public, and we can also sing,
"Is she not a dainty dame, and worthy of a King?"

She sailed from Liverpool in the same Guion Line flagship, *Arizona,* that had carried Oscar to New York. The date was October 14. She referred to the day only obliquely years afterwards when she wrote: "My many friends and relations were within easy reach, and to leave them for unknown lands gave me a feeling of utter depression."

The campaign in Egypt was over. Arabi's untrained forces were erased in a single battle by British artillery and sweating troops in solar pith helmets. Bertie had lost another chance to be a soldier. The khedive was restored to power to obey orders from London and Paris, and London streets echoed with hurrahs for parades of returning cavalrymen, with drawn sabres glinting in the grey autumn light.

On October 16, *Inconstant*, with Louis aboard, docked at Spithead. He went up from Portsmouth to Marlborough House, where his bedroom lay ready for him. "Uncle Bertie and Aunt Alix weldomed me like a lost son," he said.

X

She had nine days at sea in which to learn as much as she could about the unknown, intimidating country which she hoped would make her rich. But there was no book, nor yet a shelf of books, that promised to treat America as anything except an enigma, incomprehensible to a stranger like herself. It existed as a fact of nature and history, too overwhelming in size and the implications of its peculiar form of government to be understood by its own people. There were fifty million of them now, twice as many as in the British Isles. Every twelve months, half million newcomers poured in from elsewhere in the Western world, but not from China any longer. Congress had put up the bars against more Chinese for a trial period of ten years, despite a Presidential veto of the exclusion bill.

She had seen something of the return flow of Americans into England. Hellfire preachers like Moody and

Sankey could always draw an English congregation. Haverly's banjo-strumming Mastadon Minstrels and groups like them set music-hall audiences humming coon songs. Buffalo Bill Cody and his troupe of crack-shot cowboys and war-whooping Indians set Englishmen dreaming of adventure in a mythical Wild West. General Tom Thumb so fascinated Bertie that he had him and his midget wife to Marlborough House for closer inspection by the royal family.

Lillie knew that America would be a violent land. Its President, James Garfield, the self-made son of a frontier farmer, had been shot down in a railway station in Washington, the capital, in the summer of the previous year. His assassin was no European-style Nihilist but a disappointed office-seeker, Charles Guiteau. The present leader of the country, if that was what he amounted to in the baffling structure of American government, was a dandified lawyer. Chester Arthur was busy making over the White House, with the help of a New York artist named Louis Tiffany, and putting on the airs of an English gentleman with a dark-green landau and monogrammed blankets for the horses that pulled it.

She was going to encounter patricians whose ancestors had sailed from Plymouth more than two centuries ago and immigrants fresh from the fetid holds of the ships that ferried them like cattle across the Atlantic for a few pounds a head, excluding any food for the voyage, which steerage passengers had to bring with them. She counted on meeting the parvenu tycoons, who were accumulating fresh millions with the ruinous financial panic of 1873 done with at last, and cigar-chomping politicians, whose shabby morality had not changed since Charles Dickens caricatured them in *Martin Chuzzlewit*. She might come across an old friend or two like Moreton Frewen, out somewhere in the wilderness presumably, struggling to restore his fortunes as a rancher now that the railroad companies and the hunters they employed were wiping out the last of the buffalo herds that had covered the Great Plains.

America was supposedly the land of opportunity. She trusted that it would prove so for her. Certainly, she was arriving under the right auspices with the right credentials and introductions. She found encouragement in the fact that this new country had a high regard for the English, who came streaming in, one hundred and fifty thousand of them a year. They set themselves apart from other new arrivals, such as the despised Irish, relegated to the bottom of the social pile to fight for existence on starvation wages in sunless slums as grim as anything they had left behind.

Some working-class Englishmen restrained their enthusiasm for America. The old-established trade unions, like the stonemasons and the lithograph printers who turned out her postcard portraits, encouraged their members to emigrate. Their reasons were selfish: not anticipation of seeing the migrants grow rich but to keep the supply of their skills down and wages accordingly up at home. Letters from the New World told a different story from the tales of easy money which steamship company agents spread to drum up sales of bargain-rate tickets.

An English commission printed and circulated some of the more discouraging examples: "Tell all my friends to content themselves in England, and not ruin themselves and their families by coming to America. Dear wife, ten shillings in England is as good as nine dollars here; besides there is a surplus of men, and they seldom work more than half time." "Dear wife . . . I am sorry to say that we are deceived, for the men were all on strike when we got to Pittsburgh . . . If we start to walk to New York we must die on the road, it is so cold." "Dear wife . . . As soon as I can get the money I shall come back to you for it is no good here at all . . . Tell the children I have not forgot them; I have them in my heart."

Lillie had little time for reading in her *Arizona* cabin. Those fellow-passengers who survived the seasickness of a rough crossing stared at she made her daily entrance in a succession of eye-catching costumes to dine at the captain's table. If she appeared on the pitching deck, or in any public room, she was encircled by admiring men trying to impress themselves on her. The Americans among them, of course, were more exuberant and rather coarser than the standards of London Society permitted, but she took that to be good training for what lay ahead. Henrietta lay queasily in her bunk much of the time, terrified of the rats that infested the ship, appalled when she woke to find one on her chest.

Lillie had met enough Americans in England to know what to expect from the new plutocracy that had arisen in the United States after the end of the Civil War. Leadership of New York Society was rapidly being taken over from the old Dutch families by former stable-boys and coal-heavers. Cornelius Vanderbilt, dead for five years, started as a deckhand on the New York harbour ferryboats, but he left more than a hundred million dollars. The millions spent by Mrs. William Astor to maintain her position as uncrowned queen originated with a wily fur-trapper, old John Jacob.

Money in such accumulations worked wonders when rich Americans were infiltrating London. Of all people, an American businessman, Pierre Lorillard, had won last year's Derby with his horse Iroquois over fourteen of the finest thoroughbreds that the stables of England and Ireland could produce. American visitors were changing the forms of social life, demanding unheard-of comforts in their favourite hotels, entertaining as they did on their home territory in public restaurants, where an English gentleman would rarely have deigned to dine before.

It seemed impossible to deny a rich American anything, even a titled nobleman as a husband for his daughter. A Frenchman, an Italian, a Spaniard, or a German would do, but there was nothing to compare with having an English milord for a son-in-law. The newspaperman-financier Leonard Jerome had paved the way by settling 50,000 pounds on his delectable daughter Jennie and her bridegroom, Lord Randolph, when they were married in the British Embassy in Paris eight years ago; the prince and Alexandra sent wedding presents.

Matchmaking mothers flocked around Viscount Mandeville, son and heir of the Duke of Manchester, when he arrived in New York intent on seeing the sights. Now he had Consuelo Iznaga as his wife. Her friend, Minnie Stevens, daughter of the owner of a chain of hotels in New York, Boston, and Philadelphia, followed her example. When Minnie went to London, she found a husband in Arthur Henry Fitzroy Paget, who had no title at the time, but that was quickly remedied by a knighthood. Lady Paget was one of the prince's favourite Americans and a good friend of Lillie's.

Bertie had his own stories to tell about the welcome America had given him as an eighteen-year-old bent on pleasure, who liked to dance to everything an orchestra played until the stars faded from the sky. With his entourage, he had travelled in the guise of a student, "Lord Renfrew," but no one treated him as anything but Victoria's heir.

After watching Blondin, the acrobat, cross Niagara Falls on a tightrope, pushing another man in a wheelbarrow, Bertie wound up a two-month tour of Canada and entered the United States, with Detroit his first stop. Thirty thousand people waited to greet him. With special trains supplied by President Buchanan, the prince was received with rapture in Chicago, St. Louis, Cincinnati, Pittsburgh, and Baltimore. In Washington, he stayed in the White House as the bachelor President's guest and met his niece, chestnut-haired Harriet Lane, whose fancy for low necklines and lace berthas set a new style for American society. "A particularly nice person, and very pretty," the prince commented in a dutiful letter to Mama.

He strolled the streets of Philadelphia and rated it the most attractive city in the country. At the opera that night, the audience rose unprompted to sing "God Save the Queen" for the benefit of the eager young prince. His reception in New York "has thrown all its predecessors into the shade," one of his party reported. He rode down Broadway in a brand-new barouche beside Mayor Fernando Wood through a sea of cheering spectators.

Three thousand tickets went out for the year's most grandiose evening, a ball in his honour at the New York Academy of Music, and five thousand people jammed the ballroom. The floor collapsed under their weight just before a fanfare of trumpets announced his arrival. He waited contentedly for two hours while carpenters repaired the damage. When dancing began soon after midnight, his only complaint was that he was monopolized by dowagers instead of given his pick of pretty girls.

"Lord Renfrew" had fond memories of his four weeks in America. They gave him confidence in his ability to mix with most kinds of people on terms beyond his parents' understanding. Even the queen, for once, was impressed by his performance. "He was immensely popular everywhere," she told Vicky, "and really deserves the highest praise, which should be given him all the more as he was never spared any reproof."

So while Lillie lay in her bunk or walked the ship's corridors, sometimes with seawater swirling at her feet, she mulled over what she had heard from Bertie about the country she was heading for. Perhaps her triumph would approach his. A quarter century afterwards, when she tried her hand at writing a novel about an airstocratic couple who decide to pose as a widow and bachelor when they take ship to America, she included a private joke for his benefit. She named her hero "Baron Renfrew."

Arizona crossed Sandy Hook bar to enter New York harbour at daybreak on Monday, October 23. Lillie had not finished dressing in her cabin when she heard a brass band blaring "God Save the Queen." Outside her porthole bobbed a tug that Henry Abbey had hired to meet the liner in quarantine, bringing an army of reporters. Lillie's homesickness vanished completely. Henrietta was in a sour mood over her protégée's neglect of the rehearsals which Mrs. La-bouchère had stalwartly tried to arrange during the crossing. She was further displeased at the sight of Oscar Wilde aboard the tug.

Living in furnished rooms in Greenwich Village and disappointed by the modest impact he had made on his lecture tour, Wilde had already capitalized on his friendship with Lillie. In an interview he gave the *New York World* twenty-four hours earlier, he drawled: "I would rather have discovered Mrs. Langtry than have discovered America. She is the most beautiful woman in the world."

She waited for them all in one of the ship's public rooms, wearing dark blue unadorned with jewellery. She had decided on a similar low-key approach to this new challenge, similar to the conquest of London in a simple black dress. Packed in her luggage, there were some two dozen more splendid gowns, made to her order by an Irish seamstress of Dover Street, Piccadilly. They ran to grey satin fringed with beads with matching hat and parasol to white cream velvets and ecru lace, but the pride of the collection were her velvet mantles, one black and lined with white fox, the other brown, with a lining of Russian sable.

Oscar pressed forward with an anticipated bouquet of white lilies. She had never faced a throng of utterly shameless newspapermen before, but she handled herself like a diplomat, "in full advance of her beauty," as one of them wrote, "and added fascination of a career already marked with adventure."

The inevitable beginning: What did she think of America? "I have spent nine days aboard an American ship, so I already know your kindness and your hospitality. I am enchanted." American women? "I have often been told that they are the most beautiful in all the world, and I am sure the reports are accurate." Had she seen the Prince of Wales lately? She ignored that and waited for the next question.

What she saw of the city as she went ashore delighted her. A forest of sailing-ships' masts broke the brick and brownstone skyline over the downtown piers.

The cobbled streets there rang with the clamour of wagon-wheels and the iron-shod hooves of drayhorses. The few straggly trees that endured the chimneys' smoke glowed red with fall colour, the first she had seen.

Abbey provided an ancient carriage to carry her from the pierhead, a doleful contrast with the style in which she rode with the prince. In brisk sunlight, they drove through streets of tenements where families of ten and more huddled in a solitary room, then through blocks lit by night by the Edison Electric Company's miraculous new dynamos.

Her host would be a rarity if he could refrain from boasting about the marvels of the tumultuous city. The population had soared comfortably past the million mark. Twenty thousand of them now had a telephone for a monthly fee of ten dollars a head. The elevated railroad on Second Avenue had been open for two years now. Brooklyn Bridge was almost completed. Bicycling was a rage, with a new rink available for devotees. Lawn tennis could be played indoors at the Armoury. She was interested in the arts, was she not, so she must be sure to see the Old English, Flemish, and French masterpieces in the Metropolitan Museum, opened two years ago in Central Park, three miles away.

She listened carefully as the landau rattled along to her hotel, a rough ride as she found it compared with what the streets of London provided. She had asked to stay at the same hotel as Bernhardt had chosen, the Albemarle, within sight of the Park Theatre, where Henrietta decided that the company would open in *An Unequal Match*. Abbey had plastered the city with posters announcing the Jersey Lily's appearances. Photographs of her dominated half the store windows in the city. A carriage drive with Henrietta to Central Park that afternoon stopped all traffic on Fifth Avenue. When she tried to go shopping at Lord and Taylor's, police had to extract her from a mob.

Fresh relays of reporters waited at the hotel. She thought it best to answer every question with praise

282

for America, even the condition of the paving on the avenues, but there she was corrected. "Abuse it, Mrs. Langtry," one of her interviewers prompted. "It will be popular."

Native opportunism showed itself instantaneously in a dozen different attempts to exploit her arrival. She was deluged with dresses, hats, gloves, pairs of shoes, all of them gifts if only she would consent to wear them. Two piano manufacturers offered to make similar bargains for her endorsement. She could dine without charge in virtually any restaurant she selected as a lure for other customers. Overnight, New Yorkers started whistling "The Jersey Lily Waltz," and Lillie —usually misspelled "Lily"—became a popular name for newborn baby girls.

She was guest of honour that first night at a party given by Pierre Lorillard at Delmonico's Restaurant, one of the handful of gilded eating places, forested with potted palms, where the American rich, as she heard, elected to entertain their peers in extravagant splendour, and occasionally on horseback, as an exercise in the privileges of unrestrained wealth. Henrietta was not invited or included in the invitations pressed on Lillie at the table. To keep a promise not to abandon Mrs. Labouchère as soon as they reached New York, Lillie declined them all. In nine more days, she was to make her debut at Abbey's Park Theatre. From the window of her hotel bedroom, a wooden sign on its roof spelling out her name reminded her constantly of that.

The glimpses she caught of local Society in between rehearsals with her company occasionally amused her but caused her no surprise. New York modelled itself on London, even down to the Coaching Club, which Leonard Jerome had organized. Under the prince's tutelage, she had seen what the American invasion was doing to London. Bertie was a catalyst of change, and she had been his willing partner. Until he began opening doors for a new generation of the rich, London Society was a closed ring of landowning aristocrats under the domination of the queen and

Albert. Politicians could make their way in, so long as Victoria approved of them. Artists, writers, musicians, lawyers, scholastics, and newspapermen were unheard of. As a class, the aristocracy did not care for brains. Books were best left alone, or perhaps somebody who had read a new one might be persuaded to talk about it on occasion.

Americans and Jews were excluded from the club until Bertie's influence made itself felt. They knew how to make money, which the aristocrats by and large only understood how to spend. But the prince appreciated all manner of people, money-grubbers, moneylenders, and spendthrifts alike. His experiences in the United States left that legacy of broad-mindedness. He had ingrained wisdom about what was needed for his country to prosper, which was totally lacking in his mother, locked up in lamentations for her dead husband. Society, she lectured him in her earliest days of widowhood, was "so lax and bad" that he and Alix must "deny themselves amusement in order to keep up that tone in Society which *used* to be the pride of England." Bertie, to his credit, had not listened to her. Lillie was simultaneously a symbol of his independence, his personal pleasures, and his desire to transform and strengthen the structure of the ruling class.

He could afford to be amused at the pretensions of America's new rich as they built imitation castles and French châteaux on the refined upper reaches of Fifth Avenue, cramming them with Gobelin tapestries, English butlers, Sèvres porcelain, Chippendale dining rooms, Italian marble and Georgian silver. He liked to tease Americans about families like the Vanderbilts and the Astors, who remained beyond the pale in English Society until they began marrying off their daughters into the aristocracy.

Lillie could not indulge in any such humour. She had to make a living and, equally important, find a new place for herself somewhere in the world. She warmed to this country from the first day, even if some ladies here, more puritanical in their intolerance than anyone in London, cold-shouldered her more scornfully than the queen.

A week after she arrived, Lorillard hurried up to her Albemarle suite one evening with the news that the Park Theatre was ablaze. That made a total of seventeen theatres destroyed in the United States so far that year. Fire had broken out in the carpenters' workshop backstage and raced through the auditorium. She watched from her window as smoke darkened the red sky over Madison Square.

Flames leapt around the sign MRS. LANGTRY. Superstition and willpower clashed. Her fate depended on her name escaping destruction. "If it stands, I shall succeed," she told herself. But her determination added a correction. "And if it burns, I shall succeed without it."

When the fire faded to embers, two men were dead, the building was a ruin, but the sign survived. There were tears in her eyes and her hands were clenched as she turned from the window. "Well, we'll try again some other way," she said. The company's scenery, properties, and costumes were all gone except for her dresses, which she had the foresight to keep safely in her hotel.

Every seat for her debut except those reserved for the drama critics had already been sold in an evening auction at the Turf Club Theatre the day after she landed. Some brought seven times the usual price, with one box fetching three hundred and twenty-five dollars. This was Abbey's idea. He took the loss of his theatre in stride, and rented another, larger house, while Henrietta bustled around to the costumiers to hire clothes for the company.

Vanderbilts, Lorillards, Belmonts, and Goulds jostled together in the crowd that filed into Wallack's Theatre, the men as splendidly starched, pressed, and pomaded as any London clubmen, the women ablaze in diamond tiaras, necklaces, and stomachers. Two wagonloads of flowers stood waiting by the stage door before the curtain rose. Two hundred and fifty reviewers and reporters filled rows of the stalls, with

Oscar in his glory as guest critic for the *World*.

A cablegram arrived from Bertie, wishing her success on her opening night. That was no surprise to her. She had written it out herself before she left London, leaving him to perform this act of friendship for the woman whose courage never ceased to attract him.

Lillie had reservations about *An Unequal Match,* written by Tom Taylor, an actor in the troupe, but Henrietta was not to be argued with, and it was too late to make a change. The role of Hester Grazebrook was ludicrous, and Lillie suspected rightly that the reviewers would judge it to be precisely that. After making her first entrance as a milkmaid with a bucket on her arm, Hester climbed the social ladder to become a woman of the world, and the audience roared its approval of her.

The morning newspaper reviews were best called "mixed." It scarcely mattered. Almost seven thousand dollars in receipts set a record for any theatrical performance in America, and long lines waited at the box office. Oscar outdid himself: "It is only in the best Greek gems, on the silver coins of Syracuse, or among the marble fringes of the Parthenon frieze that one can find the ideal representation of the marvelous beauty of that face which laughed through the leaves last night as Hester Grazebrook." The most scathing of the critics dismissed her as no more than "a clever, attractive amateur."

Henrietta could find no fault with Wilde's fulsome comments, but she objected to his trying to reestablish himself with Lillie. In revenge, he planted rumours that flourished like weeds around the town. Henrietta was an evil influence. Her relationship with Lillie was much too close. Henrietta was an obstacle that Lillie would be wise to clear from her path.

The triangle of jealousies was soon contorted by a fourth figure. In old age, when Lillie assessed the victories and defeats of her life, she concluded with evident satisfaction, "I have had all that I really wanted very much." At twenty-nine, what she wanted was an infatuated millionaire to provide for her. She found him in the semiliterate, twenty-two-year-old son of a Baltimore merchant who had inherited some $5,000,000 on his father's death. In the present gilded age of Wall Street prosperity, that would give Freddie Gebhard $250,000 a year at five percent.

She was indifferent to his dark good looks when they were introduced by Leonard Jerome, so Freddie set out to court her. After she had dined tête-à-tête with him on three or four occasions, he was sufficiently encouraged to buy her a diamond necklace and matching bracelet from one of the Fifth Avenue jewellers who enjoyed a booming business in supplying such souvenirs to millionaires for a wife or a mistress. He had tried similar tactics with Jennie Jerome's considerably plainer younger sister, Leonie, who would have nothing to do with him.

He had his tribute delivered to the Albemarle hidden in a bouquet of flowers. Lillie kept both kinds of present and allowed Freddie to become her escort at the expense of rehearsing Rosalind in the company's next production, *As You Like It*.

Henrietta responded with the fury of a woman spurned. Newspaper reviews of *As You Like It* gave her good reason. Lillie's titian hair under a becoming velvet cap and her celebrated figure in a matching laced jerkin were all the critics found to praise. As an actress, they considered her, as the *New York Times* remarked, "a pretty elocutionist."

Henrietta took the slating that Rosalind received as a reflection on her own prowess as drama coach. The newspapers, which wasted no time in making Gebhard's name notorious as Lillie's purported fancy man, were rewarded the next day with a formal announcement from Henrietta. She "disapproved of Mrs. Langtry's proceedings" and "had no further connection with her, personally, or with her theatrical engagements." Mrs. Labouchère was off to Washington, to sniff out the prospects of a new career in diplomacy for Labby and herself, before she sailed home alone.

She and Lillie parted after a monumental quarrel.

In London, Henrietta placed most of the blame on Oscar's shoulders. Lillie had been content to see her go, she said, without offering her a penny for her share in the company. Lillie told a different story. According to her version of the rift, she had wanted to buy out Henrietta, but Henrietta refused.

From the dust-sheet draped house in Twickenham, Labby had the final word in a letter to his wife's liberated protégée: "I marvel at your ability to remain on good terms with that termagant, who is not happy unless she is creating misery for someone else."

The theatre fire, her two openings, the sensation she was causing in New York—there was more than enough for Bertie to write about to her, and he was anxious to stay in touch. It was the likely beginning to the correspondence that the prince maintained over an indeterminate span of years, at least until the end of the century. She saved twenty-seven of his letters in the course of her life. If he kept any of her replies, they were fed into a furnace when he died. His will ordered that all his private and personal papers, including every letter received from Alix, must be destroyed. His wife, in turn, had a similar desire, which Charlotte Knollys faithfully executed.

Bertie could not resist writing notes to women he admired, no matter what trouble might be caused if they fell into the wrong hands, as in the bruising business with Harriet Mordaunt. On the surface, his words, painstakingly penned in longhand, were usually as bland as butter. If they held hidden meaning, it was discernible only to the woman involved. Typical lines to Harriet might have come from a benevolent uncle:

"Many thanks for your kind letter. I am so glad to hear that you have made a good recovery [from measles] and to be able soon to go to Hastings, which is sure to do you a great deal of good. I hope that perhaps on your return to London I may have the pleasure of seeing you."

He wrote to Lillie wherever he chanced to be— at the Marlborough Club, aboard *Osborne,* in any number of European hotels, like the Weimar at Marienbad, where he grew furious if champagne instead of weight-reducing hock was ordered at lunch, and the furniture in his specially decorated suite was sold at doubled prices after every departure. He would use whatever notepaper was at hand, dip a steel-nibbed pen in an inkwell—he detested fountain pens—and cover three or four pages in short order.

He would address her as "Ma Chère Amie," "The Fair Lily," or sometimes "My dear Mrs. Langtry." One Sunday from Sandringham he wrote:

"Many thanks for your kind letter and good wishes for my old birthday. Please thank Jeanne for her nice little letter and the kind thought which prompted her to write . . . Ever, Yours sincerely." He signed himself, as always, "A.E."

She was sent a pet dog through his good offices, and they exchanged notes about that. "Ma Chère Amie," he wrote from the Marlborough Club, "I am glad you like the dog and don't find him too big. Perhaps you would write Lady W. a line to W. Castle and tell her you like the dog and ask the name. Take care he don't get stolen. Hoping to see you the next time I am in town. Tout à vous. A.E."

On the death of Affie on July 30, 1900, Bertie wrote from Coburg a week later: "I have 2 letters to thank you for and especially for your kind sympathy at the sad loss I have sustained. It is a dreadful blow to me not to have seen my poor Brother again but I hear he was so changed and his sufferings so great that one could not have wished his life to have been prolonged. He always liked and admired you so much. I cannot write more and remain always Yrs most sincerely, A.E."

Now and then, when she was in London between the tours she made of America, he arranged meetings with her. "Shall be charmed to call on you at five tomorrow afternoon" . . . "Shall be back in town tomorrow night" . . . "Most anxious to speak to you about something." When they were apart, he turned to matters of domesticity: news of their old friends; concern for her health; apologies for failing to send her grouse from Sandringham, a delicacy she was fond of, but he doubted whether the birds would be palatable after the rigours of an Atlantic crossing.

When he had finished, he would address the envelope, lick the stamp, and, by all the evidence, make off to the nearest post box. Alexandra, it had to be concluded, knew little or nothing of the correspondence. The letters that Lillie saved, invariably, amiable and considerate of her, extended into 1899. Shortly after he died in 1910, his heir and successor, King George V, added a personal postscript. On a sheet of black-bordered paper, he wrote, in a still boyish hand, a note of thanks for Lillie's sympathy, fondly recalling the day his father had introduced him to her thirty years back on a carefree day at Cowes.

With Henrietta disposed of, Lillie took charge of her company with the assurance of a drill sergeant. Abbey, afraid that she was too new to the business, offered to supply a substitute producer, but she brushed him aside. One of the Americans she impressed most was a promising young theatrical manager who had been acting, writing, and adapting plays for six of his twenty years. David Belasco was captivated by her on sight. "She was the most exquisite thing I ever saw," he remembered. "She needed no cosmetics, and she never used any. It was her bearing that was her most distinctive quality. She moved like a queen. Her dress was simple but of the richest material, and she wore few jewels."

"Miss Lillie," as she chose to be called, was unapproachable by any common actor or actress in the company. She had learned from the prince the techniques for maintaining distance between herself and lesser beings. During working hours, she was a business woman, exacting obedience from those who served her. She refused to be hurried or flustered by any calamity, and she seldom spoke an unnecessary word.

"Let us not fuss, please," she would say softly, with the impact of a command.

Bertie's influence showed itself in a dozen different ways. She lived by the clock, counting minutes to keep appointments. Her attention to details—costumes, scenery, makeup, contracts—was as Napoleonic as his. She was as careful as he was to listen to other people's opinions when she asked for them and as quick to come to a decision, which would be final. A succession of managers had to be taught not to question her taste for extravagance in putting on a play.

"No doubt you are right," she would tell them, "but I want it, and it *is* my money, isn't it?"

Miss Lillie was more regal onstage than off, if that was possible. A colleague was moved close to ecstasy by one talent of hers: "I never saw an actress manage a train as she did. Once on the scene, and the train 'set,' she never touched it again. It seemed a part of her end and was manoeuvred as though it were a rudder obeying its helm. And a rare exhibition of grace it made."

She was news when, even in America, it was vulgar to make news. Columns about her appeared somewhere every day. Reporters were assigned to dog her footsteps. Restaurant waiters and hotel chambermaids were constantly quizzed to provide the wisps of information, true or invented, with which to concoct tomorrow's story.

At Christmastime, London Society was not surprised to discover that Mrs. Langtry had found another means of turning her renown to commercial advantage. A full page of *The Illustrated London News* was given to an advertisement of A. & F. Pears, 91 Great Russell Street, whose soap sold in tablets or balls for one shilling, larger sizes for one shilling and sixpence or half-a-crown. GOOD COMPLEXION & NICE HANDS, read the headline, over a large boxed TESTIMONIAL FROM MRS. LANGTRY, declaring over her signature: "I have much pleasure in stating that I have used your Soap for some time and *prefer it to any other*." It was taken as no coincidence that the manufacturers proclaimed themselves to be "soap makers by appointment to H.R.H. the Prince of Wales." She had agreed to sell her name—and flout every precept for how a lady should behave—before she left for New

York. She asked a whimsical price for her condescension: one hundred and thirty-two pounds, because it chanced to be her avoirdupois weight.

One week earlier, the same magazine carried tangible evidence that Louis, too, was looking to earn a few extra guineas. Its editors had devoted columns of space to the sketches he sent back from the *Serapis* cruise after he took over the job from a staff illustrator. With *Inconstant* home again, he contributed a skilful pen-and-ink drawing entitled "Tattooing at Nagasaki, Japan." While one kimono-clad maiden plucked a samisen, two others prepared the pigments for the bespectacled sage with the needles. No signature on the illustration, but in the bearded young Englishman stretched with his head on a cushion on the floor, puffing a herbal pipe, Louis drew a self-portrait.

So far as his future as a naval officer was concerned, he was becalmed in the doldrums, making no headway toward any point of the compass. In the middle of December, he chose to go into semiretirement on half-pay again, uneasy about continuing to be no more than a pet of Uncle Bertie's. He left London to spend Christmas at Darmstadt, still home to him, where snow covered the mountains and the forests of pine on their slopes and ice sparkled on the Rhine. if he wrote to Lillie or she to him, their exchanges were as closely guarded as the existence of Jeanne-Marie.

He had time and opportunity to visit Lillie if he cared to, but no hope of marrying her. Her letters from George Lewis only repeated that there was no way of talking Edward into divorce. In Darmstadt, Louis appeared to conclude that Lillie could never be his wife, if that had ever been his ambition. A girl far more suitable for his circumstances was closer at hand. Victoria, named for her grandmother, England's queen, was nineteen. Her mother, Alice, had been killed by diphtheria four years earlier. The girl was as taken with Louis as most women were. By the time March came and he took off for Sofia to see Sandro, the thought of marriage simmered in her mind and his.

Louis went on with his brother to Moscow for the belated coronation of Czar Alexander III. Sandro's problems with his Russian masters had not yet reached breaking point. That came two years later, when Bulgarian army officers, acting for the czar, kidnapped him from his palace one August night, forced him to sign a document of abdication on threat of death, and delivered him to Russian hands. At present, it amused Alexander to treat Sandro and Louis with the hospitality blood relatives deserved. Because an aunt of theirs had married his father, they were first cousins of the czar, who remarked in private that he was entertained to watch the autocratic Sandro's struggles against his unavoidable destiny. Meanwhile, the czar courteously put a cruiser of his fleet at the two brothers' disposal so that they might see something of Palestine and Greece together.

Perhaps a sense of his younger brother's impending fate prompted Louis into proposing to his cousin Victoria immediately after he returned to Darmstadt. A link by marriage to the mightiest of the royal families of Europe would ensure that Louis was saved from the pummeling that Sandro was undergoing. The girl was overjoyed at the prospect. Her Majesty approved, and in April the engagement was announced.

Lillie made her thoughts of that another of her secrets. Possibly she had reconciled herself long since to the impossibility of being married to the father of her child. She had no more to complain about than in the past, which was being so swiftly hidden under the gold leaf of a new career. She had only one known souvenir, a photograph small enough to be easily concealed, too small to do justice to his softly bearded face and gentle eyes. He had signed it to her, "Louis Battenberg." It was another possession she saved throughout her life.

She and her troupe had just completed a two-month tour of the United States east of the Rocky Mountains, which carried them for six thousand miles in the Pullmans, day coaches, and sleeping cars of half a dozen different railroads to Boston, Philadelphia,

Chicago, St. Louis, Memphis, New Orleans, Milwaukee, Cincinnati, Buffalo, and back to New York. Watching the landscape slide past the windows planted the seed of a new desire in her. Rich Americans owned their own private railroad cars—bijou mansions equipped in sybaritic splendour with boudoirs, salons, kitchens, and bathtubs, sometimes with gold-plated fittings. One day she would lay her hands on one of these fascinating gewgaws that made travel so much more pleasant.

Reporters caught her in her suite in the Grand Pacific Hotel, Chicago, to press the inevitable question: How did she like America after four months of living there?

"It improves upon acquaintance," she answered grandly.

"Do you like the people?"

"They have been pretty kind to me."

Was there any prospect of her husband joining her?

There was no hesitation in her reply. "I am sorry to say no. Poor man, he can't spare the time to come over just now. He is in trouble and has to stay in England."

There had been fear that the timetable would be disrupted when the Ohio and Mississippi rivers rose in flood in February, swamping bankside cities, but the gravest alarm was caused by Freddie's presence. Over Abbey's scandalised protests, she had Gebhard travel with her as what she called her bodyguard. It was a coolly calculated decision in which sentimentality played no part. Knowledge of the new turn in Louis' affairs could have prompted her defiance of the rigid morality which she had been told prevailed in the Midwest. The prince had flaunted her in public; she would do the same with Gebhard. If personal circumstances compelled her to be a wanton, she would exploit the fact. Scandal sold theatre tickets, which meant money in her pocket.

The drama critics were uniformly scathing all along the route, but thousands swarmed to see her. When reporters tried to interview Freddie, he threatened to knock them down. She had second thoughts about the sense of exposing herself to verbal attack by hostile Puritans. At an early point in her itinerary, she paid the expenses of having her ingenuous sister-in-law, Agnes Langtry, cross the Atlantic to join her as a temporary chaperone. Miss Langtry's sensibilities would not permit her to stay the course. A liaison with the Prince of Wales could be condoned on patriotic grounds. Finding Lillie in a negligee and Freddie in pyjamas sharing a bottle of champagne in their hotel suite late one night convinced Agnes that she must pack immediately and make her departure before breakfast was served in the morning.

Newspaper stories heralding the events of the tour were more sensational than Lillie had bargained for. In the House of Representatives, one Congressman denounced her for degrading American morals and demanded that she be put aboard a ship for England. A newspaper editor in St. Louis went further than that and challenged Freddie to a duel.

A. B. Cunningham of the *Globe-Democrat* bore the rank of colonel from his Confederate Army days. He arrived unexpectedly at breakfast-time to interview Lillie at the Southern Hotel on the morning of her opening at the Olympic Theatre. He pushed his way in and found her with a robe over her nightgown entertaining a fully dressed Freddie. Neither of them would say a word to him, except demand that he take his leave.

His account of the incident in later editions of his newspaper was a broadside of abuse, blasting Lillie and Freddie as partners in sin and calling for a public boycott of her performances. After she set out for the theatre that evening, Freddie, swinging a cane, came across Cunningham in the hotel lobby, also carrying a stick in the fashion of the times. Spectators fancied that in his trousers, the burly editor carried a pocket pistol, too—another foible which was commonplace in the Midwest.

St. Louis had lively traditions as a center for men

of action dating back to its days as a trading post. John Jacob Astor's American Fur Company did a roaring business there then, and Mississippi River flatboats carried in immigrants to begin settling the West. The Civil War abolished the trade in slaves, who were sold in what was now the courthouse, embellished with statuary representing Law, Commerce, Justice, and Liberty. Liberty was interpreted locally as including the right to duel. No leader of Prince Albert's calming influence had arrived on the scene to put a stop to that.

"I don't want anything to do with you, sir," said Cunningham, with his hand in a trouser pocket.

"But I want something to do with you, sir," Freddie shouted. "You are an infamous liar."

Freddie kept up his tirade until the hotel clerk summoned a policeman to escort Cunningham off the premises. The following morning he sent a friend to call out Freddie to face Cunningham over pistols. Headlines on both sides of the Atlantic spotlighted the story. The Olympic was sold out for Lillie's two-week engagement. She had cause for concern, nonetheless. The death by bullet wound of either man might well ruin her. She prevailed on Freddie not to answer the challenge. "I refused to pay any attention . . . as I had already denounced him," he explained to reporters. For that, he was dismissed as a coward by a cross-section of the fire-eating male population interviewed on behalf of newspapers that could not bear to see a good story die.

She returned to New York in March, richer by more than $100,000. That came close to matching Charles Dickens' best earnings on the American lecture circuit, but of course a dollar did not buy what it had in his day. Abbey had a new venture to offer under his contract with her. Henry Irving and his beloved Ellen Terry were booked to leave the Lyceum in the coming summer to embark on an American tour of their own. Lillie would make an ideal replacement for them in London.

She deliberated over the possibilities. It could give

her the eminence she demanded in the London theatre, but perhaps at the cost of being shut out from the houses of Society like the Randolph Churchills when the uproar surrounding her United States travels was too fresh to be forgotten. This time, with the best will in the world, Bertie might not be able to protect her. She had no desire to risk humiliation. She could not hope to make the same amounts of money she had been earning here. That was the crucial factor. She negotiated to be released from her contract with Abbey. The Lyceum could manage without her.

Instead, she rehearsed her company in a production of a new play, *Pygmalion and Galatea*. First-night reviewers at the Fifth Avenue Theatre found her performance even more appalling than before. Besides, New Yorkers had a new wonder of the world to excite them. One hundred thousand of them set out to walk across the mile-long Brooklyn Bridge within twelve hours after President Arthur declared it open. *Pygmalion and Galatea*, by William Schwenck Gilbert, closed after six weeks.

If she was to make the United States her new home, she needed some time to herself on the other side of the Atlantic first. There were a number of things to attend to. She realized her failings as an actress and decided to take private lessons from the ancient comedy actor, François Régnier, who in earlier days had trained Réjane. She wanted to see the child whom she talked of as her niece. Freddie was urging Lillie to be his legal wife, so she had to discuss with George Lewis, whether some new approach could be devised to convince Edward that their marriage must be ended. Something should be done, too, about the house in Bournemouth when the present tenants' lease expired.

Possibly, she would find an opportunity to meet the prince, who had prudently put off his usual spring visit to France. French resentment ran high over what the British had done single-handedly in Egypt, and there was no knowing the kind of welcome that would await Bertie in Paris. A few minutes spent with Louis would not be totally impossible. The queen was showing her grace and favour to him by appointing him to some months of lustreless service aboard *Victoria and Albert* to keep him on hand for her granddaughter.

Lillie had been acting for fifteen months without a break. She bought souvenirs of jewellery for every member of her company before she paid them off. She earmarked a private railroad car, the *Jerome Marble,* with plate-glass windows reaching from its roof to its floor to rent as her own for her next American tour. And she went into the real estate business by investing $81,000 in mortgages on some Fifth Avenue buildings.

"America," she decided, "grows on me." She had been terrified at first, she confessed, in the Western states. "Curiosity was expressed there with a roughness of manner to which I have not yet become used. I found a lack of cultured and intelligent gentlemen." But since a fresh fortune could clearly be made every season that she cared to expose herself to vulgar curiosity, she would learn to live with it.

She asked Leonard Jerome to call on her the day before she left for England, perhaps to offer to carry messages to his wife or daughter Jennie, both of whom were in London. A general strike by seventeen thousand telegraph operators had halted all cablegrams. Her method of summoning people she clearly considered to be her social inferiors amused him. "I am going to see her this afternoon by special invitation," he wrote to his wife. Moreton Frewen had recently married their young daughter Clara. "He sails tomorrow in the *Etruria,*" Jerome explained archly, "along with this letter and Lillie Langtry." They docked in Liverpool on the second day of August.

The skill she had developed in handling publicity, turning it on or off according to her purposes, enabled her to keep her stay in London a secret from all but a handful of people during the few days she spent there. Lewis was no more encouraging than he had been over the past two years, but she had a new thought in mind. If she took out papers as an American citizen, she could probably file for divorce in one of the states that accepted grounds besides adultery.

She went to Bournemouth, where the town records registered the new occupants of the Red House as "Mrs. E. L. Langton and family." On a coping stone under the bedroom window of her old suite, she had a mason carve the date. In an obscure corner of a leaded pane in a window by the upper stairs, she scratched her initials and Bertie's with a diamond ring, then added two intertwined hearts and "1883." Those who lived in the house in years to come could only guess at the occasion that prompted her to leave this trace of her presence.

She found that Jeanne-Marie was growing up to be beautiful, even more so than her mother. There was a delicacy about her features, inherited from her father, that contrasted with the sturdier look of Lillie's face. If she saw Louis, no record was left of their meeting.

She went on to Paris to fit herself out simultaneously as a better actress and an international fashion plate. If theatre audiences were not impressed by her performances, they could certainly be drawn to goggle at her wearing a selection of the fifty gowns she ordered from Monsieur Worth. He had been a floorwalker at Swann and Edgar's London emporium before he set out to teach the French the meaning of *haute couture*. Under his purple velvet jacket and flowered waistcoat there beat the heart of a businessman. While his sewing women peeped through the velvet curtains at her, he struck a bargain with Lillie. When she was too busy with her classes to leave Régnier's *conservatoire,* the fitters brought their bolts of brocade there to cut and baste to her figure.

She was pleased with the results of her brief mission. She settled most of her account with Worth by promising him printed credit as her couturier in future programs. And Bernhardt arrived regularly at Monsieu Régnier's to help with the lessons. Lillie wrote about that to a friend she had cultivated in New York, old Dion Boucicault, the Irishman who had made a fortune as a dramatist with what he labelled "sensation drama." "I despair of becoming a real actress when I work on the stage with her," she told him, "and I would gladly exchange my beauty, such as it is, for a soupçon of her great talent. I know . . . I must emphasise as best I can my own assets. I can make you one pledge, my dear friend. When I return to America I will not disgrace you. . . . Even the assassins of the press will applaud me."

At the end of September she sailed to New York, and the prince joined Alexandra in Denmark. Lillie had recruited a fresh company for a new play; she rehearsed them every day they were at sea. Freddie met her together with the reporters, restraining his feelings about gentlemen of the press. Next month the newspaper reviewers detected some improvement in her as she tackled Daniel Frohman's featherweight comedy, *The Highest Bidders*. Back in England, the prince took his lethargic elder son to Cambridge as a Trinity College undergraduate. As material for the Royal Navy, Eddy had proved hopeless. His tutors were no more optimistic about his prospects as a student. As one of them reported, "He hardly knows the meaning of the words *to read*."

Alix was especially tearful that autumn when she left Denmark. Her sister Minnie and her brother-in-law, "poor Sasha," the czar and czarina, had been on holiday there at the same time as she and Bertie. With assassins uncurbed in Russia, Alexandra fretted that she might never see them again.

She knew something of Eddy's weaknesses. "We are neither of us blind to his faults," she confessed to the Reverend John Dalton. She yearned for the company of Georgie, who was finding that navy life fitted him as snugly as his mess jacket. He was a sublieutenant now, off at sea in HMS *Canada* with the West Indies and North American Squadron.

There was no discernible reason for her to write as she did on New Year's Eve to "my own darling little

Georgie" that "certainly 1883 was one of the happiest years of my life." Conceivably the fact that Lillie seemed to have removed herself permanently beyond the prince's reach played some part in the princess' contentment.

❧ XI ❧

The only pure, uncomplicated pleasure that Jeanne-Marie remembered of her childhood was riding in her mother's personal railroad car, listening to the muffled rumble of its sixteen wheels as it traversed the endless plains and mountains, detoured sometimes for hours on end over lonely stretches of single track through scrub and farmland because its weight threatened to crack the trestles of wooden bridges.

Between its railed-in platforms of polished Oriental teak at either end, the bright blue car stretched twenty-five yards long. Under the white roof, arching up over each platform, there ran a motif of polished brass lilies, which was repeated around the name lettered on each side. *Lalee,* according to Lillie, who chose it, meant "flirt" in some unspecified Indian dialect.

In *Lalee's salon,* where the walls were covered with cream-and-gold Lyons brocade, a grand piano stood between the bookcases and the soft-upholstered easy chairs. The *salon* opened on to a small sitting-room, with rose-coloured silk curtains, whose far door led to Lillie's dressing room. Beyond that lay her bathroom, where the fixtures were all of silver, and her bedroom, with pink silk hangings trimmed with Brussels lace. Every piece of furniture there was padded to prevent her fair skin being bruised by any sudden stop.

The kitchen, equipped to cook a full-course dinner;

the pantry with its massive icebox; the maid's room containing a sewing machine; and two guest rooms completed the pleasure dome, which lured sightseers in the hundreds to the railroad yards to which it was shunted as Lillie's itinerant hotel. She could feel satisfied that *Lalee* was much more luxurious than the private coaches she had ridden in with the prince on their Continental travels. All he wanted were comfortable leather armchairs, a thick carpet, card tables, newspapers, drinks and cigars, and never mind gilt cherubs or marquetry.

In all, there were ten rooms in the car for a child to roam in, but Jeanne-Marie had no playmates, except a governess and a maid. Friends of Lillie thought that perhaps she spoiled her niece, who seemed so close to her aunt. The girl obviously had everything a child could want—expensive clothes, a pretty face, beautiful manners. But she remembered only grey years of unhappiness.

Lalee was a gift from Freddie that cost a quarter of a million dollars. When the last strip of ornamental brass had been fitted, the overall effect was so conspicuous that he had to go on ahead by a different train to avoid arriving with Lillie at some of their destinations where her company was to play. Otherwise, the newspapers would corral him, and the scandal would never end. The car was also a special, sybaritic tribute to her from its designer and builder, the astonishing Colonel William D'Alton Mann, to whom Freddie introduced her.

The courtly colonel, a cavalry commandant in the Civil War at the age of twenty-one, patented a highly original "boudoir" sleeping car a dozen years earlier. He peddled his invention with great success in Europe, where it became the progenitor of the Compagnie des Wagons-Lits. Then he unloaded his foundering American company onto his longer-established competitor, George Pullman. *Lalee* was the climax of Mann's railroad career. He was taken up now with his part-interest in a magazine, *Town Topics,* which was a more sophisticated version of *Town Talk,* devoted to the peccadilloes of Society. The fact that Lillie and Freddie were spared his pungent, printed comments might be traced to his habit of taking "loans" from such men as Morgan and William Kissam Vanderbilt in return for a guarantee that they and their families would not be mentioned unfavourably by him.

Jeanne-Marie knew that Freddie was not her father. Her awareness of her family did not go much beyond that. She could not be certain of her identity at all. The woman she was trained to speak of as *ma tante* in public was really her mother. That was reassurance of a kind, though Mother referred to her as the daughter of Uncle Maurice, the one killed by a tiger in India. She saw something of another uncle, Clem, the barrister from London, who came over to examine her mother's finances and take a lawyer's look at the ranch Lillie had bought in California.

There was no way in the world for the child to be told that her father had been married to Princess Victoria of Hesse four years ago, in April, 1884. The queen-empress bestowed her blessings on her granddaughter and the bridegroom in person when she arrived in Darmstadt with her youngest daughter, tall, curly-haired Beatrice. The friendly little Rhine town of turreted castles and cobbled streets swarmed with relatives from all over Europe, "the royal mob," as the queen described them. Every bedroom was filled in the hodge-podge assortment of buildings that made up the Grand Ducal Palace.

Alix came with Bertie, who was in no mood for jollification. A month earlier, he had the depressing task of taking back to England from France the frail body of Leopold, whom hemophilia killed at last in Cannes. But Bertie could hardly stay away from his devoted Louis on his wedding day.

The bridegroom looked as handsome as any leading man of operetta in the dress uniform of the Hessian Artillery, frogged and braided, with a black-plumed *pickel-habue* sitting on his freshly barbered head and his legs encased in tall, spurred boots. "I have to do this as a sop . . . when I appear on State occasions," he joked afterwards to a friend. His parents and brothers joined in rejoicing over the family's auspicious link to British royalty. Two more of the Battenberg brothers were thinking in similar terms. A different young Princess Victoria, the nineteen-year-old daughter of Fritz, the German crown prince, and Bertie's sister Vicky, was blindly in love with Sandro.

The old queen was as bewitched with him as this granddaughter. She wrote later to Vicky: "I think he may stand next to beloved Papa, and he is a person in whose judgement I would have great confidence. I think him fascinating, and (as in beloved Papa's case) so wonderfully handsome."

The third romantically inclined Battenberg was Louis' brother Henry, nicknamed Liko, and happy to serve as an officer in the German emperor's Household Cavalry. Liko's choice was the queen's daughter Beatrice, whom he met at the wedding. The queen was aghast that the twenty-seven-year-old woman she had counted on keeping as her permanent companion had dared to find herself in love. Liko resolved the difficulty to Her Majesty's eminent satisfaction. As soon as he and Beatrice were married at Whippingham Church on the Isle of Wight, he and his bride would live with his new mother-in-law at Osborne.

As soon as the celebrations for Louis and his bride were over, Bertie left Darmstadt to try his hand again at matchmaking, as he had for Louis with Lillie. This time, however, he was out to do more than foster an affair. He hoped to win over Fritz to the idea of allowing his daughter to marry Sandro. Bertie escorted the sprightly Prince of Bulgaria to Berlin.

The Hohenzollerns as a whole were disdainful of the impoverished, morganatic Battenbergs. They were not worthy, in the German royal family's view, to be allied by marriage to the great reigning dynasties. More than that, the proposed marriage was suspected to be nothing more than an English plot to drive a wedge between Germany and the Russians, who were itching to have Sandro deposed—or assassinated. Old Kaiser William himself, still vigorous at eighty-seven, considered that Bertie should never have been allowed to bring Sandro to stir up family trouble. When he forbade his granddaughter to see Battenberg again, Bertie promptly arranged a secret meeting for the two lovers in Potsdam.

Louis had no reason to like Germans when they treated his younger brother so shamefully. But the problem eventually took care of itself. When Sandro was forced to abdicate as ruler of Bulgaria, he and his intended bride agreed that marriage was impossible for them. In the interim, Louis' career was steaming ahead. The queen had coaxed him into a short spell of serving again in *Victoria and Albert*. When that came to an end, as he wished it to, he was promoted to the rank of full commander. He had an understanding wife in Princess Victoria, and they had their first child, a daughter, named Alice for the dead grandmother she had never seen.

Louis' words to an ex-shipmate spoke of his contentment as a married man: "I am more keen than ever about serving on, and she is ready to go anywhere with me. We are not blessed much with earthly goods, and have to live in a small way, though we are all the happier for it, I believe." There was one hint of a problem that concerned him: "I am considered renegade by most of my countrymen."

Nothing needed to be skimped in the acquisition of earthly goods with which Lillie surrounded herself and Jeanne-Marie. No matter how trivial the play she appeared in, her looks, her clothes, and the pervasive scent of scandal surrounding her ensured that seats were always scarce. Freddie's apparently limitless affection and inexhaustible extravagance provided everything that Lillie herself could not afford when she intended to amass a personal fortune.

When they were not touring in *Lalee* for business or pleasure, there was the New York house to live in, which was another gift from Freddie. It stood at the end of a curved driveway, fifteen feet back from the sidewalk at 362 West Twenty-third Street. One of the first things she did after Freddie made over the

305

deed to her was to have the yard planted with flowers, grass, and shrubbery, then protected with wrought-iron railings and locked gates against passersby who came to see for themselves the nest that the newspapers made so much of.

Freddie also paid for the remodelling that she insisted on, from tearing walls down to enlarge the rooms, to installing marble baths and fireplaces. She engaged a young Englishman, James Mitchell, who had built a business for himself as the city's fanciest interior designer. She wanted the inside of the house finished in polished walnut that grew in only one English forest. It took a full year to install, grain, and polish with Mitchell on commission, working day and night.

"When we finished that beautiful walnut job, I was the proudest man in New York," he said when he aired his grievances in public shortly afterwards.

She took one glance at the result and said instantly, "The very latest thing in interior decoration is hard, finished white enamel. You will have to send to England for the right kind. I am sure you won't be able to get it here."

"It almost broke my heart," Mitchell lamented, "when my men set to work."

But Jersey Lily hats and gowns and accents were being copied by some New York hostessss as eagerly as though she were a pattern for all womankind. The guests who flocked to the house for supper and a few games of chance were dazzled by the glare that Lillie felt necessary to brighten otherwise dark rooms, yet dozens of other women soon had their living rooms enamelled, too.

For all her dash, Miss Lillie, a little plumper now, was still excluded from the uppermost echelons of New York Society, where Mrs. Vanderbilt and Mrs. Astor vied with each other in pretentiousness. She could discreetly drop the name of the prince as a faithful attendant at every play in her repertoire during one London season when she rented the Coventry Street theatre named for him. But she was not included in the list of the Four Hundred acceptables that Ward McAllister had drawn and kept updated for Mrs. Astor. The invitations Lillie received stopped short of the most rarefied altitudes of the tycoon class, where a million dollars was thought of as poverty, and no credentials were valid other than a personal fortune.

Her recourse was to behave more haughtily than a duchess and to teach her daughter to do the same. An impassive chilliness was common to both of them in the presence of strangers. Lillie would sit in an armchair with the splendour of the queen-empress, extending a hand to be kissed, acknowledging a greeting with a stately nod. When the crowd had gone home, she might let her defences fall. Then she would hitch up her skirt, jump up from the chair, and cry, "Thank God, that's over for a while. Now let's play." With one of the small group of survivors at the piano keyboard, the chatter and the laughter began and champagne glasses clinked.

She could be as cruel as any of her Jersey ancestors when she felt slighted. On one rainy night in London, she gave a lift in a closed carriage to another actress at the close of the evening's performance. Lillie, who liked to dabble conversationally in anything from the workings of fate to the arts of flower arranging, began to talk about the lost glories of King Louis XV and his court.

"You may be called the Pompadour of your time," her companion smiled, as they started over Westminster Bridge, which stood dark and deserted in the storm. Lillie pulled the cord to summon the coachman. "My companion gets out here," she said serenely when he opened the door. She watched in silence as the other woman walked away, her lesson learned.

If Lillie was insulted or deceived, there was no excuse for the offender. When her trust was betrayed, that was intolerable, too. "She would be hurt," said a veteran manager of her company, "for she had far more heart than she was given credit for, but she could not and would not endure stupidity or incom-

307

petence, and any lack of straightforwardness was with her unforgivable."

Her mother's insistence on precision, respect, and punctilious time-keeping rubbed off on Jeanne-Marie. Lillie rarely gave explicit instructions, but an "I wish" or "I suggest" from her must be taken as a command. Afterthoughts were not allowed. "But we have settled all that already, have we not?" she would say to cut off further, futile discussion.

Travelling in *Lalee* entailed a ritual as rigid as a coronation. Three minutes before a departure time, Lillie would appear on the platform after any guests, the staff, and, in some instances, her daughter were installed aboard. A senior railroad officer would be waiting to pay his respects. Newsboys would stand by with the day's papers. Porters would scurry to help her aboard. She had a smile and a kind word ready for everyone: "Oh, thank you so much. How kind of you!" A silver dollar might be slipped into a porter's hand: "Now you *will* buy something for yourself, won't you?" Her charm seemed as natural to her as drawing breath.

Lalee was her personal domain. The rest of her company travelled in coaches ahead, with the scenery packed in a baggage car. She was not renowned for the scale of wages she paid. A leading man engaged in England might earn sixteen pounds a week, a beginner less than two. At the lower levels, members of the troupe would trudge with their makeup boxes from the railroad station to the nearest theatrical lodgings because they could not afford the price of a cab.

They played in run-down frame buildings that dated back to the days of Junius Brutus Booth, father of the distinguished Edwin and the notorious John Wilkes, Lincoln's assassin. They performed in halls where the company handyman had to pipe in a gas supply to feed the footlights. They came to know the fantastic theatrical palaces of Western boom towns that rose in marble splendour out of the plains, surrounded by shacks that a landed English gentleman would refuse to keep his pigs in.

Now and then, a restless audience would start bombarding the stage with silver dollars. Lillie would order the curtain lowered and have her box-office manager offer refunds to anyone who asked. But such outbreaks were exceptional. Much more frequent were the stumbling strangers who were drawn by the sight of *Lalee* to introduce themselves to its owner.

She remembered a wait at one Western railroad halt while an extra locomotive was summoned to haul *Lalee*. Her private porter, black Ben, announced that "a lad in leathers" wanted to see her. He slouched in, fiddling with his Stetson.

"Then he took heart to tell me that he loved a girl who was living in one of the more distant of the wooden shanties which composed the tiny town, that she possessed my picture, had read about me in the papers. It would make them both very happy if I could be induced to wave my handkerchief in the direction of her little home, so that he might tell her later that I had done so."

She promised to do him that favour, and he left. A minute or two later he reappeared at the window. "Could you give me a bit of ribbon or something to remember you by? Here's my name and address, and if you ever need me, I will go to the end of the earth to fight for you."

"So gallant a fellow!" Lillie sighed when she retold the story.

Uninvited guests would sometimes hitch a ride aboard *Lalee*. Two shaggy mountaineers scrambled onto the rear observation platform as the train pulled out of some forgotten settlement one afternoon. She sent Ben to open the door and let them walk through to one of the public coaches up ahead. "But don't you go making any noise," he warned them, "because there's a *lady* in here."

That news kept them standing out on the teak deck until the next stop. "We've been living in the mountains for years with no sight of a woman," they told Ben, "and we've got no wish to meet one now."

On one overnight run, a coupling broke, and *Lalee*

309

was left standing alone in darkness on a single track in the middle of a forest of magnolias. Lillie slept on, unaware, until two hours later a locomotive returned in smoking haste to retrieve the lost car.

More than once, the gaudy behemoth jumped the tracks. In one Texas town, cowhands staged an improvised rodeo under *Lalee's* windows to entertain her while she waited for the work train to get her travelling palace rolling again. She quickly offered a cash prize to anyone who could ride a wild mustang that was produced, bucking at the end of a lasso. She stood on an upended barrel to watch as a dozen aspirants, including one actor in her troupe, were tossed into the dust before a seasoned *vaquero* rode the conquered horse up to her observation point to win the award.

The most singular compliment paid to her in the United States came from the self-styled "Judge" Roy Bean, a Canadian who spent most of his adult life in Northern Mexico before he arrived in the whistle-stop settlement of Vinagaroon, set among the sagebrush in a parched Texas plain, to run a saloon and serve as its mayor and officer of rough-and-ready law. After he made the journey to Chicago to see Lillie on the stage of the Haverly Theatre there, he renamed Vinagaroon "Langtry" and christened his establishment "The Jersey Lily," writing to Lillie to tell her how he had honoured her and inviting her to come to inspect his domain for herself.

Such a trip was impossible to fit into her timetable. She sent her regrets and, as a gesture of gratitude, offered to present the town with an ornamental drinking fountain. Roy Bean's reply came by return mail. A fountain would be useless in Langtry since water was the one thing nobody drank there.

The town's dignitaries repeated the invitation some years later, and Lillie eagerly accepted it. On a return run from California, *Lalee* rolled to Langtry, Texas, coupled to the rear of the Southern Pacific's *Sunset Limited*. The train would stop for thirty minutes, no more.

310

The town itself lay some distance from the tracks, so the reception centred on the wooden shed that served as a railroad station. Lillie alighted from *Lalee* to watch a welcoming procession trudging through the sand for the length of the train towards her. She was too late to meet "Judge" Bean; he had died, she learned, a few months earlier. His mild-mannered successor, Justice of the Peace W. D. Dodd, led the reception committee, with the support of Stationmaster Smith and Postmaster Fielding.

Behind them in line, the male inhabitants of Langtry, in their brightest shirts and finest leather, waited to shake her hand. Next came a group of brightly painted fifteen- or sixteen-year-old girls, who were introduced *en bloc* as "the young ladies of Langtry," and, last of all, the more soberly dressed woman identified as "our wives."

There was time to plough between the brush and cactus to call at The Jersey Lily the two-story frame shanty with a chained monkey on its piazza, where Roy Bean held court. She wanted to see the schoolhouse, but the schoolmistress had locked the door. As the *Sunset Limited's* whistle began to blow impatiently, she heard a red-bearded Langtryite mutter, "I've a great mind to kiss her, but I don't know how she'd take it."

With her calm, impregnable smile, she turned towards *Lalee*. Someone pointed out the town cemetery off in the distance. "Only fifteen of them in there died natural deaths," said one of her guides with a touch of municipal pride.

A formal presentation remained to be made to her before the train departed. A huge cinnamon bear was hoisted onto Lalee's observation platform and tethered to the rail. "Happily," she remembered, "before I had time to rid myself of this unwelcome addition without seeming discourteous, he broke away, scattering the crowd and causing some of the *vaqueros* to start shooting wildly at all angles." She stood waving farewell to Langtry as the wheels began to roll again.

As a replacement for the runaway bear, Justice of

311

the Peace Dodd sent her a revolver inscribed to her. "This pistol," was the legend, "was formerly the property of Judge Roy Bean. It aided him in finding some of his famous decisions and keeping order west of the Pecos River. It also kept order in the Jersey Lily Saloon. Kindly accept this as a small token of our regards."

On her second visit to the United States, in 1884, she announced her intention of becoming an American citizen. "I think Americans understand me much better than when I was here before." There were rumours that she was also counting on obtaining a divorce, marrying Gebhard and retiring from the theatre. She delayed for three more years.

On her first transcontinental crossing in *Lalee*, she bought a house in San Francisco and, as a resident of California, applied for United States citizenship. A year later, after a winter in London, she arrived with Jeanne-Marie and twenty-nine trunks of dresses, to begin the clandestine course of ridding herself of Edward. At a private hearing in a judge's chambers in Lakeport, California, she stated her claim for her marriage to be dissolved on the grounds that Edward had long since deserted her.

"I have always treated Mr. Langtry with affection," she declared, "never giving him cause to disregard his duty to me as a husband." Edward was unaware of the proceedings. She had no difficulty in gaining her freedom from the man she had never loved, together with custody of her child. The court papers were sealed. Her ex-husband, in England, still knew nothing of the existence of Jeanne-Marie, who was now six years old.

There was no man to occupy the role of father to her. Freddie began to live openly with her mother as soon as the divorce was completed. The girl was a focus of his attention. She went riding with him. He took her to the circus and the New York zoo, but Lillie held back from marrying him, in spite of his apparent fondness for the child. The monthly allowance to Edward continued.

The most plausible explanation was that she wanted to save her daughter from the damage they would both suffer if so much as a corner of the camouflage that concealed Jeanne-Marie were lifted. Publicity carried two edges, equally sharp, no matter how one handled it. Publicity was responsible for earning Miss Lillie something approaching half a million dollars. And it made her name synonymous with sinning on both sides of the Atlantic. She bore a deep-rooted resentment of the newspaper people who had contributed so eagerly towards making both her money and her reputation, especially if the interviewers happened to be women.

"Oh, these ghastly women reporters!" she complained. "They are so deadly in earnest, and are so naïve, and know so little about anything!" That particular outburst followed her acceptance of an invitation from one of them to go to a function "where I should meet a lot of interesting people." But when they left together, "the creature wanted to interview me on the proceedings and asked me if I was not very much impressed. That was really *too* quaint. 'My good woman,' I said, 'you forget I'm in the impressing business myself.' "

It was easier to avoid undesired publicity in London than in New York. The British press was more respectful and less probing, except for such noxious rags as *Reynold's Weekly Newspaper,* which suborned three hundred thousand readers every Sunday with a mixture of radical politics and jeers at the royal family. In England, too, the tangible aura of the prince was still effective in shielding Lillie.

She had noticed changes in him on one of her earliest visits back from the United States, nine months after Louis' marriage. "Society grows," the prince said, and he showed remarkable signs of believing that. He had become a conscientious member of a royal commission on the housing of the working classes, an unlikely topic to have interested him in the past. He tried to have Gladstone add a woman, the reformer Octavia Hill, to the roster made up of Carrington, Salisbury, and others, but with no success.

Even *Reynold's* could not fault Bertie on that score.

He disguised himself as a workingman and went with Carrington in a growler to see the slums of St. Pancras and Clerkenwell. He brushed aside their police escort to prowl unguarded through the dismal alleys. The sight of one starving woman and her three near-naked children shivering among a pile of rags in a bare, unheated room so appalled him that he pulled a handful of sovereigns from his pocket. Carrington restrained him. Once the news spread, he muttered, the neighbours on the alley might savage them for their gold. Before another week passed, the prince stood in the House of Lords to report on what he had seen and demand urgent action to rehouse the poor. It was the only major speech he ever made there.

A new mistress claimed credit for arousing his conscience. Frances, the golden-haired child heiress who had adored Lillie at first sight in Frank Miles' studio, replaced Mrs. Langtry. Her husband, the crack shot Lord Brooke, provided a flimsy screen for the relationship by travelling with her in Bertie's entourage. "Daisy," as her friends and family called her, had grown into a tempestuous, superbly dressed woman. Only a few years from now, she would be a convert to Socialism, haranguing farm labourers from the back of a wagon on the evils of private ownership of the land. Neither her place in Bertie's affections nor her later politics stood in the way of friendship with Lillie.

If anything, Daisy had the stronger will. Where Lillie had been Bertie's accomplice in loosening the chains of convention that shackled his mother's court, Daisy encouraged him to open his eyes to injustice. She convinced him of the failure of the ancient Poor Law, which set a premium on charitableness by making the rate-payers of every parish responsible for the care of its poverty-stricken. "The workhouses," Bertie agreed, "need to be reformed out of existence." At Daisy's prompting, the otherwise hedonistic prince made a point of going off to inspect the nearest work-house, when he stayed in his friends' country houses, and writing his name in the visitors' book as evidence of his escalating concern.

He yielded to the urge to write to "my own adored little Daisy wife" two or three times a week. "He expected me to write frequently," she recalled in old age, "and if I didn't, he used to say I had hurt him." Lillie could expect bread-and-butter letters from him; the onset of his middle years made those he sent Daisy more explicitly passionate. Alexandra's instinct told her what was happening. The welcome she invariably gave Lillie and her sympathy for her problems were never extended to Daisy.

While Lillie maintained her silence about her liaison with Bertie, Daisy imposed no such restraints on herself. The picture she drew of him as a bedmate was kind but temperate. "He was indeed a very perfect, gentle lover," she wrote afterwards. She thought that "anybody would have been won by him." At Eaton Lodge and the houses they stayed in together, other guests would leave them alone. The prince, said Daisy, "used to be boresome as he sat on a sofa, holding my hand and goggling at me."

As his old Uncle George, Duke of Cambridge, observed, Bertie was "taking to young girls," and Lillie was already in her thirties. She knew the prince too well to be surprised. His fancy knew no bounds. One young girl who caught his attention was the orphaned daughter of a late lady-in-waiting to Alexandra, whom the princess had made her special charge. Pretty, unaffected Julie Stonor, a commoner and a Catholic, was Georgie's declared true love, but his father came close to equalling his son's feelings towards her. But so long as the prince continued to spare time for Lillie whenever she came to London, she was content.

She found far more drastic changes in the fabric of the nation than in the behaviour of the prince. For the first time, a minister of the crown had sounded the note of war between the classes, which the Radicals had kept muted in the past. Lanky Joseph Chamberlain, ex-mayor of Birmingham before he became Gladstone's president of the Board of Trade, was attacking the very people that Lillie most admired while he electrified England with his speeches. The aristocrats, cried Chamberlain, "toil not, neither do they spin." Their fortunes "have originated by grants made in times gone by for the services which courtiers rendered kings, and have since grown and increased, while they have slept, by levying an incressed share on all that other men have done by toil and labour to add to the general wealth and prosperity of the country."

More alarming was the new, vastly increased power of the voters to put into Parliament the men they chose to carry out the transformation of England. Another extension of the franchise in 1884 made the rule a single vote for every elector. Bertie in his wisdom had embarked on a plan to win over Chamberlain from the Radicals. His chance came when Gladstone was overthrown and a government of opposition Conservatives formed, with Lord Salisbury as Prime Minister. Chamberlain was among the ninety-three Liberals who voted against Gladstone's bill to give Ireland home rule. Bertie was wholeheartedly opposed to any such madness.

The climate of political crisis did nothing to reduce the gossip that arose over Lillie, whatever she did. The fact that she had lost her place as the prince's prime favourite made her fair game for flirtatious noblemen. One of them was "the sporting earl," Hugh, the fourth Lord Lonsdale, whose interests were restricted to women and racing. His boast was that "I can always tell everything I want to know about a man by the way he sits a horse." Another pursuer of hers was the equally equine Sir George Chetwynd, of 23 Cork Street and Grendon Hall, Warwickshire, a future senior steward of the Jockey Club.

The conversation of these two fanciers centred on colts, fillies, the feats of Fred Archer, who was the foremost jockey of the times, and Monday's bloodstock sales at Tattersall's, which made as elegant a gathering as anything in London. Lillie tolerated Hugh and George, at least, largely because of her growing fascination with the money waiting to be picked up as a racehorse owner. Small talk of their kind was a major part of the equipment, too, for mingling with most old county families. She had the instincts of a gambler on horses as well as on men.

Sir George, married and the father of three children, pressed the lessons of his experience on her: "Make out your account every night after a day's racing . . . Never let your account be missing at Tattersall's." His sense of humour was more limited than hers. One of his anecdotes told how he was tempted to try out a bottle of tincture of cocoa instead of the usual swig of whisky to improve the temper of a rogue horse that he owned before he tried the animal out on the Downs.

With his brother's help, he dosed it with two teaspoonfuls of the concoction and then served his brother and himself a teaspoonful apiece. "It certainly produced an exhilarating effect on us," went the climax of his story, "and the horse ran straight as a die."

The afternoon came when a fistfight broke out between Sir George and Lord Hugh in their contest for Lillie. She still kept Redskin stabled in London for riding in the Park, though the following year Moreton Frewen reported to his father-in-law: "Everyone thinks Mrs. Langtry grown fat but pretty, Redskin is dead of the staggers."

As her riding companion this afternoon, she had chosen Hugh, whose wife had rescued the stuffed peacock from the auctioneer's hammer at Norfolk Street. George, rebuffed, promptly stationed himself at the rails alongside Rotten Row to wait for them. When Lillie and Hugh saw him, they reined their mounts to a halt. "Stay away from my Lillie!" Chetwynd yelled at Lonsdale.

The sporting earl jumped down from his horse as the baronet leapt over the rail. In the tanbark of the Row, battle began. Some spectators thought that Hugh struck the first blow with his riding crop. Others credited George with starting the fight. It was George, in any event, who went down first, his top hat rolling

317

in the dust. In seconds, he was back on his feet, exchanging punches, while the two horses shied away in fright.

Lillie's suitors were rolling on the ground, arms entangled, when two gentlemen in the crowd pulled them apart. The Duke of Portland, one of the five great landlords of London, was one; Sir William Gordon-Cummings of the Scots Guards the other. The bruised and dusty warriors were packed off to their homes in closed carriages. The newspapers and the gossips had a day to remember.

The headlines may have persuaded Lillie that she might as well abandon any further claim to Victorian respectability and bring Freddie over as evidence that she was looking for a long-term arrangement with no other man. London already knew something about Freddie and his prowess as a racehorse owner. *The Sporting Times* had printed an arch paragraph: "Mr. Gebhard's new colours, pink with gold spots, remind us of a china tea-service. Would not Lent Lily be better?"

Her cablegram urged him to pay no heed to the newspapers' account of the fight and invited him to join her in London. He could not possibly leave the United States, said his reply. The headlines produced another sequel. Dressmakers and tradesmen who had been left unpaid since her days on Norfork Street sued her for the money she owed them. At the trial, a hint of the obscure circumstances of her personal life came to light. Edward's deposition was read into the record: He could not pay the bills "because I have no funds other than the annuity allowed me by my wife on the condition that I do not molest her."

The judge ordered her to pay. The mud was slow to settle. Middle-class opinion against her hardened into the conviction that she was not only a Jezebel but perhaps a cheat as well. Jeanne-Marie, as secluded as a walled nun, was not mentioned in the case, but London was clearly far too hazardous a place for Lillie to bring her child.

When her mother stayed there, Jeanne-Marie was deposited in Jersey, in a rented house under her grandmother's care. The islanders were as sharply divided over the merits of Lillie Langtry as they were by local politics and the two parties that battled each other, Laurel and Rose. Jersey showed no more scruples in its treatment of Jeanne-Marie than in its elections, when bribery determined the winners and undecided voters were stupefied with free drink or else shipped off, drunk, for the day to Sark.

Lillie's daughter could not be protected from taunts that she was a bastard of the Prince of Wales. If she looked for the truth from her mother or grandmother they could assure her that this was a lie which she must ignore. But they deceived her before with the tale that Lillie was her aunt and she the daughter of Uncle Maurice. That pretence was steadfastly maintained in public long after she knew her true mother. Who was her other parent?

The first death she heard of in the immediate family was her grandfather's. Dean Le Breton's end came on February 28, 1888, in Kennington, an obscure corner of London, lost in the maze of working-class dwellings on the unfashionable south side of the Thames. Neither his wife nor their surviving children were with him. His last will and testament indicated his circumstances. All the money left to his name was the sum of five pounds.

Lillie was on tour in Chicago when she received the news. In her latest play, *As in a Looking Glass,* she portrayed a totally different character from her previous pert heroines. This time she played a tyrant who employed her beauty as a weapon of conquest. She could not bring herself to perform that evening. Only a handful of the company knew why. Otherwise, the death of the man whose ways with women had started her in flight from her birthplace and her origins was added to the list of secrets.

Wilde was among the few people who either learned or guessed at one of the mysteries in her background. On her next excursion to London, he paid an afternoon call on her with a manuscript under his arm. Placing it on a table, he made a sweep with his right hand: "There is a play which I have written for you."

Lillie was not sure that he was in earnest. She had never really taken Oscar seriously. His chatter sometimes amused her, but the thought that he might have pretensions as a playwright had not entered her mind.

"What is my part?" she asked cautiously.

"A woman," he said, "with a grown-up, illegitimate daughter."

If he was trying to rattle her, she would not let him. "My dear Oscar, am I old enough to have a grown-up daughter of any description?" She refused to touch the manuscript or allow him to read a line of it to her. "Put it away for twenty years" was her parting advice.

When Jeanne-Marie herself was middle-aged, Lillie wrote enigmatically in her memoirs, "Why he ever supposed that it would have been at the time a suitable play for me, I cannot imagine." The title of the manuscript she rejected out of hand was *Lady Windermere's Fan.*

That was the year when Louis' second daughter, Louise, was born. The queen's golden jubilee, which had filled London with Indian maharajahs and European princes, was a thing of the past. Bertie and the rest of the family had concluded that for once Mama should be talked into discarding her black bonnet in favour of wearing a crown. When Alix was put up to raise the subject, she received the worst snubbing of her life from her mother-in-law.

The queen continued to rail at Bertie whatever he did or omitted to do. Not long before she drove in state to Westminster Abbey to give thanks to God for her half-century on the throne, he attempted yet again to defend himself against her harassments:

> You remind me, my dearest Mama, that I am 45, a point I have not forgotten, although I am glad to say that I feel younger. You are, I think, rather hard on me when you talk of the round of gaieties I indulge in at Cannes, London, Homburg and Cowes. . . . With regard to London, I

think, dear Mama, you know well that the time we spend there is not *all* amusement, very much the reverse. To Homburg I only go for my health and to Cowes to get the sea breezes and yachting which, after the fatigue of the London Season, are an immense relaxation. Nobody knows better than I do that I am not perfect—still I try to perform the many and ever-increasing duties which lie before me to the best of my ability, nor do I shirk many which I confess I would prefer not to have to fulfill. . . .

Two days after Jeanne-Marie's seventh birthday, Bertie and Alix celebrated their silver wedding anniversary at Marlborough House. He gave the princess a diamond-and-ruby cross. The queen presented them with an enormous silver loving cup when she came to the family dinner at which her daughter-in-law wore a fresh orange fastened next to the orange blossom in her pompadour, a token, she said, that at forty-three she had ripened to maturity. *The Times'* contribution to the festivities was a leading article, advising the prince to overcome "the unfortunate weakness which has led him to patronise American cattle-drovers and prize-fighters."

Further rejoicing was cancelled on news of the death in Berlin of Emperor William I, born in the incredibly remote past of 1797. His son Fritz reigned for only ninety-nine days, with a wound in his throat where a previous tracheotomy had been performed to prevent suffocation. Then cancer of the throat killed him and put on the throne of Germany his son, William II, who derided his Uncle Bertie and rebelled against the love of England which his mother, Vicky, had tried to plant in him. The queen-empress' dreams of weaving together her country and Germany through manoeuvres of matrimony and statecraft were not to be realized. Bertie's better-founded vision of an *entente cordiale* with France held the key to the future, when the war to end wars cost nearly 900,000 British and 1,400,000 French dead.

He took Alix, Oliver Montagu, and Georgie with him to Berlin for Fritz's funeral. Then and afterwards, he tried to come to terms with "William the Great," as he labelled the quarrelsome, domineering nephew who now ruled Germany. But the Kaiser, twenty-nine-years old, had no time for the uncle he jeered at in private as "the old Peacock" or for "the old hag," the grandmother who sat on the throne of England. "William the Great needs to learn that he is living at the end of the nineteenth century and not in the Middle Ages," Bertie was fond of saying. And, "Willy is a bully, and most bullies, when tackled, are cowards." History would judge him right in two of those assessments, but not in the last.

If the prince and the Lily no longer had so much in common, Society still surmised that they occasionally shared a sofa for divertissement. Certainly, they were linked by a passion for baccarat and their involvement in separate, searing scandals.

Jeanne-Marie's adolescence might have been less insecure if her mother had married Freddie. But he disappeared from sight after the winter of 1889. He came hurrying to London when Lillie fell ill, first with measles, then with influenza, and was reported close to death. One rumour had it that he broke in on the prince when he was visiting to cheer up her convalescence. When Freddie refused to leave, Lillie, according to hearsay, was so appalled by the discourtesy that she ended her relations with him on the spot.

For whatever reason, Jeanne-Marie saw no more of Freddie, and her mother felt free to consort with a variety of other admirers. "Men are born to be slaves," Lillie used to say. When the girl was grown, she would hear a standard opening remark: "I used to know your mother." She had a stock reply: "A lot of men tell me that."

With Freddie disposed of, Lillie bought a house at 21 Pont Street in the district of Belgravia, which had superseded Mayfair as the most fashionable in town. It was familiar terrain, within a stone's throw of Eaton Place, the Park, and Buckingham Palace. Baccarat was part of an evening's entertainment there, in deference to the prince, who turned the Marlborough House clique on to the game when he gave up dancing. He carried the necessary counters in his pockets, a set of them engraved with the *fleur de lys,* a gift from Reuben Sassoon. The whisperers believed that he had to make his entry into the house over a plank laid against a side windowsill. Anyone who knew him as well as his intricate nature allowed, or saw how fat and shortwinded he was becoming, felt sure that he would see no need to be so devious.

"Baccy" lay at the root of the problem that mushroomed for him in the autumn of 1890. He accepted an invitation from one of England's new mercantile rich, the shipping magnate Arthur Wilson, to attend a three-day house party at Wilson's place, Tranby Croft, near Doncaster, Yorkshire. Daisy was automatically invited, too, but she had to cancel her acceptance at the last minute because of the sudden death of Rosslyn, her stepfather. Lillie was the second choice, but she excused herself. She was a working woman, pulling in the crowds to see her novel interpretation as the sinuous heroine of William Shakespeare's *Antony and Cleopatra* at the Prince's Theatre, London, her longest and most successful run to date.

On the first evening at Tranby Croft, the Wilsons' young son saw Lieutenant Colonel Sir William Gordon-Cummings of the Scots Guards perform some sleight-of-hand tricks with the counters on the table where he had joined the prince, Reuben Sassoon, Lieutenant General Owen Williams, of *Serapis* days, and other guests at baccarat. Bill Cummings, one of the peacemakers in the Rotten Row brawl between Lonsdale and Chetwynd, had a reputation as a brave soldier, a crack shot, and a persistent lecher whose boast was that "all the married woman try me." He had not been detected before as a cheat. The following night he tried the same legerdemain, to win a total of 225 pounds in the two sessions, most of it from Bertie, who had been accorded the privilege of keeping the bank.

Habitués of card games with the prince claimed that several of them were guilty of mild forms of deception in protest against being drawn in to play and possibly lose money to him. But Cummings' manipulations were too flagrant to be ignored. Two fellow guests were deputised to face him with the accusation. He raged that he was innocent and begged for an audience with Bertie. At dinner on the third day, the prince warned that five witnesses had spoken against him, though "we have no desire to be unnecessarily hard on you." To shield Bertie, the others solemnly drew up a pledge for Cummings to sign, swearing "never to play cards again as long as I live," in return for their promise to keep the whole incident dark. The prince was one of the nine men who added their sinatures as witnesses. Cummings left Tranby Croft early next morning, threatening to put a pistol to his head.

Too many people knew what had happened for the silence to remain unbroken. As the story spread like a contagion, Cummings was blackballed from every London club. A gentleman might cheat the tradesmen or his wife, but cards were a matter of honour. Looking for vengeance, he filed suit for slander against his five original accusers and subpoenaed Bertie as a witness.

Nothing taxed the prince's temper and health more than the five months of waiting that elapsed before the trial began. He had his wife's complete sympathy. Anxiety was making Papa "quite ill," she wrote to Georgie. "You were quite right to think that as usual Papa through his good nature was dragged into it and made to suffer, for trying to save with the others together this worthless creature, who since then had behaved *too abominably* to them all." His mother saw the opportunity to urge Bertie to renounce baccarat forever. He let her know that he would not set foot in Windsor Castle if she dared to bring up the subject.

The month of May saw the birth of his first grandchild. Louise, the second daughter of Bertie and Alix, married for almost two years to the newly created Duke of Fife, was delivered of a daughter. Her father was too glum for rejoicing. As an aggravation of his misery, he caught influenza. So did Gladstone, leader of Her Majesty's loyal opposition, and the House of Commons was promptly fumigated to guard against further outbreaks.

Meanwhile, Lillie scored a social triumph on her native island, which a considerable proportion of the civilised world's population had heard of only in conjunction with her name. For two years, she had pondered a request from the manager to appear at the Theatre Royal in Gloucester Street, St. Helier, which had historic associations with Jersey's first playhouse, built in 1802. Before then, straggling troupes performed from time to time in the Long Room over the Corn Market. She could not judge the kind of reception Jersey people would give her in public.

That spring she was convinced that they would probably like to see her. At two weeks' notice she had her trunks packed to perform the most reliable role in her repertoire, Rosalind in *As You Like It*. The current lieutenant governor, His Excellency Lieutenant General C. B. Ewart, Companion of the Bath, Royal Engineers, concluded that the time had come for him, too, to recognise the woman whom everybody spoke of as a mistress of the Prince of Wales. He invited her to appear in command performance for him and his wife at the end of the run.

She determined to provide Jerseymen with a sight to remember her by. Her costumes as Pauline Deschappelles, the heroine of Bulwer-Lytton's *The Lady of Lyons,* made the gowns of the seigneurs' ladies who crowded in to see her look almost dowdy. Nobody particularly cared whether the notorious Mrs. Langtry could act or not, so long as she was in full view, walking the stage as haughty as a queen. Hostile factions among the islanders disregarded the applause she received. So far as they were concerned, her reputation only blackened the island's name. She should be treated like any other strolling player of old and restrained to a place over the Corn Market. By coincidence, the Theatre Royal burned to the ground before the decade was over.

She sailed back from St. Helier to England to be close to the bedevilled prince if he needed consolation from her in his troubles. A deluge of them descended on him. For relaxation over a game or two of baccarat and a brandy-and-soda, Lillie was more comfortable than Daisy, who disapproved of gambling and drinking.

Daisy had landed him in a situation potentially more dangerous than the impending trial of the Tranby Croft affair, though knowledge of it was confined to a few score of people, whereas all England was being aroused by Cummings' slander suit.

Before Daisy entered Bertie's personal life, she and Charlie Beresford had been lovers. Charlie had vowed to her that, though he could not abandon his wife Mina and their only child, he would henceforth make love only to Daisy. When she learned that, after a ten-year interval, Mina was pregnant again, she exploded into anger that no smelling salts could calm. The prince tried to quell the fire by finding a new job for his old comrade. Charlie had temporarily given up seafaring to enter the House of Commons, but politics bored this restless Irishman, who considered that he deserved something better than the post of Fourth Sea Lord, the appointment given him at Bertie's urging by Salisbury, the Prime Minister. Now the prince advised Beresford to resign from Parliament and the Admiralty, to return to active service in the Royal Navy.

Charlie was away from their house at 100 Eaton Square when Mina opened an envelope addressed to him in Daisy's dashing hand. The letter inside, as Mina reported furiously to the Prime Minister, declared that "I had no right to have a child by my own husband." There were imitations, too, that Charlie had fathered Daisy's last-born son. It was perfect ammunition to be stored for use against her if she ever attempted to pursue Charlie again, or if he fell back on his promise to his wife that he would forgo the enchanting, unscrupulous Lady Brooke. Mina took the letter to George Lewis, to be deposited in his safe.

Daisy invited herself to Marlborough House one afternoon to appeal for Bertie's help in retrieving her letter. "He was more than kind," she recalled. "Suddenly I saw him looking at me in a way all women understand. I knew I had won, so I asked him to tea." At two o'clock the following morning the prince arrived at Lewis' office-home on Ely Place. The astonished solicitor had no hesitation in showing him the letter, but he refused to burn it, despite Bertie's request. Lady Charles Beresford would have to consent to that first, Lewis said judiciously. The letter went back into his safe.

Beresford was more offended by the prince's meddling in his personal affairs than by Lewis' "lickerish servility" in exhibiting the letter. He saw eye to eye with Bertie on only one aspect of the mushrooming squabble: The document should be destroyed. Mina declined to part with it to him, just as she turned down the prince when he called at Eaton Square. She would use it, she thought, to ruin Daisy's place in Society. Mina herself was a commoner's daughter. Only her marriage to Charlie, which Bertie attended, had elevated her to the prince's circle.

In a second call at the house on Eaton Square, Bertie dangled the axe of ostracism over her head. He hinted broadly that she and Charlie would both suffer his wrath if she persisted in her stubbornness. Heavy with child, Mina scribbled another complaint to Salisbury: ". . . Of course, undeterred by these threats, I refused to return the letter for obvious reasons."

The prince lived up to his warning, and Mina was banned from Marlborough House. At that, Beresford lost control of himself. On the point of leaving for the Mediterranean to take over command of the cruiser *Undaunted*, he went to confront Bertie. The prince, he raved to his face, was a blackguard and a coward. Bertie's temper flared as hot as the insolent Irishman's. One minute more, it seemed, and Beresford would start a fistfight, with every chance of winning. As it was, he stormed out, promising that if Mina suffered harm, Bertie must accept the consequences.

After she bore her second daughter, the crushing power of ostracism began to wilt Mina, as the Marlborough House enclave followed the example of its master. By the time Lillie returned to London from St. Helier, Lady Beresford had told her family and friends that the Eaton Square house was soon to be put up for sale. She would have to exile herself overseas to be spared further humiliation. Aboard *Undaunted,* Charlie nursed his grievances.

Yet another problem weighed on Bertie's shoulders. The dissipations of Eddy, next after himself in succession to the throne, alarmed both parents. Created Duke of Clarence and Avondale the previous year, Eddy was almost certainly involved in the unsavoury mess of the male brothel on Cleveland Street that sent Lord Arthur Somerset of the Blues in flight across the Channel to escape arrest. Early marriage was the remedy routinely prescribed for such troublesome young men as "Collar and Cuffs," as Her Majesty's more ribald subjects dubbed Eddy, whose photographs invariably showed his vacuous face shored up by three inches of starched linen encircling his elongated neck and with an equal width of shirt sleeve over his thin wrists.

His own first choice was Alicky, the strong-willed Princess of Hesse, a younger sister of Louis' wife. Alicky had too large a share of common sense to have anything to do with him. Instead, she waited to marry the last czar of Russia, Nicholas II, less than four weeks after he succeeded his father. She was to die beside Nicky and their five children before a Bolshevik firing squad in a Siberian cellar in 1918.

After Alicky rejected him, Eddy professed himself to be head over heels in love with Princess Hélène d'Orléans. His sentimental mother was delighted; his grandmother horrified. Hélène was an impossible choice as a future queen of England. She was a daughter of the Comte de Paris, pretender to the throne of France, which could raise permanent political difficulties with the French Republic. And, as a Catholic, she was ineligible as a wife for the heir to the British crown, under the terms of the Constitution. Nevertheless, Bertie and Alexandra acted as if any marriage were preferable to dissipation. Then encouraged Eddy and Hélène to become engaged when they stayed as guests of his sister Louise in Scotland. Alexandra was there at the time. Bertie could not bring himself to interrupt the cure he was taking at Homburg.

Eddy's interest in anybody or anything was fitful. He interrupted his courtship of Hélène to compose a number of fond letters to another pretty little creature to whom he fancied he had lost his heart, Lady Sybil St. Clair Erskine. Hélène took it on herself to appeal to Pope Leo XIII to clear the way for her to marry a Protestant. His Holiness' reply wrote the end to her romance. No matter what, he ruled, she must not abandon her religious faith.

On Lillie's return from St. Helier in May, Bertie's patience with Eddy had run out. He was so heartily tired of his elder son that he wanted to send him off to the farthest corners of the empire—South Africa, New Zealand, Canada, anywhere—to keep him out of further trouble and punish him for his transgressions. Alexandra fought against that. What a boy like Eddy needed most was his mother's care. He should go back to duty in Ireland as an officer of the 10th Hussars, the regiment into which he had been popped after his short, fruitless course of study as a Cambridge undergraduate. The queen had still another idea. The only hope of maturing her fidgety grandson lay in having him travel in Europe, which was something that Bertie would not tolerate for a moment. Eddy could never survive the temptations offered in Paris, Vienna, and Berlin.

Lillie had never known the prince so downcast. When the Tranby Croft case came up before the Lord Chief Justice, Lord Coleridge, on the first of June, she sat among the spectators. Bertie appeared in the court every day. Seldom had he been in greater need of affection from any woman. Public sentiment piled up against him in a flood tide. He might as well have been a prisoner in the dock, so far as newspaper reports dealt with him. He was not called to the witness stand, but he was exposed as an inveterate gambler, whose pastime was an illegal card game in which honour counted for nothing.

The prince complained that "the British Jury are composed of a peculiar class of society, and do not shine in intelligence or refinement of feeling." He found the newspapers "very severe and cruel, because they know I cannot defend myself." They had not revelled so enthusiastically in any story since "Jack the Ripper," three years previously, had murdered five East End prostitutes within ten weeks; he was still unidentified, and fresh killings continued to be attributed to his mutilating scalpel.

A week after the Lord Chief Justice began hearing evidence, the prince's daily torment in the courtroom went on without interruption. "This horrible Trial drags along," the queen wrote to Vicky, "and it is a fearful humiliation to see the future King of this country dragged (and for the second time) through the dirt, just like anyone else. . . . It is very painful and must do his prestige great harm. . . ."

On June 9 it took the unimaginative, unrefined jurymen less than fifteen minutes to find the five defendants innocent of slander. Within twenty-four hours Sir William Gordon-Cummings was sacked from the army, expelled from all his clubs, and married to a rich American. "Thank God!—the Army and Society are now well rid of such a damned blackguard," Bertie exclaimed. But for weeks to come, it was open season in the press and among the middle classes berating the prince. The queen grieved: "The light which has been thrown on his habits . . . alarms and shocks the people so much, for the example is so bad. . . ."

In his quarters aboard *Undaunted,* Charlie Beresford weighed his words carefully as he set them down on paper, first for Mina, then for her to show to Salisbury, and, finally, when she received her husband's telegram, deliver to Marlborough House for the prince, to whom they were addressed. "I consider that from the beginning by your unasked interference and subsequent action," Beresford wrote, "you have deliberately used your high position to insult a humbler by doing all you can to elevate the person with whom she has had a quarrel." He continued writing. The crucial point was reached: "The days of duelling are past, but there is a more just way of getting right done than can duelling, and that is—publicity."

Mina did as she was told and sent the letter to the Prime Minister along with a covering one of her own. Her husband, she said, could add one more scandal to cap the Tranby Croft affair in damning the prince. Salisbury must intervene with His Royal Highness to restore her place in Society.

Lillie chose that season to embark on a sexual adventure that reduced all Bertie's delinquencies to the level of a child's stealing pennies from a Sunday-school collection plate. She confided her reasons to no one, possibly because she did not fully understand them herself. Perhaps she was galled by Bertie's undiminished devotion to Daisy in spite of the anguish she brought him. He visited Daisy at Eaton Lodge so often that the profligate peeress had a railway station built on her estate specially for the prince's arrivals and departures and drenched him with her passion in an aura of orchids and aigrettes, diamonds, mink and nascent Socialism.

Lillie's first encounter with the sportsman who rode as an amateur jockey under the pseudonym of "Squire Abingdon" was only mildly flirtatious. He came up to her at a race meeting and pressed into her hand the bookmakers' slips covering bets he had placed on two horses which he had entered for running that afternoon. The hard-muscled little Scotsman with the quick, elastic walk and a fondness for loud checked suits could afford a stable of thoroughbreds, a string of prizefighters, and anything else he fancied. His partnership in a Glasgow firm of ironmasters and his coal mines in southern England gave George Alexander Baird half a million dollars a year to spend.

When his two horses won, Lillie was one hundred pounds better off. He brushed aside her attempt to give him the money. He was used to squandering much vaster sums on women from prostitutes to peeresses, or, a year earlier, in paying fifteen thousand pounds to settle a damage suit filed by the Marquess of Aylesbury, whose wife the Squire had seduced and abducted. Lillie agreed to the bargain he proposed: They would spend the hundred pounds on dinner together that evening.

Society treated the Squire as an untouchable. This hero of the sporting newspapers made a habit of beating women, one of whom at least had him arrested after suffering the affections of his knuckles. He fascinated Lillie. In short order, she was his acknowledged mistress and willing to let the fact speak for itself as he pawed her in public. One of his early overtures was to provide a house for them to share. On a drunken evening at Sir George Chetwynd's, the Squire bought the baronet's place on Cork Street and all its contents with a check for fifteen thousand pounds.

His demands took up most of her time that summer. They appeared at any meeting where he had a horse running. He plied her with diamonds, sapphires, and bruises, and she made no pretence to her friends that she loved him. One of them remembered finding her hiding at home with a blackened eye.

"You must think the world of him to allow him to do such things to you," said the friend incredulously.

"I detest him," Lillie replied matter-of-factly. "But every time he does it, he gives me a check for five thousand pounds."

It seemed to the diminishing number of those concerned about her that she was deliberately courting ostracism and the destruction of such reputation as she had left. Where Mina Beresford fought and schemed to cling to her position in the Marlborough House set, Lillie discarded her own privileges as though they no longer held any significance. Respectable, responsible hosts and hostesses turned their backs on the Squire and, accordingly, on Lillie. She behaved as though she were testing herself to see whether she could endure the boycott as she had lived through the challenges of the past.

If there were deeper levels in her motives, the vocabulary to identify them had not yet been invented. In Vienna, Sigmund Freud, unheard of in the world outside, was putting together his interpretations of the role of the subconscious in shaping personality. Not for four more years would he publish *Studies in Hysteria* and lay the foundations of psychoanalysis. In 1891 the complementary needs of a sadist and a masochist were as uncharted as the south polar seas.

She was marked as a bully's doxy by the time Bertie entered upon his fifty-first year in November, but there was no sign that he thought the less of her for that. The prince spent his birthday without Alexandra. She had endured all she could take of her husband for the present. A sister of Mina's had published the whole story of Daisy's letter and Bertie's blacklisting of the Beresfords in a pamphlet that circulated through Society in London and New York. Alexandra could not face the shame it created. From Denmark, where she was visiting her parents, she cancelled her plan to return for Bertie's birthday and went instead to the Crimea for the silver wedding of Sasha and her sister Minnie, Czar Alexander III and his czarina. It was a month later before Alix made her way home.

Lillie's career in the theatre came to a sudden stop. She had no new play in sight at the close of the year, when Beresford responded to a telegraphed appeal from Mina to hurry back to England to save her. He arrived, threatening to expose the secrets of Bertie's affairs unless the prince apologised. Charlie was on the point of pouring out his grievances to the news agencies when Salisbury intervened. The Prime Minister draughted one formal letter for Beresford and another for the prince, which expressed Bertie's cool regret for the "erroneous impression" Mina had formed. As part of the bargain which Salisbury arranged, Daisy was temporarily excluded from the court, and Mina at last put her precious letter into the fire.

With the Tranby Croft trial over with and an armistice declared with the Beresfords, the intimidating problem of Eddy remained, but time resolved that. Another prospective bride was found for him in Princess May of Teck, a clever, straitlaced girl who had played as a child in the nursery at Marlborough House. She was a remote cousin of Eddy's—her mother, the squat little Duchess of Teck, was one of King George III's granddaughters, like the queen herself.

Plans for the wedding were pushed at a gallop. February 27, 1892, was to be the day, only two months after Eddy proposed and May accepted him. Two weeks before that date in his closet of a bedroom at Sandringham, Eddy died of the combined effects of primary syphilis, influenza, and pneumonia. "Gladly would I have given my life for his," Bertie wrote to the queen, "as I put no value on mine." Her mother-in-law thought that Alix looked lovelier than ever in her deep mourning.

A princess as well qualified as May to serve as a future Queen of England could not be allowed to be wasted. Now Georgie, the sailor prince, was the heir of the throne. On May 3 of the following year, May agreed to marry him as a substitute for his older brother.

Bertie lightened his sorrow over Eddy's death by commissioning the building of a new three-hundred-ton racing cutter, *Britannia,* which he could not afford. Not to be outdone, Lillie simultaneously found her own means of owning a yacht that would bear comparison with his. Its price was a savage beating from the Squire that came close to breaking her bones.

He had gone to Scotland hunting stag when she took the opportunity to see something of her mother and Jeanne-Marie on Jersey, then continued on to Paris to replenish her wardrobe at Monsieur Worth's. In her hotel there, she ran across a gangling young Englishman, six feet five inches tall, who was happily engaged in dissipating what remained of the family fortune. Robert Peel, named for Victoria's Prime Minister when she was a girl of twenty-two, shared some idle days with Lillie. They were in her suite when the Squire broke in. He had pursued her to France when he found her missing from London.

First he thrashed Peel, and then he battered her into unconsciousness before he worked off his savagery on the furniture, her dresses in the wardrobes, and her lingerie in the drawers. During the ten days she spent in a hospital, she signed a complaint for the Squire's arrest, which was something Peel refused to do. It was not pity for the Squire that gave her second thoughts, but she decided to drop the charges.

The hotel suite where she passed two more weeks of convalescence had been restored at the Squire's expense. Fresh presents were delivered from him every day—a Cartier bracelet, new gowns, a ruby pendant, title to three thoroughbred colts in his stable. She still refused to allow him to see her.

The gift that restored him to her good graces was a two-hundred-and-twenty-foot yacht of twice *Britannia*'s tonnage, which he bought, cash down, from Lord Ashburton. *The White Lady* was waiting at anchor for Lillie in Cherbourg Harbour when she stepped from the train to catch the cross-channel steamer. The Squire was waiting on deck, with the papers ready to transfer ownership to her, along with a check for fifty thousand pounds for upkeep. She went aboard and stayed to sample the joys of a few days' cruising.

In June one of the two-year-old colts that the Squire gave her won its first race in her colours of turquoise and fawn. At the Squire's suggestion she listed the owner as "Mr. Jersey." She won a thousand pounds that day, which was a pittance compared with what the future brought her as she assembled her own racing stable. When she reached the age of seventy, she said contentedly, "In life, I have had all that I really wanted very much—a yacht, a racing stable, a theatre of my own, lovely gardens."

Jeanne-Marie saw the Squire for the first time aboard *The White Lady* towards the end of the season at Cowes. She left no record of her feelings and mentioned him in no known conversation. She was spared any closer acquaintance with him. He took off for New York with his latest pet of the prize ring, an aging heavyweight named Charley Mitchell, seeking to match him against Gentleman Jim Corbett for the championship of the world. Charley had just been released from Pentonville Prison. The Squire's hopes died when Mitchell was arrested on landing as an ex-convict.

Making his first visit to America, the Squire tried next to organise a tour of the West in the company of Sheriff Bat Masterson, but that dream had to be abandoned, too. He finally arrived in New Orleans, bloated by months of dissipation, to die in the St. Charles Hotel there of pneumonia, induced by a monumental drinking bout. The word spread that his will left Lillie $5,000,000. She had nothing to say.

The brief sight that Jeanne-Marie had of the Squire was more than she saw of Edward Langtry. She had to be told something about him when she was sixteen and a San Francisco newspaper unearthed the details of her mother's nine-year-old divorce.

Jeanne-Marie was reassured that her father was, in fact, the invisible Edward Langtry, no matter what was said. Now she might abandon the pretence of *"ma tante"* and openly address Lillie as her mother. She found little reason to be grateful for the change. "Father" was a word without meaning for her. She had no cause to mourn, either, when Edward, unshaven and in rags, was picked up as a vagrant and clapped into prison in the city of Chester. Doctors, whose fees Lillie paid, declared him to be insane.

Neither Bertie nor Lillie kept possession of their yachts. The prince sold *Britannia* after his nephew the Kaiser invaded Cowes with *Meteor II*, a bigger version of Bertie's racing cutter, which outclassed all the competition. Lillie chartered *The White Lady* to an American millionaire, Ogden Goelet, when the cost of running her could no longer be met by the Squire. Horse-racing was the sport now that preoccupied both the prince and his old love.

In the matter of making money at it, they were separated by no more than a few lengths. Between 1886, when his interest started, and his death in 1910, Bertie's stables earned more than 400,000 pounds in stake money and stud fees. Lillie collected close to 120,000 pounds on a single race in October, 1897, a year that brought the prince no more than 15,219 pounds from racing.

That was the year of Victoria's Diamond Jubilee, and England celebrated with a rare show of pomp, power, and solicitude for the needy. Londoners went hoarse with cheering the tottering, little seventy-eight-year-old widow who appeared in her carriage on the streets of their city, bonnet bobbing as she dozed whenever the shouting faded in her ears. Twenty-five thousand officers and men marched in review before her. Bertie stood in for his mother at Spithead, where one hundred seventy-three of her warships steamed four abreast in a five-mile parade of British might. Alexandra wrote the first check for a fund to provide dinner, as she specified, for the poorest of the poor in the slums of London.

The national mood for rejoicing made a gala day of the Cesarewitch, run at Newmarket with a field of twenty-three horses. Bertie, of course, was there, enjoying the applause he invariably was accorded nowadays as an owner whose sensational Persimmon had won last year's Derby, then romped home again in the ten-thousand-sovereign Eclipse Stakes at Sandown Park a few weeks later.

"Mr. Jersey" watched her Australian five-year-old Merman walk away with the Cesarewitch, with 10,000 pounds of her money placed to win with the bookmakers at odds of eight to one, as well as the winner's purse. Wearing a dark-brown golfing cape with dashing dignity, Bertie was the first to congratulate her. After his brother Affie escorted her to greet the flower-draped Merman, Bertie drank Lillie's health in champagne in the sanctuary of the Jockey Club. He joked that she should be the handicapper there. "No one is better qualified," he chuckled. Forty-eight hours later, she and Jeane-Marie learned of Edward Langtry's death in the Cheshire county asylum. For the rest of her days, Jeanne-Marie would insist to all but a handful of her closest friends and her own children that the man who fathered her died on October 15, 1897. Four more years passed before she herself knew for certain that this was not true.

The coroner ruled that the death was accidental, and Edward was buried at Chester. The wreath that Lillie sent bore a ribbon of turquoise and fawn, her racing colours as Mr. Jersey, which drove a *New York Times* editorial writer close to apoplexy over a "piece of insolence so utterly reckless and original, and at the same time so ingenious and effective, that its moral and social aspects tend to or toward complete disappearance. . . ."

Now that her freedom was public knowledge, Lillie toyed with the notion of making herself a princess. Paul Antonio Nicholas, Prince Esterhazy de Golantha, reputed to be the best judge of horseflesh in Austria, was eager to take her as his third wife; the first two had both died. He was Hungarian-born, rich, and well-preserved for a roué approaching his sixtieth birthday. Plans were laid for an autumn wedding, as her San Francisco attorney, Henry McPike, confirmed. But Lillie backed away, possibly because Prince Esterhazy, in pursuit of vanishing virility, applied black dye to his hair and whiskers.

❧ XII ❧

Victoria had been dead for forty-five days when Jeanne-Marie reached her twentieth birthday. The new sovereign of England and the empire was the fifty-nine-year-old fat man, wheezing from bronchitis, whom most of Society suspected of being her father. He chose to be known as Edward VII because, he said, he wished to avoid comparisons with Albert the Good. He had been obsessed with his duties from the moment he became king with adverse effect on his temper. When confusion broke out in the order of march at his mother's funeral and functionaries had conflicting thoughts for resolving it, he cut short the argument. One official alone must disentangle the chaos: "Right or wrong, let him manage everything. We shall never get on if there are two people giving contradictory orders." Within a matter of days, he named Louis, a captain in the Royal Navy now, as a personal aide.

An indisputable stepfather had come into Jeanne-Marie's life almost two years since. Hugo de Bathe, tall, attractive, and ineffectual, was only seven years older than the timid girl he was fond of squiring to dinner or the theatre with or without her mother, who was nineteen years older than he. His father, Sir Henry, disinherited him when Hugo was married to Lillie at St. Saviour's Church, St. Helier, on the same July day that Merman won the Goodwood Stakes and more thousands for his owner. "I wish I could die now," said Sir Henry, a veteran of the Crimean War, "so that the will could go into effect at once."

But her stepfather was not on the scene for Jeanne-Marie's birthday. He restored himself to his father's favour by sailing for South Africa as a volunteer in the full-scale war that for seventeen months past had matched burly Boer farmers against regiments of infantry and cavalry fighting on behalf of British *Uitlanders* for possession of the Transvaal's diamonds and gold. Sir Henry de Bathe, baronet, had six more years to live. When Hugo succeeded him, Lillie achieved one more of her ambitions. She became Lady de Bathe.

Backstage, she remained Miss Lillie. She had her own theatre, the most resplendent in London. The Imperial formed part of the conglomeration of buildings of the Royal Westminster Aquarium, where a quarter of a century ago a chance encounter with Ranelagh started Lillie's climb into Society. The playhouse was a shabby relic when she rented it, only to have it gutted and made over in marble. She furnished the interior, with its two thousand and more crimson-plush seats, in empire elegance. Every wall hanging and drapery was ordered handmade from the Royal School of Needlework. Purple silk lined the royal box, and electric light glared where gas had glowed before.

This palace of make-believe cost 55,000 pounds from her personal bank account. She considered it money well spent to have such a landmark for her own. Before the place was completed, with a deadline to be met for the opening of a new play, she told her manager, Edward Michael, "Everything is arranged at the bank. Try to leave me a little money for my hotel bills." Then she departed for a Riviera holiday, a general relaxing before battle.

Jeanne-Marie and her ailing grandmother lived with Lillie in a larger house which she bought on territory where her luck had been good before. Two Cadogan Place stood a stone's throw from Pont Street. Louis Quinze furniture set the tone in the downstairs rooms, genuine pieces this time, not the poor imitations of Eaton Place that went under an auctioneer's hammer. A stuffed grizzly bear, which Clem shot in California, snarled in the trophy room. She could seat sixty guests for dinner, then entertain them afterwards at baccarat or with dancing in the ballroom, where a permanent stage was provided for the band. Hugo's bedroom was lined in tweed, like the royal bedchambers at Balmoral, her own in satin, complementing the eiderdown on the bed embroidered with a crest of the king's "E.R." for Edward Rex.

All of it was paid for from the proceeds of another play she devised to shock the prudes and pack the theatres. Bertie and Alix saw Lillie's portrayal of a dissolute courtesan in *The Degenerates* in London. In the United States it momentarily aroused more excitement than the impending reelection to the White House of William McKinley, with a boisterous soldier of fortune named Theodore Roosevelt as his Vice President.

Lillie's daughter had not yet made her debut in Society. In the normal course, that could have taken place during the past two seasons. Among the gossips, suspicions were sounded that Lillie had not dared risk the stigma of the Court's rejecting Jeanne-Marie while the queen still lived. So Jeanne-Marie had lingered on the fringes of Society, a shy, self-effacing girl with perfect teeth and a forced smile, who flatly refused to talk about herself. Her most attentive follower was young Arthur Hill, a nephew of the Marquess of Devonshire, but he was not on hand for her birthday. The war against the Boers had claimed him, too. She thought that perhaps she loved him, but there would be plenty of time to decide that after he came home again.

One woman who knew and liked her was Margot Asquith, whose husband, Herbert, had been Home Secretary in Gladstone's fourth and last Cabinet, formed in August, 1892. With the Conservatives in power and Salisbury the Prime Minister now, Asquith was the spokesman for the group of opposition Liberals who backed the government's actions in the latest war in spite of its unpopularity with much of the population at home and the hostility it stirred in the capitals of Europe. With her shock of red hair and beak of a nose, Margot more than made up for the colour lacking in her lawyer-husband. She was an iconoclast, who delighted to startle her listeners as she spoke. She excelled herself when she approached Jeanne-Marie at a party that March.

"What did you get for your birthday?"

The girl politely went through the list of presents she had received from Lillie, Uncle Clem, and the rest.

"What did your father send you?" Margot probed.

The girl was bewildered. "But my father is dead," she said.

Margot's gaunt face wore a thin smile. "Oh, no. Your father is Louis Battenberg. Your mother must have told you that."

Jeanne-Marie's calm held firm. She made an excuse to leave as politely as possible and hurried to Cadogan Place. The confrontation with Lillie was the most painful of her daughter's life to date. She had been trained to lie for reasons that could never be satisfactorily explained. She had been brought up supposedly as the child of one dead man, Uncle Maurice, and then of another, always conscious when she grew old enough to understand of the whispers that held the new king to be her missing parent.

In later years, she spoke of the quarrel with her mother only in terms of intensity. All other details she suppressed. But she succeeded in prying the truth from Lillie. The effect was to seal off her daughter's affection for all time. Whatever love she had for her mother receded into nothing more than a recollection of some happy days aboard *Lalee*. The truth produced another consequence. The girl made up her mind to accept the first eligible man who asked her to be his wife, without waiting for Captain Arthur Hill.

But first she must observe the rules governing a young lady of her standing coming out into Society. There was no trouble about that with Bertie on the throne. He had not wasted a moment in starting some royal housecleaning to sweep away the archaic routines of the court and his mother's household, most of whose retainers were enfeebled by age. Like a new company chairman recruited to breathe life into a decaying business, he had his hands into everything, from personally opening the four to five hundred letters in his morning postbag to supervising the design of smarter livery for his servants.

He stayed on with Alix in Marlborough House while the mountainous task of modernising the accommodations in Buckingham Palace, Windsor, and Balmoral got under way. Every detail came under his inspection. His mother's rooms were dismantled, and all the busts and mementos of the drunken John Brown, dead for eighteen years, destroyed or removed. He was as pleased as a boy to discover the troves of master paintings that came to light in storerooms and basements.

"I don't know much about art," said the king, who had seldom let a week go by without visiting a gallery or a painter's studio, "but I think I know something about arrangement."

His insistence on holding all the reins irritated Alix. Unless she was at his side, she was kept away from ceremonial and social occasions, even those which she had handled without him as the princess. Her solution was to slacken her efforts to keep up with him. More and more time was passed at Sandringham with Charlotte, her dearest companion now that Oliver Montagu was lost to her; it was eight years since he died, not as a soldier but an invalid with symptoms of tuberculosis, in the futile sunlight of Cairo. One reason she dreaded moving into Buckingham Palace was her fretting over whether Charlotte could be sure of being given a suitable room there.

As for the woman who filled the principal place in Bertie's heart at the present, Alexandra certainly preferred her to Daisy, who had fallen from favour with her conversion to Socialism and wire-pulling in that cause. Dark-eyed Alice Keppel had the quality of discretion totally lacking in Daisy, as well as Lillie's ability to salvage Bertie from boredom. So the new queen tolerated this newest affair with the same good grace as Alice's strikingly handsome husband George, brother to Lord Albemarle, an infantry officer, a gentleman, and a member in good standing of

Boodle's, the Turf, and St. James's. In recognition of Keppel's forbearance, Bertie, the fountain of honour, later made him a Member of the Royal Victorian Order, an award which he enjoyed bestowing in wholesale numbers.

Only the necessary period of mourning for his mother prevented the king from making this season of 1901 what he intended the next to be: the most brilliant in his country's history. As it was, he gave the nation a foretaste of the style he planned to set by reviving the ceremonial of carriage processions to mark his state opening of Parliament in February, which Victoria had abandoned. He allowed no interruption in the presentation at court of ladies, young and old.

He had not found the time yet to change the formula, as he did before the year ended, when afternoon "drawing rooms" were replaced by evening parties in the refurnished palace ballroom. Jeanne-Marie's debut on May 16, following the same pattern as her mother's, came at the close of a fossilised age.

Her dress was plainer, her curtsey less practised and no prince had sent her a bouquet. She wore no towering ostrich plumes as a challenge to decorum as she advanced across the polished floor of the throne room, clasping the invitation to hand to the lord chamberlain. One thing had changed already at the king's touch. The orchestra played no more humdrum two-steps but romantic airs from Italian opera.

Squeezed into his uniform, he had a twitch in his blue eyes and his peppery brown beard twitched with his rogue's smile as he saw her. To have a lovely girl kiss his hand was worth the ache that prolonged standing produced in his knee ever since he fell downstairs on his way to breakfast at Ferdie de Rothschild's country place, Waddesdon, and Daisy had to summon help to pick him up. Alexandra's radiance was a sight to see, her unlined skin complemented by the darkness of her mourning. It was impossible to detect that the words Jeanne-Marie murmured to her went unheard. Alexandra was so deaf these days that she had fallen into the habit of talking to herself in private.

The girl gave her last deep curtsey, caught the train of her gown on her arm as a footman tossed it to her, and made her exit to the carriage waiting in line outside. The preliminary rites had been performed. She was ready to be married as soon as she was asked.

Several young men of shining promise sat in the House of Commons on the Conservatives' side. One of the brightest, and undoubtedly the most self-assured, was Lord Randolph and Jennie Churchill's ginger-headed son, twenty-seven-year-old Winston. He had been elected in Oldham, Lancashire, after he wrote himself into the headlines as a reporter covering the South African War for *The Morning Post* and was held captive by the Boers for a brief twenty-seven days before he scaled a wall to escape from the State Schools Prison in Pretoria.

He had been fatherless for six years, but Bertie had made his peace with the Churchills long before Randolph's death. Bertie had befriended Winston, who corresponded with him from time to time, including one letter written in captivity: ". . . I must add a few lines about the Boers, for I confess myself much impressed by their courtesy, courage and humanity. . . ."

He was one of the five young sparks who composed the entire membership of a private Parliamentary dining club named "The Malcolmtents" after its founder, Ian Malcolm. Of the five, most men of Westminster picked Malcolm as the one perhaps most likely to succeed to high office.

Ian was a Scots aristocrat, heir to 480,000 acres of the far highlands, where salmon leapt in the streams and stag abounded in the craggy hills. One day he would be the seventeenth laird and hereditary chief of the Clan MacCallum, which had provided Scotland with tribal kings. He was the model, it seemed, of a cultivated gentleman——Eton, Oxford, the Carlton Club; diplomatic service in the embassies in Berlin,

Paris, and St. Petersburg; a taste for writing poetry and translations from the Persian.

Soon after the voters of the town of Stowmarket sent him to represent them in Parlaiment in the general election of June, 1895, which swept the Conservatives back into power, Salisbury chose Ian as an assistant personal secretary. When Bertie started the Prince of Wales' Hospital Fund two years after that, Ian was the man selected to run it as secretary. At the age of thirty-three he ranked among the more eligible bachelors available in London.

He caught sight of Jeanne-Marie at a ball in Devonshire House, where Harty-tarty once scooped water lilies from a pool in tribute to her mother. Hartington had inherited a new title, Duke of Devonshire, and taken his long-term love, Louisa, as his wife after the death of her husband, the much-cuckolded Duke of Manchester. Society knew her as "the double duchess" nowadays. It could just as well have been Ian's brother Duncan who proceeded to win Jeanne-Marie. Duncan spotted her first, remote and exquisite in the crowds, and sought to be introduced, but his brother soon ousted Duncan as her suitor.

The marriage of Ian Malcolm and Jeanne-Marie Langtry was solemnized as fashionably as could be on June 30, 1902, at St. Margaret's, Westminster, in the shadow of the great abbey. The old Portland-stone church, Parliament's particular house of worship for almost three centuries, overflowed that morning with politicians and peers, the nobility and the notorious, their faces multicoloured by the light filtering in through the Flemish stained-glass windows that dated back to Henry VIII. The occasion was not of a magnitude to warrant the presence of Bertie, who, in any event, had undergone an emergency operation for peritonitis in Buckingham Palace six days earlier. His coronation ceremonies set for June 28 were postponed indefinitely, but an equerry remembered to send Jeanne-Marie a piece of jewellery, and the king himself wrote her his best wishes as soon as he felt well enough.

In the interests of diplomacy, it was Lillie who gave her daughter away. Hugo, younger than the bridegroom, was nowhere to be seen in London. Ian's father, Colonel Edward Donald Malcolm, ramrod-straight in full beard and the dress uniform of the Royal Engineers, led the contingent of his family who descended from Argyllshire. The bells pealed for the bride and groom, as custom called them to do whenever any sovereign since good King Hal drove in state past the church doors.

An orchestra of violins played in the ballroom of the house on Cadogan Place, where Lillie, matronly but dazzling, entertained two hundred guests at a champagne breakfast. Her presents to her daughter included a check, a settlement of 5,000 pounds a year, and a diamond brooch almost as magnificent as the diamond necklace that Ian had bought for his bride. After they left on their honeymoon, Lillie passed a pensive afternoon at the races and won 6,000 pounds.

The young Malcolms had two homes, a Georgian town house at 5 Bryanston Square, on the opposite side of the park at the comforting distance from Belgravia, and Poltalloch, a nineteenth-century sandstone manor house set on top of the Mull of Kintyre, on Malcolm land, ten miles from the nearest town. The date carved in the stone of the mantelpiece testified to its building in the year of his mother-in-law's birth. She saw very little of her daughter on Bryanston Square and nothing at all of her at Poltalloch. Lillie had no welcome there in the house with twenty-five guest rooms, whose central hall was hung with regimental banners and orders of Scottish chivalry. The Malcolms as a clan could abide Ian's Society bride, but not her notorious mother.

Jeanne, as she preferred to be called now, had the style of an autocrat. She seemed to have been born to wear the beautifully cut pale grey dresses and fine jewels that rapidly became her hallmark, like the hats that graced her head if there were guests for luncheon at Bryanston Square, and the tea gowns in which she presided over the silver tray in the hall at Poltalloch. The sideboard would be laden with freshly baked cakes, scones, and preserves. The air was scented with azaleas and floor wax, and daylight filtered in through the stained glass halfway up the stairs.

Her husband and the four children she bore him in the course of the years had a love for the highlands which she found it impossible to share. Poltalloch, where the bagpipes skirled for dinner guests, was synonymous with Malcolms, not with the introspective, diffident newcomer to the clan. Ian revelled in the place, from the *fraises des bois,* which the gardeners cultivated on the terrace, to the fishing, from a streamside or a boat pulled by one of the army of proud men who inhabited the surrounding cottages.

She found it easier to come to terms with the servants than with the family. There were servants everywhere. The year-round butler, housekeeper, housemaids, and pantry boy had their ranks augmented by footmen, kitchen, laundry, and still-room maids when Poltalloch filled with summer guests and for winter shooting. Then visitors would arrive in droves between the stone stags which flanked the entrance gates. Carpenters, gamekeepers, coachmen, and gillies were permanently on call.

She set about bearing a family of her own as soon as possible. Her first child, George Ian, was born ten months after the wedding. Victor and Angus followed in the next five years, then, after a decade, Helen Mary. But Jeanne still only knew of her father. She had no personal knowledge of the man who had emerged from the mysteries of her upbringing.

As Louis approached fifty, his family was complete with three daughters and an infant son, named for him. Louis and his wife Victoria had all four children with them in Darmstadt for the wedding of their eldest girl, Alice, in the autumn of the year that Jeanne became Mrs. Malcolm. Alice's eminently satisfactory marriage forged one more link with royalty. Her bridegroom was Andrew, prince of Greece and son of Alexandra's brother Willi.

The beard of Captain His Serene Highness Prince Louis of Battenberg was grizzled now. His body was thickened, like the gold-braid bands of rank on the sleeves of his uniforms. Half a year's service as aide to the king preceded his being given command of his first battleship, *Implacable*. From there, he had gone into the Admiralty as Director of Naval Intelligence. On the day of that appointment, he came close to tears. "I felt the proudest man in the Navy," said this self-determined Englishman with the German name.

Advancement closer and closer to the highest levels of service produced no noticeable effect on his nature. He was still a mixture of thinker and man of action, with sadness flickering occasionally in his warm brown eyes. Subordinates were drawn to him by his code of chivalry, which held that loyalty must be given to them in order for it to be returned. His superiors in the Admiralty and the War Office trusted him to the hilt.

The imperative demand made by his new job on Louis was to assess the strength of the fleet that Germany was frantically building to challenge British control of the seven seas. The kaiser's *Meteor II*, which drove Bertie to give up big yacht racing as Prince of Wales, was a portent of Berlin's intentions. German industrialists and landed gentry, the *Junkerthum*, envied England's commercial supremacy, based, as they knew too well, on the unexercised ability of British warships to blockade any major port in the world and ward off attack on the island itself.

At Kiel and Hamburg, the shipyards worked day and night to launch more warships, faster cruisers and destroyers, deadlier submarines. The steel mills of the Ruhr churned out cannon of every calibre, with monstrous "Big Bertha," designed to bombard Paris, in pride of place. The pace set by Germany in the arms race drove England to budget increasing millions for her fleet, to the neglect of the skimpy Brit-

349

ish army and prosperity at home. Over the first Christmas of Jeanne's married life, 107,539 Londoners depended for existence on Poor Law relief, the biggest
total for thirty years. It was no coincidence that at
the next general election the Socialists attained their
first foothold in Parliament, with twenty-nine of them
elected in a tidal change of British politics.

Somewhere in Louis' Admiralty files he could undoubtedly put his hands on United States Navy De-
partment Record 38, Volume 52. Page 558 reported
the comments of German Admiral von Goetzen made
four years earlier: "About fifteen years from now my
country will start a great war. She will be in Paris
about two months after the commencement of hostili-
ties. Her move to Paris will be but a step to her real
object—the crushing of England." Time was drawing
short if England was to meet the threat.

Louis formulated plans for updating the antiquated
schemes covering the deployment of warships for his
country's defence. He appreciated, perhaps earlier
than any other man in a similar position, that future rule of the seas must take into account the new
dangers imposed by U-boats, flying machines, and
submarine mines that could destroy or paralyse the
mightiest steel-clad battleship.

Everything he heard about the onetime sprig of
Marlborough House delighted the king. Louis was a
man to suit the First Sea Lord, Admiral Sir John
Fisher, who was equally convinced of the urgent need
to expand and reform the British Navy. Bertie's support of flamboyant Admiral Jack protected Louis, too.
Without it, Fisher, and probably Louis as well, would
have been unceremoniously deposed by jealous old-
liners in the Admiralty, whose ringleader was Charlie
Beresford. Charlie had tried repeatedly to regain the
contact with Bertie on which he had relied before the
squabble over Daisy's letter. Politely but consistently
Bertie rebuffed him.

At the House of Commons, the Malcolmtents were
disbanded when two of the club's luminaries went
their separate ways. Young Winston's ache for action

and glory carried him out of the Conservative Party, whose prospects of election victory seemed dim, to cross the floor and join the ruling Liberals. By 1910 he would have catapulted himself into the headlines again by his appointment as Home Secretary and then in the following year as First Sea Lord of the Admiralty, the supreme civilian commander of the fleet.

If Ian nursed any similar desire for national fame, he was too rich and too lacking in ambition to push himself hard enough. He also held too poor an opinion of Lillie to want anything of her company. He took four years off as Parliamentarian, partly to savour the satisfactions of Poltalloch, Bryanston Square, and 3 Pickering Place, a retreat in a little court off St. James's Street that Wellington, the Iron Duke himself, gave to an ancestral Malcolm. Books, poetry, and a good vintage champagne were as important to Ian as politics. In her late twenties, Jeanne's beauty and aura of remoteness gave no sign of fading. Her place in Society was respected and secure.

In the sunlight that warmed London on May 20, 1910, Louis marched with the gun-carriage that bore the coffin of King Edward through the streets from Westminster to Paddington Station, to be put aboard the funeral train for Windsor, where his remains would lie in the vault beneath St. George's Chapel. Behind the camion marched nine magnificently uniformed men who had no cause to doubt that, no matter what tomorrow brought, they would continue to control the world—the monarchs of England, Germany, Belgium, Bulgaria, Denmark, Greece, Norway, Portugal, and Spain. Striding along with them came Theodore Roosevelt, conspicuously different in a top hat and morning coat, President of the United States until two years ago.

Silent crowds packed the line of march. Church bells tolled an accompaniment to lamenting bagpipes and the notes of Chopin's funeral dirge played by muffled drums and silver trumpets. On Cadogan Place, Lillie hid herself away, refusing to see any reporter, shunning public appearances until she sailed for the United States that autumn to tour in vaudeville.

Now Georgie reigned as King George V, with his wife, May, as Queen Mary. His simple words in a diary entry testified to the bond he felt with Bertie, who had made certain that his son's upbringing was diametrically different from his own: "I have lost my best friend and the best of fathers. I never had a word with him in my life. I am heartbroken and overwhelmed with grief."

In December of the following year, Louis became Second Sea Lord of the Admiralty, one step down from the zenith for a serving officer. Twelve months later, his civilian commander, Winston Churchill, afforded him the ultimate honour, First Sea Lord, responsible to him for the well-being of the entire fleet.

Together, the statesman and the sailor massed Britain's warships on July 18, 1914, less than three weeks after two pistol shots fired by the Serbian Gavrilo Prinzip killed the Austrian crown prince, Archduke Francis Ferdinand, and his wife at Sarajevo, capital of the Austrian province of Bosnia. Germany had already decided that there must be war. Austria would use the pretext of the dual assassination to make such humiliating demands on Serbia in retribution that the Serbs could only reject them.

With its revolutionary new battleships, the "dreadnoughts" that Fisher had campaigned for and the emergency plans that Louis had formulated, the British fleet had been ready for ten days when Austria-Hungary, with Germany as its mentor, declared war on Serbia. Coded cablegrams from one government to another dominated the telegraph wires of Europe. The locked red boxes carrying despatches from the Foreign Office arrived around the clock on Louis' desk in his Admiralty office, where the booming of Big Ben in Parliament's tower could be heard tolling the hours. Outside his windows, the gardens were green with trees and flowers that bloomed on and on in the rare summer's heat.

352

Russia considered itself the indomitable champion of the Serbs. The day that Austrian troops crossed into Serbia, the armies of the czar would mass to do battle. France was an ally of Russia, bound to support it by the terms of the Triple Entente, and so was England, tied to the French as Bertie had hoped for. But the kaiser discounted the contemptible little British army. The German Empire's preparedness made it the supreme land power of the world. With Austria-Hungary and Italy fighting alongside them, as signatories of the Triple Alliance, the field-grey forces of the Kaiser marched to set fire to Western civilisation.

Declarations of war studded the August calendar: Germany against Russia, on the first day of the month; Germany against France, on the third, and against Belgium and Britain together on the fourth, the day that Britain and France responded against the Germans. On the sixth, when Austria-Hungary joined in against Russia, the British fleet suffered its first loss. HMS *Amphion* struck one of the mines that the Germans had planted indiscriminately in the North Sea and foundered with one hundred fifty lives lost. Forty-eight hours later, the score was even. The cruiser *Birmingham* sank a U-boat in the same waters.

British patrols of the North Sea were an essential part of Louis' original plan. Other cruisers guarded trade routes across the globe, to fend off German marauders from attacks on merchantmen, on whose cargoes his country's existence depended. The kaiser's *Emden, Königsberg, Von Spee,* and more warships like them prowled the distant oceans, terrorising unarmed ships of all but the nations of the Triple Alliance.

If the Royal Navy was prepared, the rest of the nation was not. Asquith's six-year-old Liberal government commandeered the railways on the day war began and closed the banks to stop a run on them. Hoarders besieging the food shops posed a different threat to British ability to combat a seemingly invincible Germany. A peculiar phobia swept the people, who saw the hand of German spies in every ailment afflicting the nation. Twenty-one known agents of the kaiser were thrown into prison on August 4 and two hundred suspects interned. Nine thousand Germans and Austrians in all were taken from their British homes and held as prisoners in detention camps.

At Bryanston Square, Jeanne could do little more than marvel at the overnight disruptions to living and, like the overwhelming majority of the population, approve of most of them. Food was not hard to find if one had money to pay the soaring prices, and she had three children to feed. The blackout that was imposed as darkness fell and searchlights probed the sky in search of attacking Zeppelins was a necessary nuisance. Back in Parliament with a different constituency to serve this time, the London suburb of Croydon, Ian volunteered as a British Red Cross officer in France. Lillie de Bathe gave up thought of retirement and opened in a new play, *Mrs. Thompson,* at Drury Lane, donating her salary and profits to the same organisation her son-in-law was working in.

Letters and cablegrams were censored now. Emergency legislation forbade aliens to possess a radio set or any kind of signalling apparatus, including homing pigeons. Boy Scouts armed with staves joined the Saturday soldiers of the Territorial Army in patrolling railway tracks, bridges, and waterworks as a guard against sabotage. In Europe, 80,000 neutral Americans, stranded by the exploding fury of war, sought passage home. One group of them pooled funds to buy the steamer *Viking* and sought to recoup by selling tickets at 125 pounds a head.

Spy fever mounted. A round of trials began in secret of suspected agents of the enemy, whose armies had smashed the Russians in East Prussia and driven the French government from Paris to Bordeaux. Waves of Germans had swept aside Belgium's 200,000 men in a bare two weeks of fighting. Now they surged across France, striking for the coastal ports of Dunkirk and Calais as bases for the climax, the invasion of England. The kaiser fancied that the country would make an easy prize, paralysed, as he thought, by unemployment, dissaffection among the working class, and the incurable wounds of hatred in Ireland.

Nothing, it seemed, could halt the German advance, certainly not the puny British Expeditionary Force of 175,000 soldiers hurried over the Channel to northern France. Louis' schemes for protecting the crossing had worked flawlessly. The ships of the fleet that shielded the troops were anticipating a massive naval battle, but the enemy stayed clear of the operation that landed four divisions in the course of thirteen August days.

Elsewhere at sea, it was a darker story. HMS *Pathfinder* went down with a crew of 259. The cruiser *Hela* was sunk by U-boat Number 9. The *Königsberg* captured *Pegasus*. In the Indian Ocean the *Emden* destroyed four British merchantmen, and all this before September was over.

The last bastion of Belgium's defences was the fortress-port of Antwerp, on the right bank of the Scheldt, fifty miles up from the river's mouth and impregnable against any attack, according to military textbooks. On September 28 the Germans' forty-two-centimetre siege guns began pounding the fort to pieces. Churchill rushed into a decision to ferry 8,000 ill-equipped sailors and reservists of the Royal Naval Division to reinforce the citadel's faltering defenders. Under Louis' overall direction, 30,000 men in all were put safely ashore in less than one hundred hours. Winston had to be on the scene of battle. He made for Antwerp, leaving Louis Battenberg to face the hue and cry that was arising among the public and the press, with sole responsibility for all decisions to be taken at the Admiralty.

Ten days of nonstop bombardment forced the exhausted Allied forces into flight down roads clogged with refugees with salvaged possessions loaded on to farm wagons or bundled on their shoulders. Panic-stricken horses and cattle added to the chaos as German guns continued the attack. Twenty five hundred casualties were counted in the shattered naval division. Many who survived were captured or interned in neutral Holland as they fled. The newspapers called it a national tragedy. The harshest words came from *The Morning Post* for its former employee: "A costly blunder for which Mr. Winston Churchill is primarily responsible."

One hundred thousand Belgian refugees began pouring into England, some transported by the Navy, others in sailboats and skiffs. The spy terror gained fresh momentum. Who could tell how many hundreds more secret agents of the kaiser were hidden in this flood of humanity seeking sanctuary? Shops owned by Germans were wrecked in South London. England seethed with tales of atrocities the Germans had committed, of Belgian nuns strung up inside church bells and prisoners boiled alive for rendering into soap.

The country wanted a scapegoat for disaster, and there were men of influence ready to supply one. The rumour was spread that Louis, German-born and bred, had been removed as a prisoner to the Tower of London, awaiting trial as a traitor. Among senior officers in the service clubs, gossip said that one of them, never named, had a letter, smuggled in from Germany, saying that the First Sea Lord was the kaiser's supreme spy.

One morning in October Jeanne read what *The Globe* chose to write about her father: "For the sake of the First Sea Lord himself, no less than for that of the nation . . . we ask that some authoritative statement shall be issued of a nature so emphatic and so unqualified as to remove once and for ever every cloud of doubt and to silence every breath of rumour."

Louis concealed his pain under a layer of good humour. Urged on by Beresford, his enemies increased the pressure.

At all costs they wanted Louis out. If his faith in himself and his adopted country deterred him from resigning, then somehow he must be destroyed. In the middle of October, six days after German planes dropped their first bombs on Paris, Beresford's old command, the cruiser *Undaunted,* and four British destroyers were sunk in the North Sea. In the same grey water, *Aboukir, Cressy,* and *Hogue* had been torpedoed within two hours with the loss of 62 officers and 1,397 men. Beresford added more political ammunition to his locker.

Naval invasion was reaching closer to English shores. A new rumour flared in the clubs and the public-houses, kept locked for most of the day now under the Defence of the Realm Act, which imposed a species of martial law on the land. German raiders, it was believed, had already attempted an assault on the east-coast town of Yarmouth. The fleet awaited the sight of enemy warships at the approaches to the Thames. The *Boches* were thrusting for quick victory, precisely in line with the timetables of Berlin.

On October 27 Churchill called Louis into his office to hold a postmortem on yet another reverse. Public confidence in Winston was at a low ebb. The memory of Antwerp lingered in many minds. Supporters of Louis felt that if he had a weakness, it lay in his compliance with the more forceful, nimbler-footed First Lord. *Audacious,* one of the original dreadnoughts, had struck a mine and was sinking in the Irish Sea. How could Winston still the inevitable outcry when the news was broken?

On the following day, the Prime Minister confided to his diary: "Winston pouring out his woes." "Louis," Asquith wrote, "must go and Winston has had a most delicate and painful interview with him. Louis behaved with great dignity and public spirit and will resign at once."

That night Louis composed his last letter as First Sea Lord: "I have lately been driven to the painful conclusion that at this juncture my birth and parentage have the effect of impairing in some respects my usefulness on the Board of Admiralty. In these circumstances, I feel it my duty, as a loyal subject of His Majesty, to resign. . . ."

The next afternoon, at four o'clock, he was summoned to Buckingham Palace. It had taken long argument to convince the king that the sacrifice was necessary, but time had eroded the sovereign's power that his grandmother had exulted in. A constitutional monarch had no alternative but to accept such decisions from his ministers. "At the end," he confessed in his diary, "I had to give in with great reluctance."

He waited for Louis in his little writing room. Sentimental Victorian pictures covered the walls. A naval clock on the mantelpiece rang out shipboard time. Forty-nine-year-old Georgie was as moved by their parting as the dejected man who had watched over him in days under sail in *Inconstant*, when Louis had left behind the woman whose daughter he had fathered.

The king cursed his old shipmate's enemies, and the ex-Sea Lord retained his self-control. But when his sovereign turned to praising him, he wept. He left with a promise that he would be appointed to the group which still bore the prestige of earlier days, when its deliberations concerned the innermost secrets of the crown. "I told him I would make him a Privy Councillor," said His Majesty's diary, "to show the confidence I had in him, which pleased him."

That night Jeanne met her father. He sent for the daughter he had known only as a stranger, while he kept himself informed of the turns her life had taken. He sent for her to come to his quiet high-ceilinged room in the Admiralty before he closed its door behind him for the last time. Blackout curtains would be drawn across the windows, while a fire flickered in the grate. Big Ben rang out the hours under the roving searchlight beams. What was said between them when they were alone remained her secret. The nature of Louis made it likely that tears were shed again.

It remained for Alexandra, faulty in grammar but sensitive in heart, to write a postscript after he retreated from the world. Still vigorous at sixty, Louis lived in seclusion on the Isle of Wight. "He is of noble character," said the dowager queen, who had joined Bertie in seeing to it that scandal thirty-three years ago would not tarnish the future of the princely young sprig whom they both loved, "and has sacrificed

358

himself to the country he has served so well and who has now treated him so abominably."

When the last shots had been fired in the War to End Wars, Jeanne became Lady Malcolm. For his part in the Paris conferences that set the terms of peace, Ian's reward was a title—Knight Commander of the Order of St. Michael and St. George.

Only compassion for the other, or the desire to be forgiven for what perhaps had been inevitable, could narrow the distance that separated Lady Malcolm and Lady de Bathe, and neither mother nor daughter saw the need for change.

For as long as Lillie lived, whenever she came to London, she received her own reward for discretion and loyalty—an invitation to spend an hour or so in conversation with Queen Mary, who continued the pattern established by Bertie and Alexandra. In February, 1929, Lillie died in Monaco, in the house she called Villa le Lys. The Mediterranean sparkled under its windows. Painted herons, like Jimmy Whistler's of half a century ago, soared across the interior walls. Only a woman companion was with her. Jeanne inherited her mother's silver.

Life had been over for Louis for eight years. He was Battenberg no longer. He rid himself of his alien title in 1917 in fealty to his king when the whisperers began to claim that his Hanoverian heritage made George V pro-German in his sympathies. George's answer was to erase the past by declaring that "Windsor," dependably English and reassuring, would henceforth be the name of Britain's royal family, not the Germanic "Wettin" as it was then, so far as genealogists could trace. He simultaneously invited Louis to follow his example and proclaimed his willing old friend the first Marquess of Milford Haven.

On June 20, 1924, a heart attack killed Alexandra at Sandringham. She was stone deaf by then and could no longer remember anything with clarity. "You and my darling May are in my thoughts all day long, and all your children," said Motherdear's last letter to Georgie.

The casualties of war included English Society itself. A major part of the next generation of aristocrats on which its future depended was destroyed on the battlefields of France. The survivors saw family fortunes gone in taxation that bought the victory. Now titles were bought from the politicians by the new class of rich who had made their millions selling steel, khaki uniforms, beer, and jam. The base of the pyramid was restructured, too, to provide "homes fit for heroes to live in," reforms in education and ownership of the land, old-age pensions for the poor, insurance against sickness and unemployment.

Edwardian England was washed away into the surging seas of change, but Louis, unknowingly, had a bequest to make to his adopted country in the form of a great-grandson who, unless the monarchy were overthrown, would reign one day as king.

The union of his daughter Alice and Prince Andrew of Greece produced a son, Philip, born on Corfu in June, 1921, the year of his grandfather's death, and brought up in England. In November, 1947, Philip was married in Westminster Abbey to Elizabeth, granddaughter of George V. Their first-born son and heir to the throne was Prince Charles; Philip was the Duke of Edinburgh; Elizabeth was Britain's queen.

Index

361

364

366

NEW FROM BALLANTINE!

FALCONER, John Cheever 27300 $2.25
The unforgettable story of a substantial, middle-class man and the passions that propel him into murder, prison, and an undreamed-of liberation. "CHEEVER'S TRIUMPH...A GREAT AMERICAN NOVEL."—*Newsweek*

GOODBYE, W. H. Manville 27118 $2.25
What happens when a woman turns a sexual fantasy into a fatal reality? The erotic thriller of the year! "Powerful."—*Village Voice.* "Hypnotic."—*Cosmopolitan.*

**THE CAMERA NEVER BLINKS, Dan Rather
with Mickey Herskowitz** 27423 $2.25
In this candid book, the co-editor of "60 Minutes" sketches vivid portraits of numerous personalities including JFK, LBJ and Nixon, and discusses his famous colleagues.

THE DRAGONS OF EDEN, Carl Sagan 26031 $2.25
An exciting and witty exploration of mankind's intelligence from pre-recorded time to the fantasy of a future race, by America's most appealing scientific spokesman.

VALENTINA, Fern Michaels 26011 $1.95
Sold into slavery in the Third Crusade, Valentina becomes a queen, only to find herself a slave to love.

**THE BLACK DEATH, Gwyneth Cravens
and John S. Marr** 27155 $2.50
A totally plausible novel of the panic that strikes when the bubonic plague devastates New York.

**THE FLOWER OF THE STORM,
Beatrice Coogan** 27368 $2.50
Love, pride and high drama set against the turbulent background of 19th century Ireland as a beautiful young woman fights for her inheritance and the man she loves.

**THE JUDGMENT OF DEKE HUNTER,
George V. Higgins** 25862 $1.95
Tough, dirty, shrewd, telling! "The best novel Higgins has written. Deke Hunter should have as many friends as Eddie Coyle."—*Kirkus Reviews*

LG-2